The Architecture of Richard Morris Hunt

·RICHARD·MORRIS·HUNT· AND ·RICHARD·HOWLAND·HUNT· ·ARCHITECTS·

·NEW·EAST·WING·METROPOLITAN·MUSEUM·OF·ART·

The Architecture of
RICHARD MORRIS HUNT

Edited by Susan R. Stein

The University of Chicago Press · Chicago and London

Exhibition itinerary:

The Metropolitan Museum of Art, New York: 20 March 1986–15 June 1986
The Octagon Museum, Washington, D.C.: 20 July 1986–28 September 1986
The Art Institute of Chicago, Chicago: 9 February 1987–29 March 1987

The exhibition was made possible by a gift from Stephen and Nan Swid and
the GFI/Knoll International Foundation. Publication of the book was assisted
by the William Cullen Bryant Fellows of the American Wing, the Metropolitan Museum of Art, and the Waldron Faulkner Memorial Catalogue Fund
of the American Institute of Architects Foundation.

Susan R. Stein is curator of Monticello, former director of the American
Institute of Architects Foundation's Octagon Museum, and former curator of
its Richard Morris Hunt Collection.

The University of Chicago Press, Chicago 60637
The University of Chicago Press, Ltd., London
© 1986 by The American Institute of Architects Foundation
All rights reserved. Published 1986
Printed in the United States of America

95 94 93 92 91 90 89 88 87 86   54321

Library of Congress Cataloging-in-Publication Data

Main entry under title:
The Architecture of Richard Morris Hunt.

    Includes index.
    Contents: Richard Morris Hunt, an introduction /
Paul R. Baker — Hunt in Paris / Richard Chafee —
Richard Morris Hunt, architectural innovator and
father of a "distinctive" American school /
Sarah Bradford Landau — [etc.]
    1. Hunt, Richard Morris, 1828–1895—Criticism
and interpretation—Addresses, essays, lectures.
I. Stein, Susan R., 1949–   .
NA737.H86A88   1986   720'.92'4   85-16523
ISBN 0-226-77168-7
ISBN 0-226-77169-5 (pbk.)

Contents

Contributors

Paul R. Baker is professor of history and director of the American Civilization Program at New York University.

Richard Chafee, aided by a grant from the Graham Foundation for Advanced Studies in the Fine Arts, is writing a book about the effect of the Ecole des Beaux-Arts on the architecture of the United States and Canada.

Sarah Bradford Landau is associate professor of fine arts at New York University.

Francis R. Kowsky is professor of art history at the State University of New York College at Buffalo.

David Van Zanten is professor of art history at Northwestern University.

Susan R. Stein is curator of Monticello, former director of the Octagon Museum, and former curator of the Richard Morris Hunt Collection at the American Institute of Architects Foundation.

Lewis I. Sharp is curator of American paintings and sculpture at the Metropolitan Museum of Art.

David Chase was formerly with the Rhode Island Historical Preservation Commission and is now writing a book on the social and architectural history of Newport, sponsored by the Preservation Society of Newport County.

Morrison H. Heckscher is curator of American decorative arts at the Metropolitan Museum of Art.

Acknowledgments

THE AMERICAN INSTITUTE OF ARCHITECTS FOUNDATION and the Metropolitan Museum of Art are pleased to present the exhibition and companion volume of essays, *The Architecture of Richard Morris Hunt*. Hunt, who in 1857 was among the founding members of the American Institute of Architects, served as the Institute's first secretary and third president. Since he designed the superb Fifth Avenue wing of the Metropolitan Museum of Art shortly before his death in 1895, it is fitting that this exhibition should open at the institution that serves as a monument both to him and to the Beaux-Arts classicism he so vigorously championed.

Hunt (1827–95) was one of the most influential architects of his time, and the legacy of his work in New York City, where he chiefly practiced between 1860 and 1895, is unparalleled. He was an early experimenter with the design of skyscrapers and apartment houses and added much to the overall character of the city. From the very start of his career in New York, Hunt was committed to improving the quality of American life. He was the first American to study architecture at the Ecole des Beaux-Arts and was determined to share his special knowledge with others. No schools of architecture existed in the United States at that time; consequently, Hunt established his own atelier where aspiring architects could study.

Hunt's dedication not only to the improvement of the practice of architecture but to the betterment of the cityscape was great, as his frequent collaboration with sculptors on public monuments attested. In 1892, Hunt was elected the first president of the Municipal Arts Society, an organization he helped to found, and which today is still committed to beautifying New York City.

The exhibition itself, which is drawn primarily from the Hunt collection of the AIA Foundation, reflects the growing interest in Hunt's work and in American architecture of the second half of the nineteenth century. The idea of the exhibition originated with Susan R. Stein, then of the American Institute of Architects Foundation, and was endorsed first by R. Craig Miller, associate curator, and later by Lewis I. Sharp, curator, and Morrison H. Heckscher, curator, of the American Wing of the Metropolitan Museum of Art. In addition to participating in the project as authors, Susan Stein and Morrison Heckscher organized the exhibition.

At the American Institute of Architects Foundation, Mary C. Means and Gordon Alt, president and vice president respectively, deserve mention for their recognition of the importance of this project. Curator of the Prints and

ACKNOWLEDGMENTS

Drawings Collection, Sherry C. Birk, merits special appreciation for her constant effort. A number of others have lent assistance: Judith S. Schultz, assistant curator of exhibitions, Deborah R. Dunstan, and Tony Wrenn, archivist of the American Institute of Architects.

At the Metropolitan Museum of Art, John K. Howat, chairman of the Department of American Art, supported the concept of the exhibition. The installation at the Museum was designed by David Harvey.

We are also appreciative of the care and interest given to the preparation of this volume. The photographs of many of the drawings are the work of John Tennant.

The exhibition and book would not have been possible without the exceptional generosity of Stephen and Nan Swid and the GFI/Knoll International Foundation. We also wish to thank the National Endowment for the Arts for a grant to carry out the research and writing of the book, and the William Cullen Bryant Fellows of the American Wing, the Metropolitan Museum of Art, and the Waldron Faulkner Memorial Catalogue Fund of the American Institute of Architects Foundation for publication assistance.

John A. Busby, Jr., FAIA, President
The American Institute of Architects

Philippe de Montebello, Director
The Metropolitan Museum of Art

Introduction

THE ARCHITECTURE OF RICHARD MORRIS HUNT rediscovers the distinguished career of one of the most respected American architects. Nine scholars were invited to study various important aspects of Hunt's architecture: his studies in France; the conflict surrounding his refused designs for the gateways to Central Park; the superlative Lenox Library; collaborations with sculptors that prefigured the City Beautiful movement; the late palatial houses; his drawings; and the original designs of his early and mid-career. This collective reassessment, which presents multiple points of view, has been made possible in part by the remarkable survival of Hunt's architectural drawings. Earlier scholarship was impeded by the destruction of many Hunt buildings, the usual basis for study.

This book and the exhibition that accompanies it have a long history. Glenn Brown, the historically minded secretary of the American Institute of Architects, decided in 1903 that the Institute ought to preserve the records of its greatest members. He wrote letters to prominent architects and their heirs inviting them to donate drawings and related materials to the Institute's library.[1] Few responded.

Fortunately, Richard Howland Hunt and Joseph Howland Hunt, Richard Morris Hunt's sons, shared Brown's conviction that architectural records should be preserved. When they ended their practice of architecture in 1926, they honored their mother's wish by donating their father's superb library, drawings, sketchbooks, memorabilia, collected photographs, and office furnishings to the American Institute of Architects. Some eight thousand original drawings, fifteen thousand collected photographs, and over seven hundred architectural books were crated in wooden trunks and shipped to the Institute's headquarters in Washington, D.C. The books quickly became the nucleus of the Institute's rare book collection. The drawings and photographs remained, for the most part, in packing crates for over fifty years until cataloging began in 1978.[2]

Without question, the Hunt collection of drawings, photographs, and books is the most comprehensive surviving archive of any nineteenth-century American architect. The "discovery" of this cache of documents has proved to be an exceptional resource for scholars. Using documents in the Hunt collection, Paul R. Baker of New York University wrote an authoritative biography and prepared an accurate checklist of Hunt's architectural works.[3] Perhaps most importantly, Baker recognized Hunt's achievements and established him once again as the dean of American architecture, as he was known in his own time.

Professor Baker's chapter in this book summarizes the major accomplishments of Hunt's fifty-year career and sets the stage for the analytical study of his architecture that follows.

Richard Morris Hunt was widely admired by his colleagues. Upon his death in 1895, Henry Van Brunt stated that Hunt, "by personal force and high training secured for the architecture of our time and country a standing adequate at last to represent our civilization in terms of art."[4] The Beaux-Arts classicism that Hunt had championed so eloquently, especially in his later years, was clearly in favor. However, within a short fifteen years modernism was ascendant, and eventually eclipsed Beaux-Arts architecture and its architects. The reputation of McKim, Mead, and White, Carrere and Hastings, and Richard M. Hunt suffered alike; the classicists were overshadowed by modernism and its functionalist tenets.

Although the availability of the comparatively complete archive of Hunt's work has greatly aided the reinterpretation of his career, the eight thousand surviving drawings by no means constitute all of the drawings created in Hunt's office. No single project survives with a full complement of early sketches, and presentation, conceptual, and working drawings. Many drawings were possibly loaned to clients and were not returned to the architect. Hunt's sons probably disposed of some materials prior to the gift to the AIA. It should be noted, too, that virtually all of the office correspondence has been lost, and thus was not available for research.[5] Catharine Clinton Howland Hunt's unpublished biography of her husband proved helpful in describing Hunt's involvement in particular projects. Each of the invited essayists made full use of the resources of the collection; their new interpretations are based chiefly on these drawings and photographs.

In chapter 2, Richard Chafee examines the earliest aspects of Hunt's career: his student days at the Ecole des Beaux-Arts. His close analysis of the surviving *programmes, esquisses,* and various *projets* is the most finely developed study to date of the Ecole's overall method as it was practiced in the 1840s and 1850s. Remarkably, Chafee has pieced together every *concours* in which Hunt participated and has established the foundation upon which Hunt's future endeavors were based. The chronological record of Hunt's activities reveals, as do his sketchbooks, that he traveled a great deal throughout his years at the Ecole. Professor Chafee compares Hunt's performance with that of his peers and establishes that his record, like most of his fellow students, was inconsistent. Hunt's *concours* submissions often failed. When they were accepted, however, they frequently were judged in the upper third of those accepted. Hunt must have been quite good to have won the respect of his master, Hector Martin Lefuel, who hired him to assist on the new wing of the Louvre, the Pavillon de la Bibliothèque.

What Hunt learned in France and how he put what he learned to use is the underlying theme of this book. Sarah Bradford Landau acknowledges Hunt's debt to his French training in chapter 3, and goes further to argue that he was, in fact, quite an original architect. This originality was often overlooked, as Hunt was frequently compared to Henry Hobson Richardson, who was credited with creating a new style, the Richardsonian Romanesque. Nevertheless, Hunt made a series of imaginative contributions to American design that merit his recognition as the "father of a distinctive American School." These contributions included the antecedent of the New York apartment house; a new direction in domestic architecture that fused European and American forms; commercial buildings that presaged those of Sullivan and the Chicago School in their use of tiers of arcades and the triple-window bay; and the design of one of the first skyscrapers, the New York Tribune Building.

The influence of French architecture and the Ecole des Beaux-Arts is discussed in chapters 4 and 5, on the Central Park Gateways and the Lenox Library, written by Francis R. Kowsky and David Van Zanten. In a span of fewer than ten years, prevailing attitudes toward Beaux-Arts classicism changed markedly. In 1863, Hunt was invited to design the southern gateways for Vaux and Olmsted's Central Park. His classical designs were ultimately rejected: they were considered un-American and not at all in keeping with Central Park's rustic character. A short time later, in 1870, Hunt was approached to design what was perhaps his greatest achievement, the Lenox Library, a building that Professor Van Zanten calls "a profoundly French Beaux-Arts design." Unlike the proposed Central Park gateways, the Lenox Library was well received and later was regarded as particularly important in promoting the Beaux-Arts style in America.

Hunt worked in yet another way to advance classicism: by collaborating with sculptors in the design of civic monuments to beautify American cities. Working chiefly with John Quincy Adams Ward through the 1880s, Hunt's monuments prefigured the City Beautiful movement. Hunt's involvement with sculpture, however, was not restricted to monuments. Wherever possible, he incorporated sculpture into the program of his buildings. With Karl Bitter in the 1890s, Hunt established "one of the most prolific collaborative relationships in the Beaux-Arts movement," as Lewis I. Sharp notes in chapter 7.

A group of large houses and estates completed near the end of Hunt's career overshadowed many of Hunt's earlier achievements. The opulent city houses and country estates such as Biltmore in Asheville, North Carolina, and the Breakers in Newport, Rhode Island, epitomized not only the Vanderbilts and the 1890s but Hunt's later reputation as well. I discuss the particular role that Hunt played in these later houses and in the design process throughout his career in chapter 6. It is argued that Hunt played a less influential role in the design of these later houses than his reputation suggests. The design of the great houses themselves (Biltmore, the Breakers, Marble House, Indian Spring, and the city houses for the Astors, Gerrys, and Vanderbilts) is investigated by David Chase in chapter 8.

A fitting conclusion to this collection of essays on the architecture of Richard Morris Hunt is an examination of his last commission, the Metropolitan Museum of Art, which serves as Hunt's monument. The Museum building asserts the dominance of the Beaux-Arts classicism that Hunt so vigorously encouraged. In chapter 9, Morrison H. Heckscher describes Hunt's long association with the Museum as trustee and finally as the architect who provided, as Heckscher writes, "a grand ceremonial entrance to a vast museum complex."[6] The battle for French classicism had been won.

Susan R. Stein

Notes

1. Glenn Brown to Richard Howland Hunt, 25 January 1899, Record Group 801, American Institute of Architects Archives, Washington, D.C.

2. George E. Pettengill, AIA Librarian from 1952 to 1977, saw that the drawings were protected. In 1978, the Hunt collection was transferred to the American Institute of Architects Foundation and an inventory was conducted. Grants from the National Endowment for the Arts, the Institute of Museum Services, the National Historical Publications and Records Commission, the AIA College of Fellows Fund, and the Egg and Dart Society made the subsequent cataloging and conservation of the collection possible.

3. Paul R. Baker, *Richard Morris Hunt*, (Cambridge, Mass.: MIT Press, 1980).

4. Richard Morris Hunt Eulogy by Henry Van Brunt, *Proceedings of the Twenty-ninth Annual Convention of the American Institute of Architects* (Providence: E. A. Johnson & Co., 1895), p. 77.

5. The written office records were probably discarded by Richard Howland Hunt and Joseph Howland Hunt when they dispersed the architectural collection to the AIA and family items to their relatives.

6. Chapter 9, p. 185.

Plates

PLATE I: A bandstand, the drawing
for the *concours sur esquisses* of 7
March 1849 (see fig. 2.14, p. 29).

PLATE 2: An iron bridge, elevation
for the *concours* in iron construction, 5 July to late October 1847,
première mention (see fig. 2.5, p. 20).

PLATE 3: Thomas P. Rossiter
House, 11 West Thirty-eighth
Street, New York City, 1855
(see fig. 6.8, p. 111).

PLATE 4: Sketch of a Swiss chalet
for Mrs. Mason Jones, Newport,
R.I., 1866.

PLATE 5: Sketch of the Thomas G.
Appleton house, Catherine Street,
Newport, R.I., 1870 (see fig. 6.14,
p. 114).

PLATE 6: Study for the Hitchcock-
Travers house, Narragansett and
Ochre Point avenues, Newport,
R.I., 1869.

PLATE 7: Paran Stevens town-
house, Thirty-sixth Street between
Fifth and Madison avenues, New
York City, 1870–71.

PLATE 8: Elevation of the Lenox
Library, watercolor and pencil on
paper, 1871 (see fig. 6.20, p. 117).

PLATE 9: New York Tribune Building, northeast corner of Nassau and Spruce streets, New York City, 1873–75 (see fig. 3.31, p. 56, and fig. 6.18, p. 115).

PLATE 10: Elevation proposed for
the Union League Club, New York
City, watercolor, pencil, and ink
on paper, 1879 (see fig. 6.19, p.
116).

PLATE 11: Perspective elevation of
the Yorktown Monument, watercolor and pencil on paper, ca. 1880
(see fig. 6.21, p. 117).

PLATE 12: Banquet hall mantle-piece, William K. Vanderbilt house, 660 Fifth Avenue, New York City, 1878–82.

PLATE 13: Elevation of the William
Borden house, Lake Shore Drive at
Bellevue Place, Chicago, 1884.

PLATE 14: Mrs. William Astor and
John Jacob Astor IV house, 840
Fifth Avenue, New York City,
1891–95.

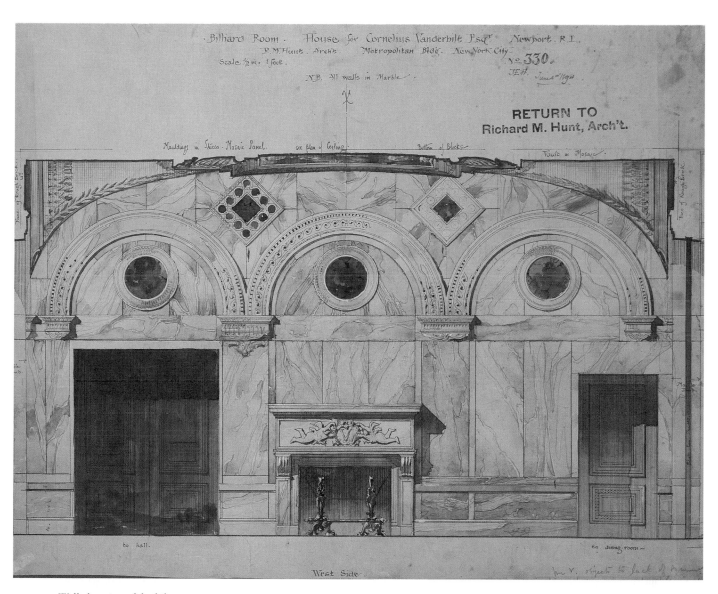

Billiard Room. House for Cornelius Vanderbilt Esq. Newport. R.I.

R.M.Hunt. Arch'ts. Metropolitan Bldg. New York City.

Scale ½ in. 1 foot.

N⁰ 330.

J.E.H. June 4ᵗʰ 1894

N.B. All walls in Marble.

RETURN TO
Richard M. Hunt, Arch't.

Mouldings in Stucco. Mosaic Panel.   see plan of Ceiling   Bottom of Blocks   Vault in Mosaic.

to hall.   to sitting room.

West Side.

PLATE 15: Wall elevation of the billiard room of the Breakers showing mosaic and marble detail, 4 June 1894 (see fig. 8.26, p. 163).

PLATE 16: Elevation of the Administration Building of the World's
Columbian Exposition, Chicago,
1892.

The Architecture of
Richard Morris Hunt

New York. D. Appleton & Co.

I

Richard Morris Hunt: An Introduction

Paul R. Baker

TO HIS CONTEMPORARIES, Richard Morris Hunt was popularly known as the "dean of American architecture," and recognition of his position as a pathbreaker and leader of a flourishing new profession permeates journal articles, public speeches, and private correspondence of the late nineteenth century. The critic Mariana Griswold Van Rensselaer believed that "it would be difficult to overestimate the good influence Mr. Richard Hunt has had both upon the profession itself and upon its status with the public." Hunt, she suggested, was especially able "to lay hold of the stolid, indifferent, obdurate, or timid client, and lead him whither he would have him go." For Stanford White, it was "to a certain extent from [Hunt] and through him that the real modern artistic advance in architecture in New York and America can be traced." And his partner, Charles F. McKim, asserted bluntly: "Mr. Hunt was the pioneer and icebreaker who paved the way for recognition of the profession by the public."[1]

Hunt was awarded countless professional honors and indeed was one of the most highly acclaimed of all nineteenth-century Americans. The esteem in which his colleagues held him was evidenced by his election to the presidency of the American Institute of Architects in 1887 and his reelection to that office in the reorganized Institute two years later. Hunt had been a founding member and the first secretary of the Institute, and over the years he had worked tirelessly to strengthen this national professional society. Election to many international societies, award of the first honorary doctoral degree to an architect from Harvard University, and the first award to an American of the Royal Institute of British Architects' gold medal in 1893 affirmed his position toward the end of the nineteenth century as the leading American architect. Time and again Hunt served as a spokesman for his profession.

In addition to the professional recognition he enjoyed, Hunt was widely held in warm personal regard. He was, one commentator wrote, "perhaps the most beloved by the greatest number of his own profession."[2] He was admired for his vigor, enthusiasm, and wit, and for his judiciousness, intelligence, and scholarly knowledge. His manner was vivacious and affable; he expressed himself forcefully and was noted for his picturesque, expletive-filled language. Hunt was admired by some, as well, for his high social position; his family was respected, he had excellent social connections, and his fortune was sufficient to support a very comfortable way of life. Moreover, he had firm ideas about good taste in architectural matters and had the ability to communicate his ideas readily to others. He had a reputation for always dealing candidly with colleagues and clients.

Hunt was born in Brattleboro, Vermont, on 31 October 1827. His family had long been distinguished for public service and leadership in business. Shortly before Richard's birth, his father, Jonathan Hunt, a prosperous lawyer and landowner, had been elected to Congress and served in the House of Representatives until his sudden death from cholera in 1832. The congressman's young widow, who was well provided for, subsequently devoted herself to the care and education of her five children, one of whom was William Morris Hunt, who became a noted painter. After living several years in New Haven, the family moved to Boston to be near William, who was preparing for Harvard College. When as a Harvard student William later became chronically ill, Mrs. Hunt decided to take the entire family to Europe for a few months in the hope of bettering his health. In October 1843, they sailed for France. What was planned as a brief trip, however, turned out to be a stay of twelve years, interrupted for Richard by a single short visit back to the United States in 1848.

Italy especially delighted the Hunt family, but it was Paris that became their home, and there, on his second attempt in December 1846, Richard successfully passed the admissions examinations to the Ecole des Beaux-Arts. He was the first American to study there. He entered the atelier of the noted architect Hector Martin Lefuel, and his work in the atelier, at the Ecole, and later with Lefuel on the Pavillon de la Bibliothèque of the Louvre gave him a wide-ranging architectural training such as no other American of his time had received. During these years of study in Paris, Richard also kept up a full social life, collected antiques and architectural books, and traveled extensively throughout England, Ireland, the Continent, and the Middle East. Despite his cosmopolitan experiences, however, Richard always remained very much an American at heart, devoted to his own country. When he returned to the United States in September 1855, he was not only well prepared for his profession, but also highly committed to creating well-designed buildings for his rapidly developing homeland.

Hunt believed that the best opportunities for a professionally trained architect were to be found in New York City, and he soon established himself in a studio in the old Gothic Revival building of New York University, on the east side of Washington Square. There in the University Building he gathered together his "spoils of foreign travel," the many antiquities and books he had collected in Europe, and there he also began to provide architectural instruction to a few pupils, modeling his teaching on the system of the Ecole. His first New York design was for a townhouse with studio space for the painter Thomas P. Rossiter, whom he had known in Paris. Commissioned by Rossiter's father-in-law, a dentist named Parmly, Hunt's design and his work on the house became a subject of dispute over fees. The subsequent court case was important in helping to establish fixed charges for work done by professional architects. While engaged on the Rossiter house, Hunt was also briefly employed by Thomas U. Walter in the enlargement of the Capitol in Washington, D.C.

Far more significant was Hunt's first major project, the Studio Building on West Tenth Street, New York City. This was the earliest structure in the United States designed specifically to provide studios and gallery exhibit space for artists. Upon completion in the spring of 1858, it almost immediately became the center of New York artistic life. Painters and sculptors opened their workrooms regularly to guests and occasionally to the public at large in general receptions. Such well-known painters as Frederic Church, Winslow Homer, John La Farge, and William Merritt Chase maintained studios in the building, and Hunt himself for some years kept a studio that served simultaneously as his working office, his home, and his classroom. His atelier instruction expanded, his pupils now including Henry Van Brunt, Charles Gambrill, Frank Furness, William R. Ware, and George B. Post, all of whom later became prominent architects. Ware later organized professional schools at the Massachusetts Institute of Technology and at Columbia University and became the most influential figure in nineteenth-century American architectural education; Ware often acknowledged the formative influence of Hunt's atelier instruction.

By the early 1860s, Hunt was well established in New York. He became widely known in artistic circles for his Tenth Street studios, was active in the recently founded (1857) American Institute of Architects, was outspoken in support of the Republican Party, and was prominent in the social life of the city. Commissions in Newport brought him regularly to that seaside resort, to which his brother William had already moved, and there Richard became acquainted with and courted young Catharine Clinton Howland, who came from a wealthy and socially respected New York shipping family. Richard and Catharine were married in New York early in April 1861 and shortly after their wedding they sailed to Europe, where they remained for a year and a half. The first of their five children, Richard Howland Hunt, was born while they were living in Paris. As during his earlier stay in Europe, Hunt traveled extensively, visiting architectural sites and doing considerable sketching and painting. Following their return in November 1862, the Hunts moved into a house on West Thirty-fifth Street, which was to be their home for a quarter of a century. Their residence was said to be "one of the early strongholds of taste and culture" in New York.[3] Hunt also purchased a house, known as Hill Top Cottage, on Bellevue Avenue in Newport, not far from the highly influential J. N. A. Griswold house, an early stick-style residence, that Hunt had been commissioned to design when he was still in Paris.

Back in New York, Hunt was deeply involved in designs for and controversy surrounding the southern gateways for Central Park. Hunt conceived the gateways as transitional from the city streets to the park, which he envisioned as a recreational pleasure garden, to be filled eventually with architectural additions of all sorts. Planned in a French manner with formal gates, elaborated piers and pedestals, and considerable statuary, the Central Park gateway designs, however, were roundly attacked by critics as inappropriate to American conditions and alien to the rural character of the park that Frederick Law Olmsted and Calvert Vaux, its creators, had intended. Hunt's gateways were never constructed, but the controversy helped establish his reputation as one committed to civic beautification.

Hunt again visited Europe in 1867, having been invited to serve as an American commissioner and juror for the Paris Exposition of that spring and summer. Richard had many duties in connection with the exposition, but he and his wife also enjoyed the lavish entertainments provided for foreign representatives in Paris, including an imperial ball honoring the czar of Russia. Departing from Paris, the Hunts and their young son made an extensive tour of Scandinavia and Russia, but a threat to kidnap their son forced them to leave Moscow abruptly.

Following his return to New York, Hunt saw his career gather momentum, and by the close of the 1860s he was occupied with a large number of major projects, which varied widely in type of building and stylistic approach. The architect's domestic buildings of the late 1860s and the early and mid 1870s encompassed summer cottages at Newport and townhouses in Chicago, Boston, and New York. The Travers Block of shops in Newport, which had bachelor apartments above, dates from this period. In Chicago, on Prairie Avenue, the Marshall Field mansion, with its fairly conventional mansard-style street facade, was Hunt's largest residence up to this time. In Boston, the two Martin Brimmer houses on Beacon Street were widely admired. Hunt's New York houses provided elegant touches to city streets that were dominated by drab and uniform brownstone fronts.

Hunt's several public commissions from this period posed important challenges. In New York, he designed for James Lenox the Presbyterian Hospital, including an administration building, a substantial ward building, and a heating plant, as well as the neighboring Lenox Library, one of Hunt's most important structures, an elegantly monumental building with *néo-grec* ornamentation, which fronted on Fifth Avenue at Seventieth Street, across from Central Park. In New Haven, East Divinity Hall, the Marquand Chapel, and the Scroll and Key Society clubhouse were prominent additions to the Yale College campus. Academic buildings at the Hampton Institute in Virginia and a handsome library and a church in Matteawan, New York, provided other tests of the architect's ability to adapt his ideas to special needs.

His New York commercial structures, however, brought him the greatest notice in these years. The Stuyvesant Apartments on East Eighteenth Street constituted the first New York building to embody "French flats" or multifamily housing for "respectable" people of means. The five-story building, completed in 1870, was an immediate success, and apartment living quickly caught on and soon transformed city life. Hunt also designed the Stevens House on Twenty-seventh Street for multifamily living. Two strikingly original iron-front stores on lower Broadway were outstanding examples of a type of construction that dominated commercial development in New York in the 1870s. Among Hunt's other commercial structures, the most notable was the Tribune Building, erected on Newspaper Row facing City Hall Park and completed in 1876. For some years this was the tallest edifice in New York and it thus plays an important role in the historical development of the skyscraper.

The architect's intense commitment to his many commissions brought on a deterioration of his health, and for some months in 1873 he was almost completely incapacitated. In early 1874 his doctors ordered him to take a long rest. Thus in 1874–75, Hunt and his family once again visited Europe, where he found both a respite from professional chores and much-needed aesthetic nourishment, though he continued to offer advice about the ongoing Lenox Library and Tribune Tower projects. Following his return to America, Hunt was involved for a time as a juror for the architectural exhibits at the Philadelphia Centennial Exhibition, while his own work moved in some new directions.

Toward the end of the 1870s, Hunt commenced the first of many projects for the Vanderbilt family; indeed, he undertook so many substantial commissions for this family that critics sometimes dubbed him "the Vanderbilt architect." William K. Vanderbilt, a grandson of the Commodore, first commissioned Hunt to design a large and rambling Queen Anne–style country residence at Oakdale, Long Island, followed by the Scandinavian timberwork-style Saint Mark's Church at Islip, Long Island. Far more important, however, was a chateau-like mansion for William and his wife Alva on Fifth Avenue at Fifty-second Street, created in a late French Gothic–early Renaissance mode. For several years this house was the most widely admired residence in New York City and, probably to a greater extent than any other American dwelling of the Gilded Age, set a goal for Americans of wealth and fashion to emulate. The mansion was opened to guests in March 1883, with a great housewarming costume ball, one of the most lavish parties of the time and an affair that established the preeminence of the Vanderbilts in New York society. Hunt also designed a large mausoleum on Staten Island for the Vanderbilt family, as well as a small, Flemish-style library on West Thirteenth Street for George W. Vanderbilt, William's brother. A chateau-style mansion for William Borden in Chicago echoed the design of the Fifty-Second Street residence.

As a leading architect, Hunt was increasingly invited to design public monuments as well as private memorials. In an age that accepted the importance of statuary monuments for civic embellishment and moral inspiration, Hunt's designs were among the most significant for Americans, and in a few major works he created emblems of shared nationality that helped heal the bitter divisions of the Civil War and Reconstruction. Many of his monuments were joint endeavors with the sculptor John Quincy Adams Ward, who usually worked in a naturalistic vein. Two early collaborations were on a statue of Commodore Matthew Calbraith Perry, the naval hero noted for opening the ports of Japan to the Western world, erected in 1868 in Touro Park, Newport, and the large Seventh Regiment Monument, raised in New York's Central Park in 1873, in honor of the state national guardsmen who gave their lives in the Civil War. Hunt's first commission from the United States government and another collaboration with Ward was the imposing Yorktown Monument in Virginia, commemorating the 1781 victory of General Washington over Lord Cornwallis. Hunt was especially proud of the 150-foot columnar monument, which was unveiled in October 1884, although he realized it received less notice than many of his other works. Two other New York City statues by Ward and Hunt were completed in the mid-1880s: the prominently placed, larger-than-life figure of Washington in front of the old Subtreasury Building (Federal Hall) on Wall Street and the severely restrained Pilgrim Statue in Central Park. The dignified Garfield Monument, located near the west front of the Capitol in Washington, D.C., was completed in 1887 by the two artists, whose joint work also included portrait statues of Horace Greeley and Henry Ward Beecher. Another substantial Hunt-Ward collaboration was the large Belmont tomb complex located in Island Cemetery, Newport.

The most important of Hunt's monumental work, however, was the base and pedestal for the Statue of Liberty. Frédéric-Auguste Bartholdi's conception of a huge statue of the goddess of Liberty, to be a gift from the people of France to the people of the United States, took many years for its realization; however, by 1876, the right arm and torch were already completed and sent for exhibit at the Philadelphia Centennial Exposition and subsequently in Madison Square. After a site on Bedloes Island in New York Harbor was selected, Hunt, as architect-in-chief for the project, developed his conception of a base to be set within the star-shaped walls of Fort Wood on the small island. The pedestal, as ultimately realized, provided a dignified and harmonious setting for the huge statue. The Statue of Liberty was dedicated on 28 October 1886.

Shortly after his plans for the Liberty project had been completed in 1885,

Hunt, his wife, and their younger children once more sailed for Europe, where the architect remained for a full year. Hunt's life thus fell into a regular pattern of intense periods of work followed by extended sojourns in Europe, which seemed to provide him with aesthetic sustenance and spiritual renewal. As before, Paris was the family's European home: there they were near the eldest son, Richard Howland Hunt, who was now attending the Ecole des Beaux-Arts and preparing to follow in his father's footsteps. And in Paris Hunt participated in activities of the Institut de France, of which he had been elected a corresponding member. Upon their return from abroad, the Hunts made their New York home on Washington Square North, close to Catharine's childhood home and near the University Building, which had been the architect's first New York residence. Another journey in 1889 to collect furnishings and art objects for George Vanderbilt's mansion, then being planned in Asheville, North Carolina, brought Hunt and his wife back to Europe for a brief two months. In 1893 they made a final trip to Europe, when Hunt was awarded the Royal Institute of British Architects' gold medal.

From 1888 through 1891, as president of the American Institute of Architects, Hunt actively promoted the interests of his profession. His public speeches embodied his view of the importance for present-day architects of serious study of the great work of the past. Although contemporary architects faced different and often unique problems in building design, Hunt believed that inspiration and guidance could best come from the achievements of the past. And for Hunt, architectural work of the highest quality had always to embody harmony, dignity, and repose.

From the mid 1880s, Hunt became increasingly involved in commissions for very large houses. These great residences were among his most noteworthy work and contributed importantly to his subsequent historical reputation. By this time, Hunt was well known as the most fashionable architect in the country, and no doubt some clients sought his services to reinforce their claims for social position and acceptance. Of the many types of building he designed, Hunt seemed to find large private houses especially congenial. Several of the great Hunt houses were erected in New York, on or near Fifth Avenue, the earliest of them the Henry G. Marquand and Ogden Mills mansions, executed in the 1880s, and mansions for William V. Lawrence, Elbridge Gerry, and Mrs. William Astor, built in the early 1890s. Among these dwellings, the most distinguished were the Gerry mansion on Fifth Avenue at Sixty-first Street, decorated with motifs from the early French Renaissance, a house that the architectural critic Montgomery Schuyler called "so distinctly an ornament to the city [as to be] one of the public possessions," and four blocks to the north on Fifth Avenue, the double residence for Mrs. William Astor and her son John Jacob Astor IV, based on later French Renaissance sources, a structure more formalized and regular than the Gerry house.[4] Both of these important houses were razed little more than thirty years after their erection.

Newport, Hunt's summer residence, however, was the place where his creative hand in very large houses was most evident. A quiet summer retreat for New England merchants and intellectuals before the Civil War, Newport, by the 1880s, had burgeoned into the ultrafashionable resort of the New York superrich, who demanded ever grander "cottages" for their brief summer visits. Hunt's early remodeling of Château-sur-Mer, for some years the largest house in Newport, helped to establish his credentials for great domestic projects in the resort town. The large Busk house was perhaps Hunt's most "organic" house, built of rubble-coursed masonry and rooted to its rocky site overlooking the ocean. Ochre Court, a sumptuous mansion for Ogden Goelet, a New York real estate developer, was created in a free adaptation of late French Gothic and early Renaissance elements; but this very large house, like Hunt's other New-port mansions, was squeezed onto disproportionately small grounds. Marble House, for Alva Vanderbilt, designed in a highly formal, neoclassical manner, included the most lavish interiors of any of Hunt's buildings and has long been a showplace of Newport. Belcourt Castle, erected for Oliver H. P. Belmont, who later married Alva Vanderbilt, was created, in effect, as a magnificent stable and carriage house with living quarters attached. The exterior includes a mixture of English, Italian, and French elements. The Breakers, the largest of these Newport "cottages," was for yet another Vanderbilt, Cornelius Vander-bilt II. This great house, which has more than seventy rooms, was modeled upon sixteenth-century Genoese *palazzi*. Like others of Hunt's houses, the Breakers is today a prominent tourist attraction.

Yet another mansion, Biltmore House, in Asheville, North Carolina, which Hunt erected for George W. Vanderbilt, was the architect's most spectacular domestic commission. Set in some 125,000 acres of grounds landscaped by Frederick Law Olmsted, Biltmore House, with some 255 rooms, is the largest private house in the United States. Originally conceived as a country seat for winter and spring occupancy, Biltmore estate developed into the earliest signifi-cant center for scientific forest management and education in the country. The several large public rooms of Biltmore House were decorated in diverse styles, which was typical of Hunt's great houses. The grandest room of the mansion, the huge banquet hall, dominated at one end by a massive triple fireplace, rises to a height of seventy-five feet. Like the other great Hunt houses, Biltmore House was created to provide a suitable setting for the ostentatious personal display so characteristic of fashionable American society of the Gilded Age and after. These great mansions have often been excoriated by social critics as an appalling and tasteless extravagance, especially when viewed in light of the all-too-evident and widespread poverty in slums and ghettos. Yet these great houses embodied architectural elements from the European past that provided aesthetic pleasure for Hunt and others, and Hunt hoped that they might become in effect public possessions and influence the general refinement of American taste.

For the World's Columbian Exposition in Chicago in 1893, Richard Hunt was invited, along with other prominent architectural firms, to design one of the principal buildings around the Court of Honor, the primary architectural assemblage of the fair. Hunt was chosen chairman of the Board of Architects and was assigned the Administration Building. The high, gleaming gold and white dome of the Administration Building, visible from all over the fair-grounds, served as a symbol of the "White City" Exposition; Hunt's building brought him widespread notice and popular acclaim.

As the preeminent American architect by the 1890s, Hunt was invited to design a variety of major buildings. He contributed a large academic building, a gymnasium, and a small guardhouse for the United States Military Academy at West Point and a group of diverse structures for the United States Naval Obser-vatory in Washington, D.C. The Fogg Art Museum at Harvard University and a classroom building at what became Case Western Reserve were added to his extensive collegiate work, among which the earlier Seminary Library and

Marquand Chapel at Princeton were especially important. Designs for decorative doors for Trinity Church, New York, were master achievements of a different character. Finally, shortly before his death, Hunt created the entrance wing of New York's Metropolitan Museum of Art, which was built by his son Richard Howland Hunt. The Hunt entrance wing established the character for later additions to the museum, and it serves ultimately as a splendid monument to his artistic genius. Hunt died at Hill Top Cottage in Newport on 31 July 1895.

In the forty years of his architectural practice, Richard Morris Hunt created a body of work remarkable both for its wide variety of building types and its use of several styles. Many of his buildings are today national treasures. He served his profession well in the American Institute of Architects and as a public spokesman. As an individual he was almost universally admired, and these personal qualities helped lend status to the profession. Indeed, Hunt was the most influential figure in the development of architectural professionalism in the United States in the nineteenth century. As a teacher, he had a strong influence on others, and through his pupil William R. Ware he significantly influenced the character of late nineteenth- and early twentieth-century architectural education.

After Hunt's death, several New York art associations joined together to erect a Hunt Memorial. A site was chosen opposite the Lenox Library on Fifth Avenue between Seventieth and Seventy-first Streets at the edge of Central Park. The architect Bruce Price and the sculptor Daniel Chester French collaborated on the Memorial, a semielliptical seat at the base of an Ionic colonnade of polished, detached columns, surmounted by an ornamental entablature. A central pedestal holds a larger-than-life bust of the architect, and at each end stands a bronze allegorical figure. The Hunt Memorial was dedicated on 31 October 1898, and remains today an elegant civic testimony to a man who did so much to enrich the city and the nation.

Notes

1. Mariana Griswold Van Rensselaer, "Recent Architecture in America: Country Dwellings," *Century Magazine* 32 (May 1886): 15; Stanford White to Mrs. Harrison, 19 March 1896, Press Book 15:337, White Collection, Avery Library, Columbia University; Charles F. McKim to Lawrence Grant White, 21 April 1909, McKim Papers, Library of Congress. For a full biographical study of Hunt, see Paul R. Baker, *Richard Morris Hunt* (Cambridge, Mass.: MIT Press, 1980).
2. Alfred Stone, "The Early History of the American Institute of Architects," *Proceedings of the Fortieth Annual Convention of the American Institute of Architects* (Washington, D.C., 1907), p. 175.
3. M. E. W. Sherwood, "New York in the Seventies," *Lippincott's Monthly Magazine* 42 (Sept. 1898): 393–94.
4. Montgomery Schuyler, "The Works of the Late Richard M. Hunt," *Architectural Record* 5 (Oct.–Dec. 1895): 131.

References

Baker, Paul R. *Richard Morris Hunt*. Cambridge, Mass.: MIT Press, 1980.

———. "Richard Morris Hunt." *Macmillan Encyclopedia of Architects* (New York: The Free Press, 1982), 2:436–44.

Burnham, Alan. "The New York Architecture of Richard Morris Hunt." *Journal of the Society of Architectural Historians* 11 (May 1952): 9–14.

De Kay, Ormonde, Jr. "Richard Morris Hunt." In *Three Centuries of Notable American Architects*, edited by Joseph J. Thorndike, Jr., pp. 88–109. New York: American Heritage Publishing Co., 1981.

Ferree, Barr. "Richard Morris Hunt: His Art and Work." *Architecture and Building* 23 (2 Dec. 1895):271–75.

Ganelin, Susan Stein. "The Drawings of Richard Morris Hunt." *American Preservation* 2 (April–May 1979):18–25.

Jordy, William H., and Christopher P. Monkhouse. *Buildings on Paper: Rhode Island Architectural Drawings, 1825–1945*. Providence, R.I.: Brown University, 1982.

Landau, Sarah Bradford. "Richard Morris Hunt, the Continental Picturesque, and the 'Stick Style.'" *Journal of the Society of Architectural Historians* 42 (1983):272–89.

Paris, William Francklyn. "Richard Morris Hunt: First Secretary and Third President of the Institute." *Journal of the American Institute of Architects* 24 (Dec. 1955):243–49; 25 (Jan. 1956):14–19; 26 (Feb. 1956):74–80.

Schuyler, Montgomery. "The Works of the Late Richard M. Hunt." *Architectural Record* 5 (Oct.–Dec. 1895):97–180.

Van Brunt, Henry. "Richard Morris Hunt:A Memorial Address." *American Architect and Building News* 50 (2 Nov. 1895):53–56.

Van Pelt, John Vredenburgh. *A Monograph of the William K. Vanderbilt House, Richard Morris Hunt, Architect*. New York: John V. Van Pelt, 1925.

Wallis, Frank E. "Richard M. Hunt, Master Architect and Man." *Architectural Review* 5 (1917):239–40.

2

Hunt in Paris

Richard Chafee

RICHARD MORRIS HUNT was the first American to study architecture at the Ecole des Beaux-Arts in Paris. Many of the drawings he did as a student are extant, and a chronology of his activity at the Ecole can be made.[1] That he trained in Paris is one of the reasons why hundreds of his younger countrymen went to that city to learn architecture. How Hunt himself happened to get there is a curious story.[2]

After the death in Washington in May 1832 of Hunt's father, Congressman Jonathan Hunt, Mrs. Hunt devoted her energies to the education of her five children, of whom Richard (born in 1827) was the second youngest. She did not return with them to Brattleboro, Vermont; instead, that fall she took the family to New Haven, Connecticut. There, in the summer of 1837, Mrs. Hunt was introduced to an Italian political refugee named Spiridione Gambardella, who was a painter. To help him earn a living, she had him teach art to her eldest child, William (born in 1824), to her daughter, and to herself. Gambardella left New Haven after a few months, not knowing that he had sounded William Morris Hunt's calling.

In 1838 Mrs. Hunt moved with her children to Boston, in the hope that William would enter Harvard College. He did so in the fall of 1840, but, as his sister-in-law Catharine was later to write, "his heart was not in classical studies."[3] That autumn Richard entered the Boston English High school.[4] After his freshman year at Harvard, William was "rusticated," in the words of the college, but a year later he was readmitted. The next summer (1843) he caught cold and developed a cough so persistent that physicians in Boston advised Mrs. Hunt to take him to a warmer climate, such as Italy's. In the spring, John, the second son, had completed his sophomore year at Harvard, and Richard had graduated from his school, first in a class of twenty-two.[5] Mrs. Hunt would not let the Atlantic divide her family, and thus early in the fall of 1843 she and her five children sailed on the *Duchesse d'Orléans* from New York to Le Havre. She planned to have the family return to Boston a year later. In fact, twelve years were to pass before Richard Morris Hunt would again reside in America; and thereafter through his buildings, his teaching, and his leadership of the profession, he changed American architecture. Such were the results of William's cough.

From Le Havre the Hunts traveled to Paris, where for several months they saw the sights, and where Richard and his brother Leavitt (who was slightly more than two years younger, the baby of the family) were temporarily put in a boarding school. Richard learned French quickly. Late in February 1844, they all departed for Rome. William's health, which had begun to improve while they were crossing the Atlantic, continued to get better and ceased to be a worry. The six Hunts toured Italy for three months, going south as far as Naples and north again, at a leisurely pace, through all the famous cities, and on to Geneva. The Swiss city was known as a center of education, and by the end of May Richard and Leavitt were enrolled at Alphonse Briquet's boarding school for boys. The student body included French, English, and a score of American pupils.

Dick Hunt, as he was called, had expected to prepare for West Point and a career in the army. But at Monsieur Briquet's, during his seventeenth and eighteenth years, he discovered another interest. He began taking lessons from an architect in Geneva named Samuel Darier. Hunt saved some of the drawings he made under Darier. What seems to have been the earliest is a copy of J. G. Heck's map of the United States and the Missouri Territory; what may have been Hunt's first architectural drawing is a comparison of various columns (see fig. 6.2).

By May 1845, Hunt's plans were changing. In a letter to his mother dated 5 May, he wrote that he had decided that if he was not admitted to the military or naval academy, he would study architecture. "Getting a good ground work" in Geneva, he would afterwards "endeavor to take a degree at the 'Ecole Centrale' at Paris, or some other *first rate* academy in Europe." Then he would "return to America where an architect of the *first* quality would be much sought for."[6]

Hunt's immediate goal at the time appears to have been practical. The Ecole Centrale des Arts et Manufactures, which was (and continues to be) a school of engineering, had been privately established in 1829 to train engineers, mainly for private industry. During the French Revolution a school of engineering had been founded—it was called the Ecole Centrale des Travaux Publics—but after only two years, in 1795, its curriculum was made more abstract and it was renamed the Ecole Polytechnique. The founders of the Ecole Centrale des Arts et Manufactures believed that the education at the Ecole Polytechnique was too far removed from practical requirements and that their new school would fill a gap that had existed since 1795. At the Ecole Centrale des Arts et Manufactures, the course in civil engineering was sometimes referred to as construction or as architecture. The focus of the course was on utilitarian structures such as railroad stations, hospitals, bridges, and canals; the long-time professor was Louis-Charles Mary (1791–1870), who had been a pupil of J.-N.-L. Durand at the Ecole Polytechnique. The Ecole Centrale did not teach architecture as a fine art; that was the concern of the Ecole des Beaux-Arts.[7]

Hunt was not to go to the Ecole Centrale but rather to the Ecole des Beaux-Arts. It would seem that he was directed to the latter by his teacher, Samuel Darier, who had been a student there. (Darier's drawings for the *construction générale* requirement, in which he got a *troisième médaille*, were kept by the Ecole; they show him to have been able, if not extraordinary.) On 1 August 1845 Hunt left Geneva for Paris, and after getting settled he sought admission to the school. On 4 September the chargé d'affaires of the United States in Paris wrote, signed, and sealed a note at the request of "Monsieur Richard Morris Hunt" to certify that the "natif de l'Etat de Vermont" was a citizen of the United States. Hunt forwarded the note to the Ecole. (Each foreign applicant customarily presented such a letter from the representative of his nation—the United States did not yet have an ambassador in France—whereas each

French citizen presented a birth certificate.) On 12 September the architect Hector-Martin Lefuel stated in a form provided by the school that "le sieur Richard Morris Hunt . . . Etudiant en Architecture . . . est en état de se présenter aux examens d'admission." The form recorded that Hunt was in the atelier Lefuel.

A few words about the relationship between the ateliers and the Ecole are appropriate here. Each applicant to the school chose his own master or *patron*; and in Hunt's time every master's studio for teaching, or atelier, was outside the school. Each pupil had his drawing board in the atelier; there he acquired his education in the discipline, guided by more advanced colleagues and by the *patron* himself. The Ecole itself offered lectures, a library, and casts of sculpture and ornament for study. More important, it was at the Ecole that programs were issued and the results judged and graded. All graded schoolwork was organized as competitions or *concours d'émulation*. Judgment was rendered by the professors of the *section d'architecture* (that is to say, the four architects who lectured at the Ecole), assisted by the *commission*, a body of twenty distinguished architects elected for life terms by the professors of the whole school.[8] In reality, however, nearly all the judgments were handed down by the professors and a few members of the *commission* at most. A student could advance through the school only through success in the *concours*, and to do so he needed the teaching he got in his atelier.

Why, one might ask, did Hunt choose the atelier Lefuel? It was new and small; Lefuel, winner of the Grand Prix de Rome in 1839, was just back from his years at the French Academy in that city. The best-known ateliers in 1845 were those that had recently produced winners of the Grand Prix: students of L.-H. Lebas had carried it off in 1840, 1841, 1843, and 1845; a pupil of G.-A. Blouet in 1842; and a man in Achille Leclère's little atelier in 1844. Also well known, though they won no prizes, were the ateliers of the *néo-grecs*: Henri Labrouste, J.-F. Duban, and Léon Vaudoyer. Lefuel's atelier never grew large or particularly famous, and it lasted only about a decade.

Probably Hunt went to Lefuel because of Darier. While at the Ecole, Darier (1808–84) and Lefuel (1810–80) had been colleagues in the atelier of J.-N. Huyot.[9] Lefuel stayed with Huyot longer: he was enrolled in the atelier by 23 September 1828, admitted to the Ecole on 28 December 1829, promoted to the school's first class on 7 December 1832, and awarded the Grand Prix de Rome in September 1839. Darier was in the atelier by 23 July 1830, the second class of the Ecole on 6 January 1832, and the first class on 6 June 1834. Shortly thereafter he evidently went home to Geneva. At the end of the decade he surely learned that Lefuel had won the Grand Prix. He may have read early in 1845 in the *Revue générale de l'architecture* of Lefuel's fifth-year *envoi de Rome*, a project for the *mairie* of an arrondissement in Paris.[10] (The *Revue* praised the design for its practicality but regretted that it was not more artistic.) In the summer of 1845, Darier could not advise his pupil Hunt to study with Huyot, for in 1840 Huyot had died, the atelier had closed, and most of the students had gone to old Lebas. Thus the *patron* in Paris to whom Darier was closest was Lefuel, and it is not surprising that Hunt attached himself to the latter.

Once in Lefuel's atelier, Hunt began in September 1845 to prepare for the annual sequence of Ecole entrance exams, each of which was a *concours*. In October he took the test in mathematics, an oral questioning of each candidate by the professor; Hunt was thirty-third of the sixty-three who passed. On 3 No-

vember he took the written exam in descriptive geometry and in the middle of
the month attended the oral exam; again he passed but barely, forty-eighth of
fifty-one. The *concours* in architecture was held on 17 December; that day he
designed a portico with benches for reading and with a kiosk for the sale of
newspapers. The number of students entering the competition was 122; at the
end of the day, 109 of them submitted sketches; and two days later the jury
accepted sixty-two of the designs. Hunt's was rejected, and thus he was not one
of the forty-three applicants received by the Ecole on 19 December 1845. (In
the group, the man ranked first was H.-A. Revoil, who was later to restore
churches in the south of France and to write a book, *L'Architecture romaine du
midi de la France.* Among the others were G.-A. Ancelet, who was to win the
Grand Prix de Rome in 1851 and afterwards became a professor of drawing at
the Ecole, and E.-J.-B. Guillaume, Grand Prix de Rome winner in 1856, who
ultimately became professor of theory at the school. All of the forty-three new-
comers were Frenchmen.[11]) On admission day, when he learned that he had
not got in, Hunt wrote in his diary, "Aujourd'hui nous commençons bien
étudier l'architecture."[12]

So he did. In 1846, apparently as an exercise, he copied renderings Lefuel
had drawn in Rome; for example, on 21 January 1846 Hunt imitated a study by
Lefuel of the Doric order (fig. 2.1). In that year Hunt also followed the custom
of using programs from the school to make designs, as if he were taking part in
school *concours.* A *salle d'asile* (primary school), the drawings of which (figs.
2.2, 2.3, 2.4) Hunt dated 2 and 3 February 1846, looks old-fashioned, having
the blocklike shapes, smooth surfaces, and austere decoration of the neoclassical architecture prevalent in France in the first third of the century.

As soon as he could, which was the autumn of 1846, Hunt again tried for
admission to the Ecole. As was then done, he was given credit for the exams he
had already passed. On 9 December 1846 he was one of the 107 candidates
presenting themselves for the *concours* in architecture, and he was one of the
ninety-eight who submitted sketches of a chapel for an orphanage. Two days
later the jury approved fifty-eight of the designs, ranking Hunt's as thirty-fifth.
It then admitted fifty-six *aspirants* to the school; Hunt was thirty-seventh.

Several of the new students of 1846 were later to become well known in
France. Honoré Daumet, who won the Grand Prix de Rome in 1855, became
one of the most respected *patrons* at the Ecole, founding an atelier in 1862 and
conducting it for more than thirty years. (Among his pupils would be Charles
Follen McKim and also Richard Morris Hunt's sons, Richard Howland Hunt
and Joseph Howland Hunt.) Daumet was also an architect of note: in its grandeur and use of the late Gothic and early Renaissance style, his château of
Chantilly, built in 1875–82, is akin to the large houses Hunt did in the late
1870s, '80s, and '90s.[13] Also admitted to the Ecole in 1846 were A.-S. Diet,
who won the Grand Prix de Rome in 1853 and subsequently practiced in Paris,
and Henri Espérandieu, a native of the south of France who later returned
there to become the most important architect in Marseilles until his death in
1874. Among the new students of 1846 were several who were foreign-born:
besides Hunt, there were four Swiss.[14] Switzerland provided the largest group of
non-Frenchmen to the *section d'architecture* of the Ecole in those years; whereas
no foreigners were accepted in 1845, in 1846 all five of the non-French contingent came from or through that country. It is not known whether Hunt was
the only one of these young men to have associated with Samuel Darier in Ge-

2.1 A study of the Doric order, dated 21 January 1846 and copied from a study by H.-M. Lefuel of the propylon at Delos.

neva. It is a fact, though, that Hunt was the first citizen of the United States to enter the *section d'architecture*.

Once in the school, Hunt became very active. Great importance was placed on the competitions in architectural design, and within the week that he joined the second class, he took part in one of these, the *concours des places*, a one-day sketch problem that had been given annually since 1819. It was required of all students in the second class, except for a small number of the most advanced, and the jury ranked all the competitors, including those whose entries were judged unsatisfactory. The assignment on 16 December 1846 for the eighty-three students who presented themselves was to design the elevation and cross-section of a courtyard in a building for a ministry of war. The next day another eighty-six students competed using a different program, for in all there were too many people to meet together in the building where the sketches were made. The jury, however, ranked all the competitors as a single group. With a "fixed place" in the second class and thus exempted from the *concours* were twenty-four students; of the further 169 who competed, Hunt was ranked fifty-seventh, a respectable position for somebody newly admitted.

The *concours des places* was held but once a year. More frequent were the

architectural *concours* requiring either *projets rendus* (rendered projects) or *esquisses* (sketches). These two types of competition were the very center of architectural studies at the Ecole. Every year there were six *projets rendus* and six *esquisses*, assigned alternately one a month. In the *concours sur projets rendus*, each competitor had twelve hours at the Ecole to make a preliminary sketch that then had to be submitted, and afterwards two months in the atelier to prepare for judgment a set of drawings (usually plan, elevation, and section, all drawn with pencil and pen and rendered with watercolor washes). The *concours sur esquisses* were like the beginning stage of the *concours sur projets rendus*: competitors submitted for judgment sketches they made in no more than twelve hours at the school. All submissions to the jury were identified by number, not by name, so as to avoid partiality; and the jury met without students present. Judgment was severe: most of the *projets rendus* and nearly all of the *esquisses* were rejected. Students got no credit whatsoever for their failures. But as both *projets rendus* and *esquisses*, when accepted, brought the student the same number of *valeurs* or credits, a specified number of which were needed for promotion to the first or upper class, and as a *projet rendu* took two months and an *esquisse* twelve hours, the latter could be very rewarding. Hunt, like most of his colleagues, entered each kind of competition many times. In fact, in his years at the school, December 1846 to September 1854, he registered for twenty-eight *concours sur esquisses* and thirty-one *concours sur projets rendus*.[15]

Unlike most of the other students, however, Hunt kept his schoolwork. He brought home with him to America not only final drawings and many preliminary sketches but also nearly all the programs for his *concours* and even other programs as well—materials that were often kept in the ateliers for the use of beginners. Did Hunt from the first think of himself as a teacher, a *patron* in America, bringing the method of the Ecole des Beaux-Arts to his countrymen? Just as he had copied drawings by Lefuel, he may have imagined his own drawings being copied one day by his pupils, and probably they were. Nevertheless, the value of these early drawings is that they let us see what he did while he was learning architecture.

During his first two years of school, between which he took no vacation, Hunt entered an architectural competition every month but one for sixteen months, January 1847 to April 1848. He made seven *esquisses* and eight *projets*

2.2 A primary school, elevation dated 2 October 1846.

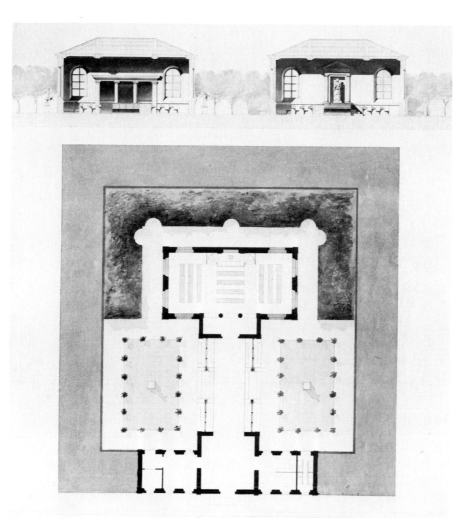

2.3 A primary school, plan and transverse section.

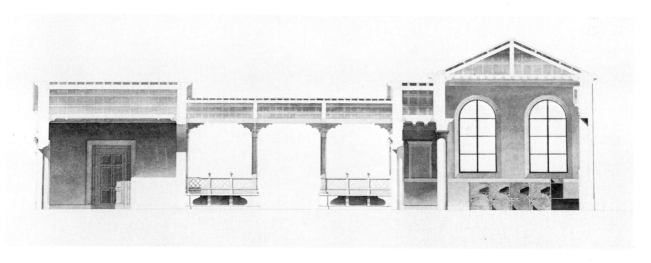

2.4 A primary school, longitudinal section.

rendus. Among the *esquisses* are a communal oven, the decoration of a well, and a workshop for a public scribe; among the *projets rendus* are an almshouse, a public square, a naval academy, an observatory, and a rectory. In none of these *concours* did he gain credit. Indeed, it was not architectural designs that most occupied him during his first two schoolyears, but rather the *concours* in construction. In Hunt's time there were four such *concours*: in masonry, wood, iron, and *construction générale*. Before a student could be promoted to the first class, he had to get credits in all of the construction *concours*. They were long—each ran for four months—and demanded drawings more specific than the *projets rendus.* Construction drawings were marked with dimensions.

As soon as was possible after he was admitted, Hunt took part in a construction competition. On 4 January 1847 the annual *concours* in masonry was held. The program called for the "application of the science of stonecutting to the construction of works of architecture," and the drawings were due in late April. On 30 April the jury accepted Hunt's project, awarding him a *première mention,* an adequate grade though not the highest. (There were six *médailles* and twenty-five *premières mentions* for the thirty-eight students who submitted drawings.) Even before the end of the competition, on 5 April, Hunt had registered for the *concours* in wood construction: the subject was "the details of different wood joints used in civil construction, and the application of these details to the carpentry of foundations partly in water." On the day judgment was rendered, 30 July, he again got a *première mention.* (There were seven *médailles* and twenty-seven *premières mentions* for the forty-two submissions.) On 5 July he had enrolled in the *concours* in iron construction, and when it was judged on 30 October it brought him another *première mention.* (There were six *médailles* and twenty-six *premières mentions* for the thirty-seven projects under consideration.) The program called for an iron bridge across a river at an angle of sixty degrees to the axis of the flow. Hunt's drawings (figs. 2.5, 2.6, and 2.7) show his increased proficiency: the hand and eye are sure. His bridge obviously owes something to a nearby iron bridge, the Pont des Arts, which since 1803 had spanned the Seine between the Louvre and the Palais des Quatres Nations, a short walk from the Ecole des Beaux-Arts. It also owes something (if only the circular rings between the arch and the roadway) to several English iron bridges that Hunt may have seen in a well-known book of the time, J.-B. Rondelet's *Traité théorique et pratique de l'art de bâtir.*[16] Hunt's fourth and final construction project was in "general construction," and again its schedule overlapped with the preceding *concours.* On 4 October 1847 the program for an exhibition hall for metal sculpture was issued, and on 4 February 1848 the thirty-seven entries were judged. Hunt again got a *première mention.* (The jury bestowed twenty-seven *premières mentions* and four medals.) Success in this competition fulfilled Hunt's requirements in construction.

In December 1847 Hunt took a day off from his drawings for *construction générale* in order to compete in the annual *concours des places.* The *concours* for Hunt's group was held on the twenty-first of the month, and the subject was a studio for a sculptor. Two sketch problems were assigned, one to half of the students in the second class on one day, and the other to the other half on the next. In all, twenty-one people had fixed places, and 189 had to be placed. The jury ranked Hunt sixty-second of the 189 (among whom Espérandieu was fifth and Daumet fortieth).

2.5 An iron bridge, elevation for the *concours* in iron construction, 5 July to late October 1847, *première mention.*

2.6 An iron bridge, detailed plan of half an arch.

Élévation
à l'échelle de 0,02 p.

Coupe
Transversale

Plan
de
l'extrémité
du
Pont.

Coupe
Longitudinale

Détail
des Entretoises.

Détails
des Rotules.

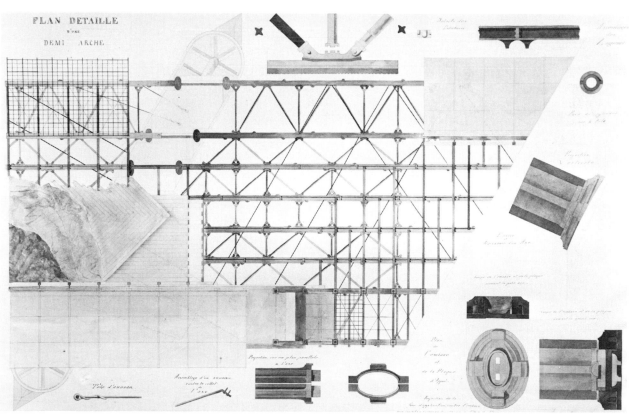

PLAN DÉTAILLÉ
D'UNE
DEMI ARCHE

Détails des
Entretoises.

Dimensions
des
Longerons.

Tête d'anneau.

Assemblage d'un anneau
contre le collet
de
l'arc

Projection vue en plan parallèle
à l'arc

Plan
de
l'embasse
et
de la Plaque
d'appui.

21

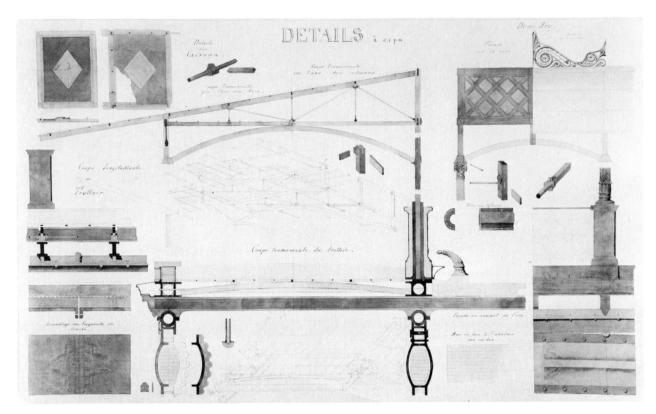

2.7 An iron bridge, details.

In the 1847–48 school year Hunt also attended lectures on mathematics (i.e., statics, trigonometry, and geometry), and on 21 April 1848, when the math exam was judged, he gained a *mention*. (Thirty-two students were examined. The jury awarded two medals and seventeen *mentions*, Hunt's being thirteenth of the seventeen.) Soon thereafter Hunt left Paris for a lengthy trip. It was not the first time he had taken a vacation from his studies in order to travel; in August 1846 he had interrupted his preparation for the school's entrance exams to join his family on a tour of the British isles.[17] Now, two years later, having accomplished a body of work as an *élève de l'Ecole*, he took half a year off to travel in the United States. With his mother, sister, and brother Leavitt, he voyaged for four months by train and riverboat into the South and over the Appalachians. The itinerary included New York City; Philadelphia, where they inspected new Greek-revival buildings such as Thomas U. Walter's Girard College and Federick Graff's waterworks; Baltimore, where they went to church in Benjamin H. Latrobe's Roman Catholic cathedral; Hampton Roads, Virginia, for a few weeks by the sea; Staunton, Virginia, for its natural bridge, which they sketched; the western part of Virginia for six weeks near the hot springs; down the Ohio river by steamboat to Cincinnati, with a side trip to Ashland, Kentucky, to call on Henry Clay; Nashville, Tennessee, where they admired William Strickland's Greek-revival capitol; Saint Louis; and then homewards via Chicago, Detroit, Buffalo, and Niagara Falls to Brattleboro, Vermont, a couple of weeks before Richard Morris Hunt's twenty-first birthday. Not since 1843 had he been in his own country, and during the long journey in 1848 he saw more of it than ever before.

Hunt reached Paris in time for the *concours des places* of 19 December 1848, for which he designed the "entrée principale d'un palais." Twenty-one students had fixed places, and in all 159 deposited their sketches at the end of each of the two days of *concours*. Of these 159, Hunt was ranked seventh, Daumet thirty-seventh, and Espérandieu one hundred thirteenth. Although Hunt had been away for more than half a year, he did much better than he had in the preceding *concours des places*. During the winter he registered every month in a *concours* in architecture, as he had done in most every month in his previous years in the school, and in the spring he rid himself of one more requirement: perspective. The one-day *concours* was on 17 April 1849: seventy-four students enrolled, and forty-three submitted *esquisses*. Three days later the jury bestowed two medals and thirty-six *mentions*, of which the sixth went to Hunt.

With this success, Hunt had fulfilled his requirements in every subject except architectural design. As has been said, from December 1846, when he entered the school, he had taken part in architectural *concours* without gaining a single credit in the judgments. Unfortunately for us, the minutes of the juries in Hunt's years at the Ecole give no hint of the standards for acceptance or rejection of students' work; these standards seem to have been so completely taken for granted that they were not discussed. What is reported for each *concours* is little more than the decision as to how many of the competitors passed and the names of those who did, ranked by number. One wishes that more were told. The pages of numbers do reveal, however, that the standard of judgment for the *concours* in construction, mathematics, and perspective was very different from that for the *concours* in architectural design. In construction, mathematics, and perspective, most of the work was accepted; in architectural design, most *projets rendus* and *esquisses* were rejected. Perhaps that is the reason why students in Hunt's time tried as soon as they could for credit in subjects other than architectural design. Sixteen months of work in the four construction *concours* were likely to bring results, whereas there might be nothing to show on the record after as many months of work on *projets rendus* and *esquisses* during the early years in the second class. The sequence of Hunt's accomplishments is far from unique: his colleague, Daumet, for example, has a somewhat similar record. Both had entered the school in December 1846, and by the end of April 1849 both had gained credit in the four construction *concours*, mathematics, and perspective. The order of successes was not identical, and by May 1849 Daumet had one further achievement: in the sketch *concours* of February 1847, which Daumet, Hunt, and sixty-nine others entered, Daumet got a *seconde mention*, one of the four passing grades. He was therefore a few credits nearer promotion than Hunt.

In the fall of 1849 Hunt also began to get favorable results in architectural *concours*. On either 7 or 8 August that year (the records are ambiguous) he registered for a *concours* of *projets rendus* due at the beginning of October. The subject was a funerary monument for three families, and on 5 October 1849 the jury looked at thirty-two projects. The jurors excluded eleven as *hors de concours*, in most cases because the students had ignored the program's requirement that construction be shown in cross-section. Of the remaining twenty-one projects, seven were accepted, six with *première mention* and one with *seconde mention*. Hunt was second among *premières mentions* (see fig. 7.1); Daumet was fifth. (The jurors then considered a one-day sketch problem that had taken place on 5 September: the arrangement of a large city house on an irregularly shaped site. The number of *esquisses* shown was twenty-four, one most probably by Hunt. Three *secondes mentions* were bestowed, one to Daumet, and it gained him enough credits for the jury thereupon to promote him to the first class.) Six months later, on 5 April 1850, the jury evaluated forty-three *esquisses* of a churchwardens' stall designed on 6 March. The jury awarded three *secondes mentions*. The second of them went to Hunt for his proposal (fig. 2.8).

Toward the end of the next school year, there were two more *mentions* for Hunt, one for "un théâtre pour une petite ville," which was a *projet rendu* (figs. 2.9, 2.10, 2.11, 2.12) and the other for "une crèche" (fig. 2.13), an *esquisse*. He worked on the theater from 2 April until early June, and he designed the nursery on 7 May. Both were judged on 6 June 1851. The jury had

2.8 A churchwardens' stall, the drawing for the *concours sur esquisses* of 6 March 1850, *seconde mention.*

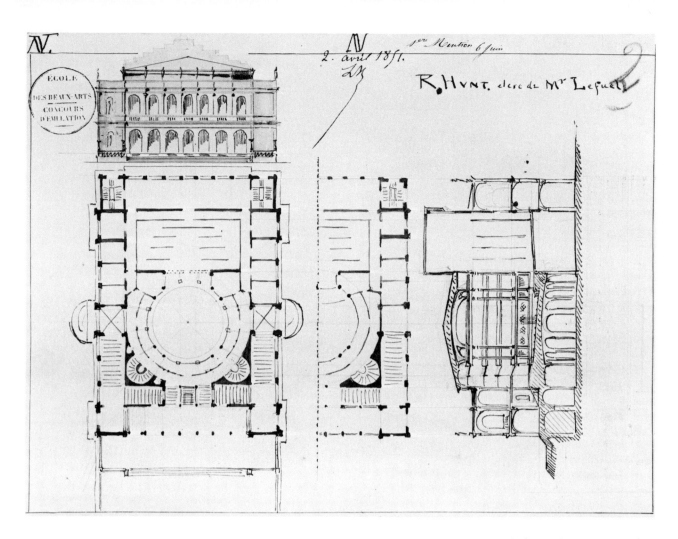

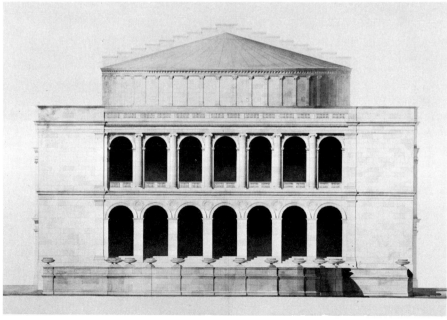

2.9 A theater for a small city, the preliminary *esquisse* of 2 April 1851 for the *concours sur projets rendus* of 2 April to early June 1851.

2.10 A theater for a small city, final elevation for the *concours sur projets rendus* 2 April to early June 1851, *première mention*.

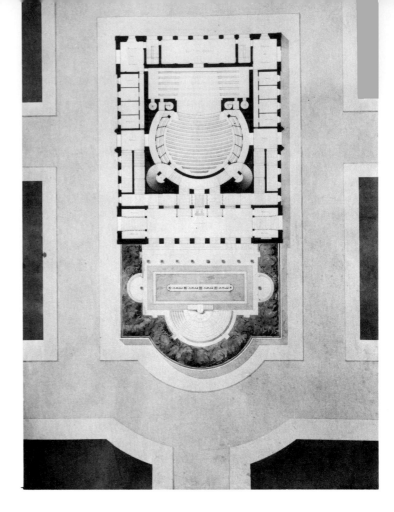

2.11 A theater for a small city,
final plan.

2.12 A theater for a small city,
final section.

2.13 A nursery, the drawing for
the *concours sur esquisses* of 7 May
1851, *seconde mention*.

before it thirty-four theaters, and it bestowed seven *premières mentions* and three *secondes mentions*. Hunt got the fourth *première mention*. After looking at forty-six *crèches*, the jury gave only two *secondes mentions*; Hunt got the first. These *mentions* gave him sufficient points for promotion that day to the first class.

These four successes in *concours* in 1849–50 and 1850–51 did not come easy. In his first two school years at the Ecole, 1846–47 and 1847–48, Hunt had enrolled in seven *concours sur esquisses* and eight *concours sur projets rendus*, fifteen of the monthly competitions in sixteen successive months. In the two school years following his American trip of 1848, he registered for an architectural competition every month but one for nineteen successive months, January 1849 to July 1850. In the summer of 1850 he had toured England again with his brother William, going by way of Normandy. The next school year Hunt took part in nine more architectural *concours* in the nine months from October 1850 to June 1851. Between January 1849 and June 1851, then, Hunt made thirteen *esquisses* and fourteen *projets rendus*. Among the *esquisses* are the entrance to a prison, a bandstand (fig. 2.14), a streetlamp, a small summerhouse, a telegraph station, and the two for which he got credit, the churchwardens' stall (fig. 2.8, above) and the nursery already mentioned (fig. 2.13, above). The *projets rendus* include an old-folk's home, a slaughterhouse, a village church, a lithographic printshop, a pavilion in the center of the facade of a presidential palace, two versions of a railway station (figs. 2.15, 2.16), a hostel for visitors to Algeria, and the two that won the jury's approval, a funerary monument (see fig. 7.1) and a theater. In sum, in the second class Hunt got favorable results in four of forty-two architectural *concours*. Is it entirely coincidental that these four successes came after he gained credits in all the other required subjects? One wonders if the *concours* were as truly anonymous as they were meant to be. A student's name was not on his drawings. Nevertheless, did the jury know who had done what, and did it ultimately reward years of effort?

Hunt traveled (fig. 2.17) during the summers of both 1851 and 1852. In June 1851 he went with his brother Leavitt to England for the Great International Exposition in London, and, recrossing the Channel, he passed through the north of France to Germany, where in July he visited Düsseldorf and Heidelberg (fig. 2.18). In June 1852 he visited his brother William, the painter, at Barbizon, and in July he saw the châteaux of the Loire with his mother and sister (figs. 2.19, 2.20). On 1 August 1852, he and William set out on a year-long expedition, which Lefuel seems to have encouraged. The itinerary took Richard and William through Belgium and Holland to Düsseldorf, Berlin, Prague, Vienna, Trieste, and Venice. For three months they slowly made their way south through Italy and Sicily, and beyond to Malta. On 3 January 1853 they landed in Egypt, at Alexandria, and for more than three months they were in the valley of the Nile, sailing up river as far as Philae (fig. 2.21) and downstream again to Alexandria, whence they embarked for Gaza. Then, on horseback, they rode across rocky terrain to Jerusalem, reaching the city at the end of April; and after seeing Bethlehem and the Dead Sea, they headed their horses north to Beirut. From there, in late May, they took to sea again, stopping along the way at Tripoli, Rhodes, Smyrna, Constantinople, and Piraeus, the last on 10 June. After almost a month in Athens, they set sail across the Adriatic to Trieste and Venice. Finally, they journeyed by rail via Graz, Vienna, Salzburg, and Munich to Paris. On 29 July 1853 Richard Morris Hunt was back in his apartment on the Left Bank.

2.14 A bandstand, the drawing for the *concours sur esquisses* of 7 March 1849.

2.15 A railway station, a sketch on tracing paper during the *concours sur projets rendus* of 4 December 1850 to early February 1851.

2.16 A railway station, a study of alternate versions.

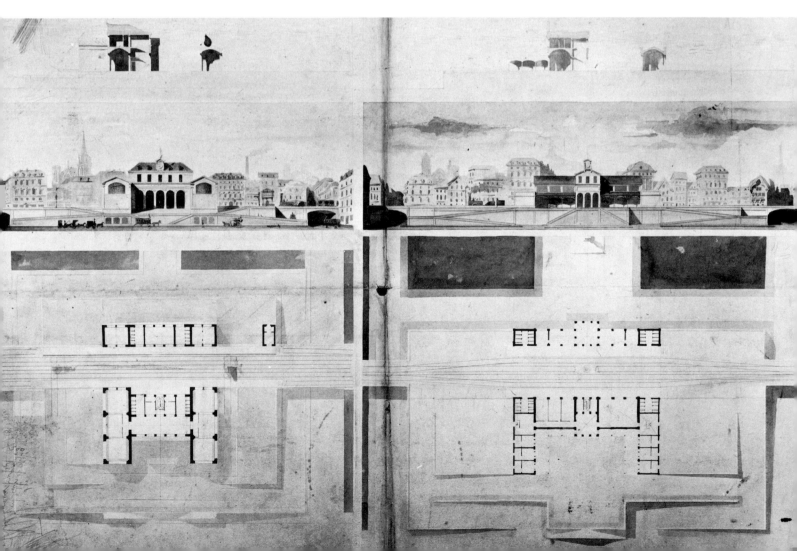

2.18 Heidelberg, 1851.

2.17 "Ham, Bill and I on the road
to Angers." Hunt, his brother
William Morris Hunt, and their
American friend Hamilton Wild,
sketched in the late 1840s or early
1850s.

2.19 Blois, probably sketched in
1852.

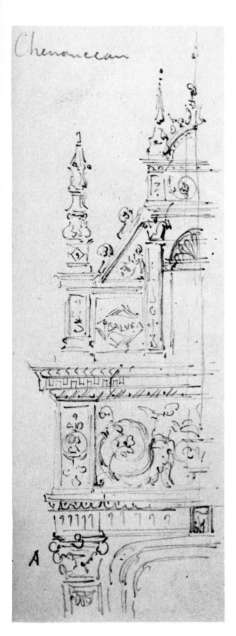

2.20 Chenonceau, sketched during the same trip to the Loire valley, probably in 1852.

2.21 The temple of Kneph at Esneh, 21 February 1853.

Within the week he was at the Ecole. He devoted 2 August to designing an *arc de triomphe* for a one-day sketch competition. In both September and October he entered an architectural *concours*, each without success. He then began to travel again, this time with his mother and sister, to Nîmes and Avignon and onward to Rome for the winter. By 4 April 1854 he was again in Paris; that day he took part in another *concours sur esquisses*, the subject of which was a pier for gondolas. From April through September 1854, Hunt participated in every monthly competition but one, that in August, and all to no avail. The *concours* that began on 5 September 1854, the subject of which was a small, suburban tavern, was his last activity at the Ecole. In the first class from October 1851 through September 1854, Hunt had entered seventeen *concours*, requiring eight *esquisses* and nine *projets rendus*. For none was he awarded credit.

Among these *projets rendus*, however, are some of his most interesting student designs. A large public greenhouse ("un jardin d'hiver"; figs. 2.22, 2.23, 2.24) was the subject of a *concours* held on 4 November 1851. Obviously this airy interior, enclosed by iron and glass, owes much to the Crystal Palace that had been built in London for the Great Exposition earlier in the year. Hunt himself had been in the Crystal Palace. There is, however, no sketch of it in the book Hunt carried with him on that trip; as an example of architecture it seems not to have caught his eye. What the *jardin d'hiver* most likely reveals is Paxton's influence on G.-A. Blouet, the professor of theory of architecture at the Ecole from 1846 to 1853, who wrote the programs for the *concours*.

A building for the archives of the national audit office ("des archives pour la cour des comptes"; figs. 2.25, 2.26, 2.27) of 1852, an attempt in the *néo-grec*

2.22 A winter garden, interior section.

2.23 A winter garden, perspective for the first-class *concours sur projets rendus* of 4 November 1851 to early January 1852.

2.24 A winter garden, plan.

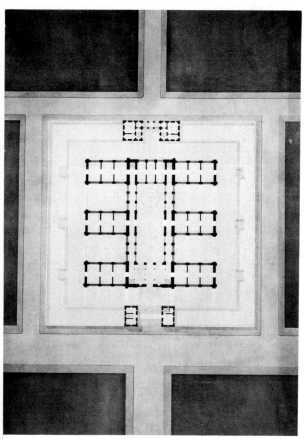

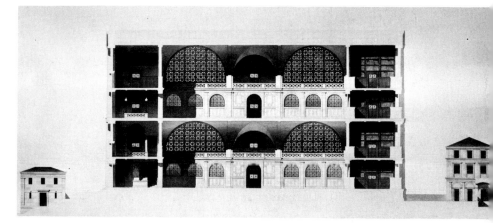

2.25 *Top:* The archives of the national audit office, elevation for the first-class *concours sur projets rendus* of 2 March to early May 1852.

2.27 The archives of the national audit office, section.

2.26 The archives of the national audit office, plan.

2.28 A ministry of justice, elevation for the first-class *concours sur projets rendus* of 6 September–5 November 1853.

style, is small in scale and obviously derived from Henri Labrouste's Bibliothèque Sainte Geneviève. Hunt followed Labrouste's example by making the principal decoration of the facade consist of rows of names inscribed on panels, each beneath the arch of an arcade. For Labrouste, this monumental catalog of authors' names was symbolic of the books within and therefore of all knowledge.[18] For Hunt the names seem to have been little more than a pattern, and are even treated playfully: some are of members of the atelier Lefuel.[19] The design, very different from nearly all of Hunt's earlier work, reminds us that in Hunt's years Labrouste was a *patron* at the Ecole.

A ministry of justice done in 1853 is very different in spirit (figs. 2.28, 2.29, 2.30). The mood of Bonapartism, revived in the early years of the Second Empire, inspired the new professor of theory of architecture, J.-B. Lesueur, to call for homage to the creator of the French code of laws. Lesueur's program specified that the ministry building be imagined on the Ile de la Cité, filling the place Dauphine. In front of the main (west) facade was to be a statue of a seated Napoleon, one or two stories tall. Hunt's Napoleon would have been colossal; it would have dwarfed the existing statue of Henri IV, which Hunt would have kept. Behind the Napoleon, Hunt placed a facade that is a variation of the Loggia dei Lanzi in Florence: five huge arches, raised high above the ground and supporting a richly decorated cornice and attic. Beyond the gigantic arches Hunt situated a building in a subdued and academically correct style. The jury rejected the scheme.

In Hunt's last year at the Ecole, 1854, he was also busy with the important

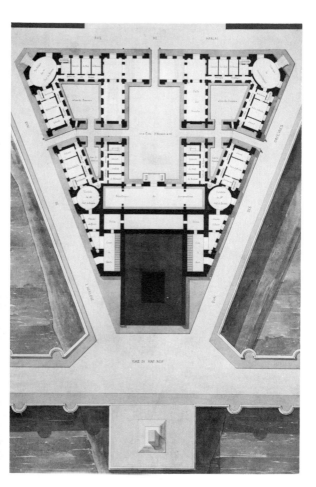

2.29 A ministry of justice, plan.

2.30 A ministry of justice,
elevation and section.

2.31 Pavillon de la Bibliothèque,
the Louvre, Paris, by L.-T.-J. Visconti and H.-M. Lefuel. Hunt
made studies and full-size drawings
of details for Lefuel in 1854–55.

task of assisting the architect in charge of the completion of the palace of the
Louvre. At the beginning of 1852, Louis Napoleon named L.-T.-J. Visconti
architect of the Louvre and charged him with planning a long-considered
project, the linking of the Louvre and the Tuileries. Visconti quickly came up
with a design, and that summer three thousand men began the construction.
On 29 December 1853 Visconti died. As his successor, Napoleon (by then the
emperor Napoleon III) promptly appointed Hunt's *patron* at the Ecole, Hector-
Martin Lefuel.[20] In April 1854 Lefuel invited Hunt to join the office of the
architect of the Louvre as an inspector of works, fifth class, and in December
Hunt was promoted to inspector fourth class. He seems to have been what today is called a "job captain," responsible for the achievement of Lefuel's ideas in
one part of the large complex. Specifically, to quote what may have been a
paraphrase of Hunt's own description of his duties, "he was put in charge of the
Pavillon de la Bibliothèque, opposite the Palais Royal, and had the honour of
making, under Lefuel, all the studies and full-size drawings of that Pavillon."[21]
The Pavillon de la Bibliothèque (fig. 2.31) is one of the tall, mansarded,
square-domed blocks that are the most prominent feature of the Louvre of
Napoleon III. Probably Hunt developed Lefuel's general scheme for the pavilion, designed some of the details, and supervised the construction.

It is surprising to think that part of the Louvre is by an American architect,
for that palace was, in the words of the *Revue générale de l'architecture* (1855),
"the most important of all the great works presently being executed in Paris."[22]
One would not expect to find a foreigner entrusted with any part of a national

monument. But after a decade in France, Hunt must have been virtually a Frenchman. His future, though, lay on the other side of the Atlantic. In the spring of 1855 he made yet another visit to London, and in August of that year, having consigned to a shipper his library of several thousand architectural books, his collection of as many photos of historical buildings, his furniture, art objects, and bric-a-brac, he took passage westwards. In September 1855 he set forth on his American career.

What, it might be asked, did Hunt learn at the Ecole des Beaux-Arts? A brief answer would be, to design quickly and to design monumental public buildings. The school's curriculum—in particular, the requirement that every design competition begin with a sketch to be submitted within twelve hours, and the fact that equal importance was given to the *concours sur esquisses* and the *concours sur projets rendus*—taught future architects how to grasp at once the requirements of a commission and conceive of an architectural arrangement likely to fit those requirements. Since the Ecole des Beaux-Arts was the national school of architecture (and charged no tuition), its first purpose was to train architects for the needs of the state, which were for public buildings, not private houses. It was assumed that these public buildings would be commissioned by the state, and further that they would for the most part be built of lasting materials such as stone or brick. It had been assumed for decades that this public architecture would be classic in style, not Gothic; but during Hunt's time in Paris, the buildings of Labrouste, Duban, and the other *néo-grecs* were stretching the definition of the classic, and the writings of Viollet-le-Duc were prompting a reevaluation of the Gothic.

Hunt was to find that few of the Ecole's assumptions held true in America. The Neo-Gothic was as highly esteemed as the neoclassic. He would build most often in wood. His commissions would come not from the state but from private individuals. He would design many houses and only a few public buildings. Nevertheless, the habits of thought that he learned at the Ecole and the atelier Lefuel were to serve him well in the years to come. What he would do during those years in America is another story.

TABLE 2.1 · HUNT'S ADMISSION CONCOURS

Date	Subject	Number of enrollments	Number of submissions	Date judged	Number accepted	Hunt's rank
1–21 Oct. 1845	Mathematics	129	116	31 Oct. 1845	63	33
3 Nov. 1845	Descriptive geometry	112	89	12 Dec. 1845	51	48
17 Dec. 1845	Architecture: a portico ("un portique pour la lecture dans une promenade publique").	122	109	19 Dec. 1845	62	Failures not ranked

Immediately after this judgment, the jury fixed the number of *aspirants* admitted to the Ecole in 1845 at forty-three. Hunt was not included.

As the minutes of the judgments determining admission in 1845 and 1846 reveal, candidates who passed one or two of the three exams were required in the following year to attempt only what had been failed.

Date	Subject	Number of enrollments	Number of submissions	Date judged	Number accepted	Hunt's rank
9 Dec. 1846	Architecture: a chapel ("une chapelle pour un hospice d'orphelins").	107	98	11 Dec. 1846	58	35

In 1846 the number of *aspirants* admitted to the Ecole was fifty-six. Hunt was ranked thirty-seventh.

TABLE 2.2 · HUNT'S STUDENT CONCOURS[a]

Enrollment	Type and subject	*Esquisse* by Hunt	*Rendu* by Hunt	Date due	Date of Judgment	Result
16 Dec. 1846	*Concours des places*: the elevation and section of an arcade in a courtyard ("La coupe du portique et la façade du retour d'angle de la cour de l'hôtel d'un ministère de la guerre").	yes		16 Dec. 1846	18 Dec. 1846	57 of 169
4 Jan. 1847	Construction, masonry: stonecutting ("L'application de la science de la coupe des pierres à la construction d'ouvrages d'architecture").	yes	yes	Apr. 1847	30 Apr. 1847	1ère *Mention*
6 Jan. 1847	Architecture, *esquisse*: a communal oven ("Un four banal").	yes		6 Jan. 1847	5 Feb. 1847	
3 Feb. 1847	Architecture, *projet rendu*: an almshouse ("Une maison de charité").	yes	?	early Apr. 1847	9 Apr. 1847	
3 Mar. 1847	Architecture, *esquisse*: the decoration of a well ("La décoration d'un puits").	yes but not submitted		3 Mar. 1847		

TABLE 2.2 · HUNT'S STUDENT CONCOURS[a] (*continued*)

Enrollment	Type and subject	*Esquisse* by Hunt	*Rendu* by Hunt	Date due	Date of Judgment	Result
22 Mar. 1847	Perspective: a hall in a bath building ("La mise en perspective d'une des salles du palais des thermes de Julien [in Paris]").	yes		22 Mar. 1847	?	
5 Apr. 1847	Construction, wood: details of joints ("Les détails de différents assemblages en usage dans les constructions civiles").	yes	yes	Jul. 1847	30 Jul. 1847	1ère Mention
7 Apr. 1847	Architecture, *project rendu*: a public square ("Une place publique sur la déclivité de la côte de chaillot en face de l'école militaire").	yes	probably	early Jun. 1847	4 Jun. 1847	
5 May 1847	Architecture, *esquisse*: a public shelter ("Un chauffoir publique avec portique").	no		5 May 1847		
2 Jun. 1847	Architecture, *projet rendu*: a naval academy ("Une école navale pour une ville maritime de deuxième ordre").	yes	?	early Jun. 1847	6 Aug. 1847	
5 Jul. 1847	Construction, iron: a bridge ("Un pont biais formant angle de 60° avec l'axe de la rivière").	yes	yes	Oct. 1847	30 Oct. 1847	1ère Mention
7 Jul. 1847	Architecture, *esquisse*: a tomb for two brothers ("Un tombeau pour deux frères").	no		7 Jul. 1847		
4 Aug. 1847	Architecture, *projet rendu*: a prison ("Un prison cellulaire pour le chef lieu d'un département").	yes	possibly	early Oct. 1847	8 Oct. 1847	
8 Sep. 1847	Architecture, *esquisse*: a workshop for a public scribe ("Une échoppe d'écrivain publique").	yes but not submitted		8 Sep. 1847		
4 Oct. 1847	General construction: an exhibition hall for metal sculpture ("Un édifice public destiné aux expositions temporaires des monuments de sculpture et des produits de l'industrie des métaux").	yes	yes	31 Dec. 1847	4 Feb. 1848	1ère Mention
6 Oct. 1847	Architecture, *projet rendu*: public baths ("Des bains publics sur un terrain irrégulier").	yes	?	early Dec. 1847	10 Dec. 1847	
3 Nov. 1847	Architecture, *esquisse*: a piggery ("Une porcherie").	no		3 Nov. 1847		
8 Dec. 1847	Architecture, *projet rendu*: an observatory ("Un observatoire pour une grande ville départementale").	yes	?	early Feb. 1848	11 Feb. 1848	

TABLE 2.2 · HUNT'S STUDENT CONCOURS ª (*continued*)

Enrollment	Type and subject	*Esquisse* by Hunt	*Rendu* by Hunt	Date due	Date of Judgment	Result
21 Dec. 1847	*Concours des places:* a sculptor's studio ("Un atelier de sculpteur statuaire").	yes		21 Dec. 1847	24 Dec. 1847	62 of 189
2 Feb. 1848	Architecture, *projet rendu:* a rectory ("Un presbytère ou maison curiale").	yes	yes	early Apr. 1848	7 Apr. 1848	
1 Mar. 1848	Architecture, *esquisse:* a butcher's shop ("Une boutique de boucher").	no		1 Mar. 1848		
12 Apr. 1848	Architecture, *projet rendu:* a national assembly hall ("Une salle d'assemblée pour les représentants de la nation").	no	no			
14 Apr. 1848	Perspective a tilted capital ("La mise en perspective d'un chapiteau incliné et oblique").	yes		14 Apr. 1848	12 May 1848	
Apr. 1848	Mathematics: an examination on statics, trigonometry, and geometry				21 Apr. 1848	*Mention*
19 Dec. 1848	*Concours des places:* the entrance of a palace ("L'entrée principale d'un palais").	yes		19 Dec. 1848	22 Dec. 1848	7 of 159
10 Jan. 1849	Architecture, *esquisse:* the entrance of a prison ("L'entrée d'une prison").	yes		10 Jan. 1849	9 Feb. 1849	
7 Feb. 1849	Architecture, *projet rendu:* an old folk's home ("Un petit hospice").	yes	yes	early Apr. 1849	6 Apr. 1849	
7 Mar. 1849	Architecture, *esquisse:* a bandstand ("Un orchestre pour des bals en plein air").	yes		7 Mar. 1849	6 Apr. 1849	
4 Apr. 1849	Architecture, *projet rendu:* a slaughterhouse ("Un abattoir pour une ville chef lieu de département").	yes	yes	early Jun. 1849	8 Jun. 1849	
17 Apr. 1849	Perspective: a grindstone ("La mise en perspective d'une meule appuyée sur un bloc de forme parallélépipède").	yes		17 Apr. 1849	20 Apr. 1849	*Mention*
2 May 1849	Architecture, *esquisse:* a bridge in a garden ("Un pont dans un jardin d'agrément").	yes		2 May 1849	8 Jun. 1849	
6 Jun. 1849	Architecture, *projet rendu:* a pavilion in a park ("Un pavillon de plaisance dans un parc").	yes	?	early Aug. 1849	Aug. 1849	
7 or 8 Aug. 1849	Architecture, *projet rendu:* a funerary monument ("Un monument funéraire pour trois familles").	yes	yes	early Oct. 1849	5 Oct. 1849	1ère *Mention*

TABLE 2.2 · HUNT'S STUDENT CONCOURS [a] (*continued*)

Enrollment	Type and subject	*Esquisse* by Hunt	*Rendu* by Hunt	Date due	Date of Judgment	Result
5 Sep. 1849	Architecture, *esquisse:* the plan of a large cityhouse ("La distribution d'un hôtel sur un terrain irrégulier").	yes		5 Sep. 1849	5 Oct. 1849	
3 Oct. 1849	Architecture, *projet rendu:* a teachers' college ("Une école normale primaire pour 40 élèves").	yes	yes but prob. not submitted	early Dec. 1849	7 Dec. 1849	
7 Nov. 1849	Architecture, *esquisse:* a streetlamp ("Un candélabre pour un réverbère à gaz").	yes but not submitted		7 Nov. 1849		
5 Dec. 1849	Architecture, *projet rendu:* a village church ("Une église de village").	yes	yes	early Feb. 1850	8 Feb. 1850	
9 Jan. 1850	Architecture, *esquisse:* a dairy ("Une laiterie").	no		9 Jan. 1850		
6 Feb. 1850	Architecture, *projet rendu:* a lithographic printshop ("Un établissement pour l'impression et la vente de lithographies").	yes	yes	early Apr. 1850	5 Apr. 1850	
6 Mar. 1850	Architecture, *esquisse:* a churchwardens' stall ("Un banc d'oeuvre pour une église paroissiale de petite ville").	yes		6 Mar. 1850	5 Apr. 1850	2*ème* Mention
3 Apr. 1850	Architecture, *projet rendu:* the entrance pavilion in a palace ("Le pavillon milieu d'un hôtel de la présidence").	yes	yes	early Jun. 1850	7 Jun. 1850	
8 May 1850	Architecture, *esquisse:* a fountain for a village ("Une fontaine avec abreuvoir").	no		8 May 1850		
5 Jun. 1850	Architecture, *projet rendu:* an orangery ("Une orangerie").	yes	?	early Aug. 1850	9 Aug. 1850	
3 Jul. 1850	Architecture, *esquisse:* a small summerhouse ("Une bastide").	yes but not submitted		3 Jul. 1850		
9 Oct. 1850	Architecture, *projet rendu:* a monument to the Trinity ("Un monument à la trinité").	yes	yes	early Dec. 1850	6 Dec. 1850	
6 Nov. 1850	Architecture, *esquisse:* a guardhouse by a railroad ("Une maison de garde sur une ligne de chemin de fer").	yes		6 Nov. 1850	6 Dec. 1850	
4 Dec. 1850	Architecture, *projet rendu:* a railroad station ("Une station de chemin de fer").	yes, twice	yes, twice	early Feb. 1851	7 Feb. 1851	
8 Jan. 1851	Architecture, *esquisse:* the doorway of a guardroom ("La porte d'une salle de gardes").	no		8 Jan. 1851		

TABLE 2.2 · HUNT'S STUDENT CONCOURS [a] (*continued*)

Enrollment	Type and subject	*Esquisse* by Hunt	*Rendu* by Hunt	Date due	Date of Judgment	Result
5 Feb. 1851	Architecture, *projet rendu*: a hostel in Algeria ("Une maison hospitalière pour l'Algérie").	yes	yes	early Apr. 1851	4 Apr. 1851	
12 Mar. 1851	Architecture, *esquisse*: a telegraph station ("Un télégraph").	yes		12 Mar. 1851	4 Apr. 1851	
2 Apr. 1851	Architecture, *projet rendu*: a theater ("Un théâtre pour une petite ville").	yes	yes	early Jun. 1851	6 Jun. 1851	1ère Mention
7 May 1851	Architecture, *esquisse*: a nursery ("Une crèche").	yes		7 May 1851	6 Jun. 1851	2ème Mention
4 Jun. 1851	Architecture, *projet rendu*: a school for poor children ("Une crèche avec salle d'asile et ouvroir").	no	no			
2 Sep. 1851	Architecture, first class, *projet rendu*: a spa ("Un établissement thermal").	no	no			
7 Oct. 1851	Architecture, first class, *esquisse*: an exhibition building ("Un édifice provisoire pour des expositions d'horticulture").	yes but not submitted		7 Oct. 1851		
4 Nov. 1851	Architecture, first class, *projet rendu*: a winter garden ("Un jardin d'hiver").	yes	yes	early Jan. 1852	9 Jan. 1852	
2 Dec. 1851	Architecture, first class, *esquisse*: a birdcage ("Un volière dans un jardin d'hiver").	no		2 Dec. 1851		
6 Jan. 1852	Architecture, first class, *projet rendu*: the headquarters of a prefecture ("Un hôtel de préfecture").	no	no			
3 Feb. 1852	Architecture, first class, *esquisse*: a family tomb ("Un monument sépulcral pour une famille").	no		3 Feb. 1852		
2 Mar. 1852	Architecture, first class, *projet rendu*: the archives of the national audit office ("Des archives pour la cour des comptes").	yes	yes	early May 1852	7 May 1852	
6 Apr. 1852	Architecture, first class, *esquisse*: the entrance to a racecourse ("L'entrée d'un hippodrome").	yes		6 Apr. 1852	7 May 1852	
4 May 1852	Architecture, first class, *projet rendu*: a cemetery ("Un campo santo").	yes	?	early Jul. 1852	9 Jul. 1852	
2 Aug. 1853	Architecture, first class, *esquisse*: a triumphal arch ("Un arc de triomphe").	no		2 Aug. 1853		

TABLE 2.2 · HUNT'S STUDENT CONCOURS^a (*continued*)

Enrollment	Type and subject	*Esquisse* by Hunt	*Rendu* by Hunt	Date due	Date of Judgment	Result
6 Sep. 1853	Architecture, first class, *projet rendu:* a ministry of justice ("Un hôtel pour le ministère de la justice, avec portique en l'honneur de Napoléon Ier").	yes	yes	5 Nov. 1853	11 Nov. 1853	
4 Oct. 1853	Architecture, first class, *esquisse:* an open-air theater ("Un théâtre dans un bosquet").	no		4 Oct. 1853		
4 Apr. 1854	Architecture, first class, *esquisse:* a pier for gondolas ("Un petit port pour les gondoles").	no		4 Apr. 1853		
2 May 1854	Architecture, first class, *projet rendu:* an opera house ("Un théâtre de l'académie impériale de musique").	yes	?	early Jul. 1854	14 Jul. 1854	
6 Jun. 1854	Architecture, first class, *esquisse:* a pulpit in a cathedral ("Une chaire à prêcher pour une église cathédrale").	yes but perhaps not submitted		6 Jun. 1854	14 Jul. 1854	
4 Jul. 1854	Architecture, first class, *projet rendu:* a parish church ("Une église paroissiale pour une grande ville").	yes	?	early Sep. 1854	8 Sep. 1854	
5 Sep. 1854	Architecture, first class, *projet rendu:* a suburban tavern ("Une guingette").	?	?	early Nov. 1854	10 Nov. 1854	

a. The information in this table is based on the documents cited in note 1 to the text.

The books of registrations (vols. AJ-52-160, 163, 164, and 167) provide the dates of enrollment, the types of *concours* and their subjects, and the names of each participant. The registrations show whether or not each competitor submitted an *esquisse* at the end of the first day of the competition.

Hunt's *concours* record, which is in his dossier (vol. AJ-52-369), shows when and for which types of *concours* he got credit. The minutes of the jury (vols. AJ-52-107 and 108) confirm these credits and name the subjects of the *concours*, thus tying judgments to enrollments.

However, none of the documents records whether or not students in Hunt's time submitted their final drawings for the *concours* that required *projets rendus*. Obviously, credit for a design is evidence that all the required drawings were before the jury. But the minutes of the jury do not name the students whose entries were submitted and rejected. Thus, for this table, evidence of Hunt's final drawings is mostly provided by the drawings that have been kept. For some of the *concours* requiring *projets rendus*, the final drawings are incomplete or entirely lacking. It cannot be determined, therefore, whether Hunt failed to make a full set of renderings and thus did not submit what he had made, whether part of the submitted set has been lost, or whether a whole set has been lost. The column "*Rendu* by Hunt" thus shows many question marks.

Notes

1. Hunt kept things: his drawings by the thousands, his notebooks, his large library; and we can be thankful that so much has survived.

The Ecole des Beaux-Arts also kept things, in particular detailed records of its students. In the 1950s and 1960s, when the school had high enrollments and insufficient funds and when its past no longer seemed relevant to the present, the *sous-directeur*, Robert Cassanas, made sure that the records were preserved. In 1972 the records were transferred to the Archives Nationales, where they were cataloged by Brigitte Labat-Poussin. This excellent catalog has been published: *Inventaire des archives de l'Ecole Nationale Supérieure des Beaux-Arts et de l'Ecole Nationale Supérieure des Arts Décoratifs* (Paris: Archives nationales, 1978).

The documents on which this chapter is based are as follows:

—At the AIA Foundation, Hunt's drawings and the programs, preserved almost in full by Hunt, issued by the Ecole for the *concours* he entered. These programs are dated.

—Archives Nationales vol. AJ-52-160, *Ecole d'Architecture: concours communs aux 2 classes*, registrations for *concours* in construction, in perspective, and for admission, from 7 April 1842 through 7 April 1857.

—Archives Nationales vol. AJ-52-163, *Section d'Architecture—concours—2 ᵉᵐᵉ classe*, registrations for the monthly architectural *concours* from 8 November 1843 through 8 December 1848.

—Archives Nationales vol. AJ-52-164, *Section d'Architecture, Concours de 2 ᵉᵐᵉ classe*, registrations for the monthly architectural *concours* from 19 December 1848 through 8 October 1856.

—Archives Nationales vol. AJ-52-167, *Section d'Architecture, concours, 1 ᵉʳᵉ classe*, registrations for first-class *concours*, 1848–63.

—Archives Nationales vol. AJ-52-107, *Ecole Royale des Beaux-Arts, section d'architecture, registre des procès-verbaux des jugements des prix délivrés dans l'école d'architecture [commençant] au 9 janvier 1846, registre treizième*, minutes of the jury.

—Archives Nationales vol. AJ-52-108, *Ecole Nationale des Beaux-Arts, section d'architecture, quatorzième registre: registre des procès-verbaux des jugements des prix délivrés dans l'école d'architecture commençant au 18 octobre 1850, finissant le 27 juin 1857*, minutes of the jury.

—Archives Nationales vol. AJ-52-369, *Ecole des Beaux-Arts, élèves d'architecture, présences antérieures au 31 décembre 1895*, vol. 17, pp. 212–15, Hunt's dossier. To be specific, p. 212 is the front of what was a folder in a file, p. 213 the record of *concours* for which Hunt got credit, p. 214 a note from Lefuel on 12 September 1845 presenting Hunt to the Ecole, and p. 215 a note from the American legation giving Hunt's place and date of birth and certifying him to be a citizen of the United States.

2. For a definitive biography of Hunt, see Paul R. Baker, *Richard Morris Hunt* (Cambridge, Mass., and London, 1980). Among Baker's sources is an unpublished biography of the architect by his widow, Catharine Clinton Howland Hunt (n.d., but Baker, p. viii, puts the date ca. 1907). The late Alan Burnham had a typewritten copy of Catharine Hunt's manuscript, which in 1975 he kindly let me read. In the following paragraphs, information about Hunt's family and youth is from the Burnham copy of Catharine Hunt's biography, pp. 1–32, or from Baker's book, pp. 2–62, unless otherwise noted.

3. Catharine Hunt, unpublished biography, p. 17.

4. *Catalogue of the Past and Present Members of the English High School of Boston* (Boston: The English High School Association, 1868).

5. Ibid.

6. Partly quoted and partly paraphrased by Baker, *Richard Morris Hunt*, p. 24.

7. On the Ecole Centrale des Arts et Manufactures, see the *Cinquantième anniversaire de la fondation de l'Ecole Centrale des Arts et Manufactures: compte rendu de la fête des 20 et 21 juin 1879* (Paris, 1879). Also published in 1879 was a history of the school by Comberousse; I have neither seen the book nor learned its exact title. On the formation of the Ecole Polytechnique and on the short-lived Ecole Centrale des Travaux Publics, see my essay, "The Teaching of Architecture at the Ecole des Beaux-Arts," in *The Architecture of the Ecole des Beaux-Arts*, ed. Arthur Drexler (New York and London, 1977), pp. 72–73.

8. This arrangement had been brought into existence by the regulations of 22 July 1819 (articles 6 and 7). Later the makeup of the jury changed: the decree of 6 May 1874 (title III, articles 22–26) established a jury of thirty members, namely the eight architects in the Académie des Beaux-Arts of the Institute; the ten or twelve professors in the *section d'architecture*; and as temporary members, outside architects, five of whom were to be elected every year by the entire faculty of the Ecole.

In Hunt's time, the four professors in the *section d'architecture* of the Ecole were:

1. Theory: L.-P. Baltard until his death in 1846, then G.-A. Blouet until his death in 1853, and then J.-B.-C. Lesueur.
2. History of art: L.-H. Lebas.
3. Construction: A.-M.-F. Jäy.
4. Mathematics: I. Francoeur.
5. Perspective, nominally in the *section de peinture et sculpture* but in fact active in the *section d'architecture*; S.-C. Constant-Dufeux.

In Hunt's time, the other twenty members of the jury, that is, the *commission*, consisted of (each until his death, unless otherwise noted):

1. P.-F.-L. Fontaine until 1853, then H.-M. Lefuel.
2. Vignon until 1846, then J.-B.-C. Lesueur until he became professor of theory in 1853, then L.-T.-J. Visconti for five days, then A. Paccard.
3. A.-P. Ménager.
4. F. Debret until 1850, then J.-J. Clerget.
5. Ach. Leclère until he became secretary-archivist of the Ecole in 1847, then P.-J. Garrez until 1852, then P.-E. Lequeux.
6. A.-M. Chatillon.
7. Vallot until 1847, then L.-T. Van Cleemputte.
8. H. Rohault de Fleury until 1846, then E.-N.-J. Gilbert until 1854 when he succeeded Leclère as secretary-archivist of the Ecole, then F.-J.-B. Guénepin.
9. Gauchon until 1846, then F.-E. Callet until 1854, then (30 September 1854) Théo Labrouste.
10. Lahure until 1854, then A.-I.-E. Godeboeuf.
11. J.-B.-A. Labadye until 1850, then A.-H. de Gisors.
12. J.-L. Provost until 1846, then C.-E. Isabelle.
13. A.-N. Caristie.
14. E.-J.-L. Grillon.
15. J.-J.-M. Huvé until 1852, then A.-M. Garnaud.
16. M.-P. Gauthier.
17. C.-J. Hittorff.
18. J.-J.-B. de Joly.
19. G.-A. Blouet until he became professor of theory in 1846, then V. Baltard.
20. L.-N.-M. Destouches until 1850, then J.-F. Bouchet.

9. On Lefuel and Darier, see Thieme and Becker, *Allgemeines Lexikon der bildenden Künstler* (Leipzig, 1907–50). E. Delaire's *Les Architectes élèves de l'Ecole des Beaux-Arts, 1793–1907* (Paris, 1907) also has short biographies of these two men (and of all other former students in the *section d'architecture*). Delaire gives Darier dates as 1800–1880, thus disagreeing with Thieme and Becker. That the latter are correct is confirmed by Darier's Ecole dossier, which is in Archives Nationales vol. AJ-52-361.

10. *Revue générale de l'architecture* 6 (1845, 1846), col. 86.

11. Delaire, *Les Architectes*, lists by rank the names of students admitted to the Ecole's second class, pp. 13–53.

12. Entry for 19 December 1845, quoted by Baker, *Richard Morris Hunt*, p. 30.

13. On Chantilly, see Ann Van Zanten's contribution in Drexler, *The Architecture of the Ecole des Beaux-Arts*, pp. 444–47.

14. They were D.-L. Braillard, who while at the Ecole was a pupil of Henri Labrouste and later practiced in Geneva; Charles Dahler, born in Berne, and in Paris a pupil of Lebas; J.-E.-H.-D. Franel, from Vevey, and later an architect of some importance in Switzerland, among whose buildings was the Grand Hotel in Vevey and who served as president of the Société des Ingénieurs et Architectes Suisses; and J.-J. Stehlin of Basle, another pupil of Labrouste, who later designed the *palais de justice* and post office in Basle.

15. After Hunt, the next important American architect to study at the Ecole des Beaux-Arts was Henry Hobson Richardson. From December 1860 to August 1865 Richardson registered for eighteen *concours sur esquisses* and twenty *concours sur projets rendus*. Hunt, in his ninety-four months at the Ecole, took part in fifty-nine architectural *concours*; Richardson, in his fifty-seven months there, took part in thirty-eight. Thus both men entered an architectural *concours* in approximately two of every three months. On Richardson's architectural education, see my essay, "Richardson's Record at the Ecole des Beaux-Arts," *Journal of the Society of Architectural Historians* 36 (October 1977): 175–88.

16. Hunt acquired a copy of the eleventh edition (Paris, 1842). Pages 320–40 of the *tome troisième* are about iron bridges. In its atlas, plates CLVII, CLVIII, and CLIX show the bridges at Coalbrookdale, Sunderland, and Staines.

17. On Hunt's travels during his Paris years, see Baker, *Richard Morris Hunt*, pp. 39–61.

18. For a description of the Bibliothèque Sainte Geneviève, for illustrations, and for a statement by Labrouste, see the *Revue générale de l'architecture* 10 (1852), cols. 379–84, and

0

plates XXI–XXVII; 11 (1853), cols. 392–99, and plates XXX–XXXII. See also Neil Levine's essay, "The Romantic Idea of Architectural Legibility: Henri Labrouste and the Neo-Grec," in Drexler, *The Architecture of the Ecole des Beaux-Arts*, esp. pp. 334–57.

19. Two of the men in the atelier were Americans who followed Hunt into the Ecole des Beaux-Arts. Thus Francis Peabody (1831–1910) and Arthur Dexter (1830–97) were the second and third American citizens to study architecture at the Ecole (the fourth was Henry Hobson Richardson). Both Peabody and Dexter were from Massachusetts, and it seems likely that Peabody entered the atelier Lefuel because Hunt was there and that Dexter followed Peabody. Francis Peabody's older brother, Joseph (1824–1905), and Hunt's older brother, William, were both in the class of 1844 at Harvard College. Francis Peabody was born in Salem, Massachusetts, and did not attend a college. He became a pupil of Lefuel in September 1850, got into the Ecole in November 1852, and met with success in only one *concours*, in April 1853. Arthur Dexter was born in Boston, was graduated from Harvard College in the class of 1851, and joined the atelier in August 1852. He was admitted to the Ecole on the same day as Peabody and got no credit for *concours*. Neither man practiced architecture in later life. Francis Peabody was employed as Lloyd's agent in Boston; Arthur Dexter led the life of a dilettante in Rome and Boston. I am grateful to the late Right Reverend Malcolm E. Peabody for his letters of 3 and 28 July 1969 about his grandfather. Francis Peabody's Ecole dossier is in Archives Nationales vol. AJ-52-377; Arthur Dexter's is in AJ-52-363. On Dexter, see also the *Class Book of the Class of 1851 of Harvard College*, in the Harvard University archives.

20. On the work by Visconti and Lefuel on the Louvre and Tuileries, see Louis Hautecoeur, *Histoire de l'architecture classique en France*, tome 7: 1848–1900 (Paris, 1957), especially pp. 1–10.

21. So said J. Macvicar Anderson, president of the Royal Institute of British Architects, when introducing Hunt to that body on 19 June 1893. Hunt had probably provided information about his career to Anderson. A few moments after Anderson spoke, Hunt himself said, "the Pavillon de la Bibliothèque . . . was entrusted to my care" (*The R.I.B.A. Journal* 9, n.s., [22 June 1893]: 426, 429.

22. *Revue générale de l'architecture* 18 (1855), cols. 85–87.

3

Richard Morris Hunt: Architectural Innovator and Father of a "Distinctive" American School

Sarah Bradford Landau

But I cannot help thinking that if Fergusson [James] were to see some of the work done here in the last decade, he would at least modify his opinion, and own that there is growing up a distinctive school of American architecture, and that Hunt, more than anyone else, may be considered its father.

A. J. Bloor, "Annual Address," *Proceedings of the Annual Conventions of the American Institute of Architects*, 10 (12 October 1876): 29–30.

3.1 Studio Building, 15 West Tenth Street, New York City, 1857; demolished.

FOLLOWING Richard Morris Hunt's death on 31 July 1895, laudatory obituaries and reviews of his distinguished forty-year career poured forth from the press and architectural journals. The extent to which these have determined, to this day, critical opinion of his architecture is remarkable. In 1895 Hunt's reviewers regarded him as the most widely renowned American architect of his time, the "doyen" of his profession, and the man who almost singlehandedly elevated the status of the architect in America. In the words of his former pupil George B. Post, Hunt was "almost the first trained architect of American birth to practice with distinction in this country."[1] The list of honors awarded him is a lengthy one, and includes the coveted Victoria gold medal, bestowed by the Royal Institute of British Architects in 1893; his election in December 1893 to associate membership in the Académie des Beaux-Arts in Paris; his memberships in the Society of Saint Luke in Rome and in the major professional organizations of Paris, London, and Vienna; and his participation as a founder and third president of the American Institute of Architects.

Every account of Hunt's career points out that he was the first American architect to be trained at the Ecole des Beaux-Arts in Paris. Hunt's New York atelier, in existence from 1857 to 1860, is credited with transmitting to America the Ecole's rigorous system of training. (The Ecole tradition was carried on by Hunt's pupil William R. Ware, who headed the first American school of architecture, founded at MIT in 1868, and went on to head the Columbia University School of Architecture.) The excellence of Hunt's teaching, described by *New-York Daily Tribune* critic Royal Cortissoz as "healthily academic," is frequently recalled.[2]

Hunt's reviewers were quick to acknowledge his fame, honors, and professional commitment, and some even refer to his material success, but most also expressed reservations about the quality of his architecture. Many found it lacking in originality—an opinion that has endured. P. B. Wight put it bluntly: "Hunt was not a great architectural genius. . . . His work was not novel or inventive. . . . He never laid claim to originality, and often said that you could not show him anything modern, but that he would show you its counterpart and of higher degree in the works of bygone ages." According to the *Real Estate Record and Builders Guide*, Hunt's buildings were "deficient in, but not destitute of, power, imagination, spontaneity, delicacy and charm. The touch of inevitableness—the result of the complete fusion of the artist's processes, perceptions and individuality in the accomplished work—was rarely his. . . ." Henry

47

Van Brunt, who had studied with Hunt, explained, "His pencil in hand was a magic wand, which chastened the buoyancy of his imagination and made him a scholar. Thus he founded no new school." The inference was usually that Hunt's admiration for historic architecture had inhibited his imagination, though Van Brunt maintained that Hunt's early work in the spirit of the "Graeco-Romantic movement in France under Labrouste" betrayed a "natural vivacity of temperament."[3]

In 1895 the critics acknowledged Hunt and H. H. Richardson as the two most important figures in American architecture. Inevitably, and usually to his detriment, Hunt was measured against Richardson. Richardson had invented a new style, and his work had attracted a large following, neither of which, according to Hunt's reviewers, could be claimed by Hunt. Rather defensively, Van Brunt attempted to find some virtue in these failings: "Unlike Richardson, Hunt did not leave upon his work an expression of strong personality, and for that reason his leadership . . . is far safer against the dangers of aberration among his followers." Bloor alone argued positively the virtues of Hunt over Richardson, asserting that "the well balanced and conscientious architect works from the inside to the outside—which Richardson did not do and Hunt did."[4]

Like Van Brunt, Montgomery Schuyler believed that Hunt's youthful efforts demonstrated individuality and imagination. But even in this work, in Schuyler's judgment, Hunt had not achieved "a new and comprehensive style." Robert Craik McClean, editor of the *Inland Architect and News Record*, was exceptional in noticing that Hunt's French-château style had attracted many followers. McClean also pointed out that recently there had been an attempt to "found a modern school" based on Hunt's work in the "modern French style"— by which he meant Beaux-Arts classicism. However, rather less perspicaciously, and doubtless swayed by loyalty to the Chicago school, McClean predicted that the attempt would not be successful.[5]

Hunt's critics were men of their time. Though effectively at an end by 1895, the Richardsonian era was everywhere in evidence. The work of the Chicago school was still drawing favorable comment, and Beaux-Arts classicism was obviously in the ascendant. Hunt's early work belonged to a bygone era, the war and depression-wracked years of the late 1850s to the mid 1870s. Not surprisingly, then, his more recent work, especially the palatial residences in New York, Newport, and Asheville, drew more attention from his reviewers. Even Schuyler, who devoted a generous portion of his long and thorough review to the early work, considered Hunt's later architecture to be his best. Hunt's most admired building was the W. K. Vanderbilt mansion in New York, his first essay in his François I style and the building that, in 1885, had been third in the list of the ten best buildings in the United States published in the *American Architect*.[6] The critics also liked his later houses in that mode, especially Biltmore. The Administration Building at the Columbian Exposition of 1893 was generally regarded as one of America's greatest monumental buildings.[7]

With the advent of twentieth-century modernism, Hunt's late work fell out of favor, as indeed did all of his architecture, and until quite recently it was more often cited for its conspicuousness and ostentation than for any positive qualities of design.[8] But now, with so much attention being paid to American Beaux-Arts classicism and the houses of the well-to-do in the late nineteenth century, interest in Hunt's work has revived. Yet neither the Vanderbilt mansion nor the Administration Building has regained its former status. Estimations of Hunt's early work have hardly been revised since 1895, although a great deal more is known about that work and about Hunt's career as a whole, chiefly because of the efforts of Paul R. Baker.[9]

All along, Hunt's early work has both fascinated and perplexed—and at times even repelled—his critics. Today, as in 1895, the preeminence of the Tribune Building, the Stuyvesant Apartments, and the Griswold house in the context of their specific genres is acknowledged if not fully understood. Hunt's Lenox Library, today recognized as a singularly pure expression in this country of mid-century French architectural style, also appealed to the academic taste of 1895. Nevertheless, present-day historians find it as difficult to appreciate the restless red and white color scheme and vigorously active design of some of the early buildings, particularly the Presbyterian Hospital, as did Schuyler.[10] Somewhere along the way, the concept of Hunt as the father "more than anyone else" of a school of American architecture, as A. J. Bloor expressed it, has been forgotten. It was buried by the Richardsonians in the 1880s as well as by Hunt himself, who abandoned the innovative and sometimes gawky designs of his early career for the grander work and the mansions that characterized his late career. The implications of Bloor's comment, however, deserve further discussion.

The Tenth Street Studio Building

The first landmark in Hunt's career was his Tenth Street Studio Building of 1857 (fig. 3.1). The building, Hunt's first independently realized large commission, the site of his famous New York atelier and of the studios of many well-known American artists, was also highly significant architecturally. It introduced a new type of building to New York, one in which studios, living accommodations, and gallery space were combined in one structure designed specifically to satisfy the needs of artists. Hunt's previous experience—his student project for an archives building (see figs. 2.25–2.27), his work for Lefuel on the Pavillon de da Bibliothèque of the Louvre (see fig. 2.31), and the studios and exhibition space provided in his just completed Thomas J. Rossiter House (see fig. 6.8)— as well as his close association with artists had prepared him for this unique undertaking. The design of library and picture galleries and artists' studios would remain a specialty of his.

The Studio Building presented New Yorkers with a bold and practical version of the "Graeco-Romantic," or *néo-grec* work of those architects associated with Henri Labrouste and the Romantic-rationalist movement in France. Its long brick facade was "rationally" articulated by sharply projecting moldings between stories and raised brick bands around segmental-headed windows and the door. Repeated across the ground story, a circle-in-the-square motif reinforced the geometry and rectilinear design of this front; and, strategically placed, light brown stone or possibly terra-cotta trimming relieved the monotony of the red brick. The use of ornamental brickwork was exceptional at this date; only in the 1870s and 1880s, with the growth of the architectural terra-cotta industry and the development of light-colored brick, would the all-brick or brick and terra-cotta front become prevalent in the city. Hunt's inspiration for the facade may have been the inner forecourt facades of Félix Duban's Palais des Etudes (1834–40) in the Ecole des Beaux-Arts complex, a logical choice of model; but his use of brick rather than stone, his avoidance of such explicitly Renaissance-derived motifs as pilasters, and his imaginative brickwork ornament, correspond to contemporary French vernacular architecture.[11]

The four-story Studio Building was planned in the form of a hollow square about ninety-eight by ninety-four feet. At the center was a courtyardlike enclosed space roofed over by a skylight at the second-story level, the exhibition gallery. Of the twenty-five studios in the building, twelve had adjoining sleeping rooms at the half-level.[12] In essence these were duplex studio apartments, although none had kitchen facilities. Here, all in one building, were precedents for the New York apartment house, apartment hotel, duplex apartment, and courtyard apartment house. But it would be years before these ideas were fully implemented, and others besides Hunt would contribute to their realization.[13]

Struggles with the High Victorian Gothic

In the 1860s the preferred style for New York cultural and institutional buildings was the English-imported High Victorian Gothic. That preference, along with the financial depression of the late 1850s and the Civil War that followed in the early 1860s, accounted for Hunt's difficulty at first in getting commissions of this kind. His expertise in studio and gallery design brought him an invitation in 1861 to compete for the National Academy of Design in New York. However, his warehouselike project, with its huge, unmolded ground-story windows (see fig. 7.3), impressed the Academicians less favorably than did P. B. Wight's "Ruskinian" adaptation of the Ducal Palace in Venice, although Hunt's design was Gothic and had bichromatic arches over the windows.[14] Van Brunt later recalled that Hunt "inspired the classic camp with ardor" in the "battle of styles" waged in the early sessions of the AIA, but the "strongest and best equipped men in the profession" were on the side of Gothic. Schuyler, however, recognized the latent Gothicist in Hunt. Asserting Hunt's fundamentally romantic nature, he speculated that "it was only Mr. Hunt's exceptional training that prevented him from being among the pioneers in this country of the Gothic Revival."[15]

Certainly Hunt resorted to the Gothic several times in the 1860s. He used it for his National Academy of Design project, his proposal for the New-York Historical Society Museum (ca. 1865), and his competition design for the Brooklyn Mercantile Library (1865; fig. 3.2). But in each instance his interpretation

3.2 Elevation proposal for the Brooklyn Mercantile Library Competition, October 1865.

3.3 Presbyterian Hospital, Administration Building, East Seventieth Street between Madison and Fourth (later Park) Avenues, New York City, 1869–72; demolished.

of the High Victorian Gothic idiom was unorthodox, which surely explains, at least in part, why none was ever executed. In the case of the Mercantile Library project, symmetry and an unusual openness imparted by large, closely set windows distinguish an otherwise reasonably "Ruskinian" facade. In that competition, Wight's more subdued and thoroughly English Victorian Gothic design was, again, selected over Hunt's.

Several of Hunt's urban and institutional designs made soon after his trip to Paris in 1867 reveal a fusion, in varying proportions, of the Gothic and the *néo-grec*. The Presbyterian Hospital (1869–72), the Yale Divinity School (1869–70), and the Stuyvesant Apartments (1869–70), which fall into this category, have been severely criticized. They have been described as "confused," "frenzied," "awkwardly composed," "overly fussy," and worse[16] (figs. 3.3 and 3.19). Hunt was probably trying to align his work with the High Victorian Gothic, then approaching its peak of popularity in America, and in doing so trying to arrive at a style that would also reflect his affinity for modern French architecture. Viollet-le-Duc, whom he had seen in Paris, had obviously influenced Hunt; but polychromy and a certain medieval rationalism, or, as Neil Levine has described it, a "crypto-Gothic" quality,[17] also characterized the work of architects directly associated with the *néo-grec* movement, e.g., Léon Vaudoyer and Louis Duc. (Hunt, of course, knew their work as well.) Under the influence of Hunt, who was his teacher, Frank Furness devised a powerful and highly personal style from just this sort of compromise. The outcome for Hunt himself may have been less impressive, but his work of the late 1860s encouraged the rise of a modern urban style in America described in the 1870s as "Neo-Greek" or "Neo-Grec."[18] His Presbyterian Hospital featured the unmolded triangular and rectangular lintels associated with the secular Gothic by Viollet-le-Duc.[19] In America these lintels, often decorated with simple incised designs, as in the case of the hospital, became the hallmark of the American Neo-Grec.

The Early Newport Villas

Assisted greatly by his social connections, Hunt had no difficulty obtaining domestic commissions in the 1860s. His simulated half-timber J. N. A. Griswold house in Newport, Rhode Island, commissioned while he was on his honeymoon in Paris in 1861, encouraged the building of picturesque suburban and resort houses in Newport and elsewhere in the northeast for the next fifteen years or so (fig. 3.4). The Griswold house and subsequent houses with similar characteristics have been called examples of the mature and late "stick style" by Vincent Scully, Jr., who has identified this mode as predominantly American and as having originated in designs published in English and American pattern books.[20] Scully notwithstanding, Hunt and the several architects who followed his lead were inspired by the contemporary revival in Germany and France of half-timber houses, the Swiss chalet, and other vernacular styles of wood architecture. In France this romantically motivated revival was represented by the picturesque garden pavilions and country and resort houses built during the Second Empire. Hunt's vast architectural library included foreign publications illustrating this work, and of course he knew it at first hand as well. As the chief American practitioner of the European vernacular revival, he set an example that was followed by such architects as the French-trained Robert Swain Peabody and the Newport firm of George Champlin Mason (fig. 3.5).[21]

The recent rediscovery of several Hunt-designed wood-frame houses, principally the Hitchcock-Travers (ca. 1862; 1869–71), Mrs. William F. Coles (1869–70), and Charlotte Cushman (1871–72) houses—none, unfortunately, extant—further confirms Hunt's stature as a domestic architect (fig. 3.6). William Ralph Emerson's Sanford-Covell house (1869–70) in Newport and Dudley Newton's Cram-Sturtevant house (1875–76) in nearby Middletown adhere to precedents set by this group of houses and by the Griswold house.

In the early 1870s, Hunt designed several highly picturesque "cottages" with polychrome brick or slate-hung walls, prominent stickwork, and big, overhanging gables—features derived from the Swiss chalet and other European vernacular types. This group, which includes the T. G. Appleton (1870–71) and H. G. Marquand (1872–73) villas in Newport and the Howland Circulating Library (1871–72) in Beacon, New York (fig. 3.7), compares with the contemporary *chalets normands* at the Norman resorts in France. Bloor placed Hunt at the head of a movement in which "old forms and modern sentiment have . . . produced combinations . . . suggestive of vernacular shades of expression in architectural art," and he also observed that in Newport

> Hunt was one of the first to invest comparatively inexpensive cottages and villas with some of the attributes of an indigenous and coherent art; and from the firm of a pupil of his [Charles Gambrill], Gambrill and Richardson, we have had some of the latest and best developments in this kind. . . .[22]

Bloor rightly credits Hunt with having stimulated a new development in American domestic architecture, a development that would culminate in the vernacular expression known as the Colonial Revival.

3.4 John N. A. Griswold house, 76 Bellevue Avenue, Newport, R.I., 1861–63.

3.5 *Above:* George C. Mason, Jr., architect, Thomas F. Cushing house, Newport, R.I., 1869–70. Photograph reprinted from G. C. Mason, *Newport and Its Cottages* (Newport, 1875).

3.6 *Left:* Mrs. William F. Coles house, Bellevue Avenue and Dixon Street, Newport, R.I., 1869–70; demolished.

3.7 Howland Circulating Library, 477 Main Street, Beacon (formerly Matteawan), N.Y., 1871–72.

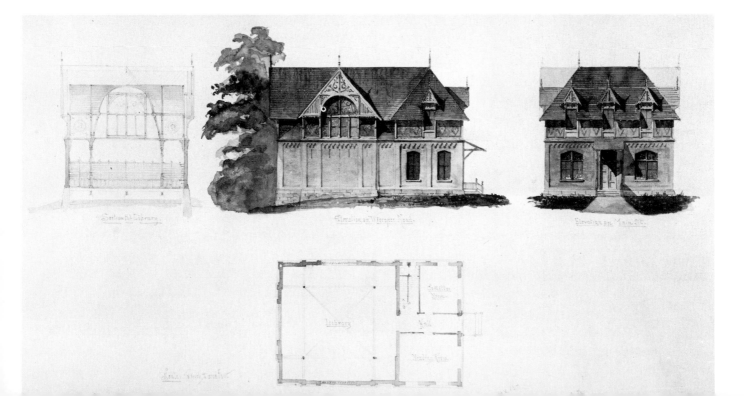

Commercial Buildings

Along with the economy, Hunt's career began to flourish on all fronts after the Civil War. He did, however, continue to lose out in competitions from time to time. He lost an important one in 1867, that for the Equitable Building, to Gilman and Kendall, who were assisted on engineering matters by George B. Post. As the first office building to incorporate an elevator as part of its initial design, the Equitable has been called the first skyscraper.[23] The increased height of the new "elevator building" presented architects with unprecedented and difficult design problems; the several variations of Hunt's Equitable project reveal that he proposed a pair of tall arches subsuming three stories on the main Broadway front and a two-story arcade on the long Cedar Street side of the building (fig. 3.8). Hunt and Richardson, whose competition project for this same commission includes arcades embracing two stories, were early to realize how effective the device could be as a means of organizing the stories of a tall commercial building. Though not published, their proposals undoubtedly impressed other New York architects, especially Post, whose arcaded buildings of the 1870s transmitted the motif to others. Hunt's designs include strongly demarcated bays and boldly detailed arches—pointed in the perspective illustrated here—that define big mullioned and transomed windows, features that would appear in more developed form in the Lenox Library. Curiously, the general scheme of the front and side walls, in which vertical rows of windows frame each facade, foreshadows Babb, Cook, and Willard's remarkable De Vinne Press (1885–86) in New York.[24]

Even more significant in the development of the late nineteenth-century commercial style is Hunt's office and store building commissioned by the merchant and banker Royal Phelps and built on Union Square in 1872 (fig. 3.9).

3.8 *Left:* Perspective proposal for the Equitable Life Assurance Society Building, Broadway and Cedar Street, New York City, ca. 1867.

3.9 *Below:* Royal Phelps Building, 25 Union Square West, New York City, 1872; demolished.

3.10 Elevation proposal for the Western Union Telegraph Company Building, Broadway and Dey Street, New York City, ca. 1872.

3.12 Preliminary elevation, Coal and Iron Exchange (Delaware and Hudson Canal Company building), 17–21 Cortlandt Street, New York City, ca. 1873.

3.11 Preliminary elevation, New York Tribune Building, ca. 1873.

In the narrow stone and cast-iron front of this five-story building, Hunt achieved an early version of the commercial formula traditionally ascribed to Louis Sullivan: a tripartite scheme, an arcaded midsection, and a facade that seems more glass than masonry. Sullivan could easily have seen this building as well as other commercial work of Hunt's; in 1873 and again in 1874 he visited Hunt's office in New York.[25] In fact, the Royal Phelps Building closely anticipated Adler and Sullivan's early commercial designs, for example, the Jeweler's (1881–82) and Troescher (1884–85) buildings.

Hunt's preliminary designs of about 1873 for the Western Union Building (a commission awarded to Post), the Tribune Building, and the Coal and Iron Exchange disclose his experiments with different rhythms of arcading (figs. 3.10, 3.11, 3.12). In these structures Hunt used segmental arches, probably because they were currently favored by French architects for utilitarian brick architecture. Hunt's studies for the Tribune Building and the Coal and Iron Exchange, as well as the completed buildings, presage the formula made famous by Richardson's Marshall Field Wholesale Store in the mid 1880s: a quickening rhythm utilizing tiers of arcades. The rhythm of the Coal and Iron Exchange as constructed (1873–76)[26] prefigured that of Post's highly influential Produce Exchange, built from 1881 to 1885 just a few blocks away. Hunt's commercial work was also early to utilize the triple-window bay, yet another feature commonly associated with Chicago buildings of the 1890s.

The Tribune commission offered Hunt the opportunity to design a building twice as high as any commercial structure yet built in New York (fig. 3.13). As completed, the ten-story building was 260 feet from the sidewalk to the top of the tower finial, taller by thirty feet than Post's contemporary Western Union Building. The Tribune (1873–75) is third in the sequence of elevator buildings today considered to be the "first skyscrapers." Although completed in the same year, the Western Union was begun earlier, in the fall of 1872.[27]

The faults of the Tribune Building have often been pointed out. Even Bloor, a contemporary observer, found the color contrast of the light stone trim and the brick—red with black brick patterns—"too violent" and the form of the building "somewhat extravagant and outré" as well as lacking in "repose." But, as Bloor acknowledged, Hunt was working at quite a disadvantage with regard to the contour of the site (fig. 3.14).[28] On the side of the main front, on Print-

3.13 New York Tribune Building, northeast corner of Nassau and Spruce streets, New York City, 1873–75; demolished.

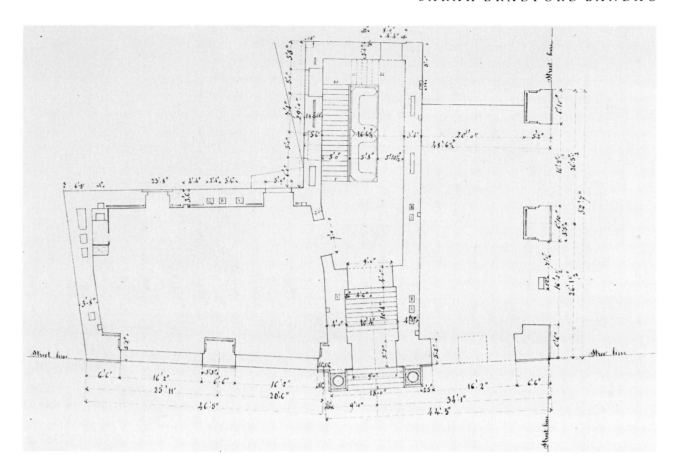

3.14 Plan of first story (lobby floor), New York Tribune building.

ing House Square, the property line was oddly angled. Hunt tried to overcome the problem by positioning the main entrance and the tower at the point of the obtuse angle. By beginning the tower midway up the front rather than at the base of the building, he made it an integral part of the structure. A letter written to Hunt on 19 January 1875, signed "H. C.," explains the cause of the most severe defect of the final design: the low height of the base in respect to the heavy proportions of the mansarded top resulted from the owners' belated decision to increase the height of the building. In the preliminary design, which called for eight stories including a one-story mansard, the base and top are in scale. (Ironically, an alternative proposal called for a well-integrated, ten-story building; see fig. 6.18.) Even in what is probably the penultimate design (published after construction had begun), where the mansard embraces two stories, the proportions are not bad. The decision to add a third story at the mansard level, apparently made after the building was under construction, resulted in an awkward and unbalanced composition.[29] But the added height increased the significance of Hunt's building. With its soaring clock tower, the Tribune Building prefigured the tower-skyscrapers of the future.

Just how technically innovative Hunt's commercial buildings were is not entirely clear, but several elements of the Tribune Building's construction were decidedly avant-garde. These include the composition of its concrete-bedded foundation, the structure of its giant relieving arches (seen in the first and fifth stories), and its fireproof floor construction. According to P. B. Wight, who was an authority in fireproofing technology as well as an architect, the fireproof construction of both the Tribune Building and the Coal and Iron Exchange was the most advanced type available. The floors, manufactured by the Fire-proof

Building Company of New York according to a system recently patented in France, were constructed of flat arches made of hollow terra-cotta blocks resting on iron beams. Wight credits Hunt with having recommended to this company the substitution of terra-cotta for the hollow concrete blocks normally used in the French method—a great improvement because the lighter weight of the terra-cotta permitted the use of lighter-weight iron beams. Hunt's were among the earliest American buildings with "hollow tile" arches, earlier examples having been the Kendall Building (1872–73) in Chicago and the New York Post Office (1869–75; Hunt had collaborated on the design of the latter).[30] Hunt's Lenox Library (1870–77) and Roosevelt Building (1873–74) were also constructed with hollow-block floor arches supplied by the Fire-proof Building Company.[31]

As further insurance against fire damage, no upright iron supports were used in the Tribune Building; the iron floor beams were purposely not left exposed, and brick or cement partitions were used between rooms. The red brick exterior walls, characteristic of much of Hunt's commercial work, provided added protection against fire; in the early 1870s hard brick was favored for commercial buildings for just this reason.[32] These precautions had been prompted by the catastrophic devastation caused by the recent fires in Chicago and Boston.

The number and convenient side-by-side location of the two public elevators and the provision of at least one exterior window in every room distinguished the plan of the Tribune Building. Rental tenants occupied most of the seven floors below the roofline, and the newspaper's offices were on the top two floors. Taking full advantage of the prestige and view afforded by its lofty height, the paper's editor, Whitelaw Reid, had his office in the tower. At least two major rooms, the banking and counting rooms on the ground floor, were decorated by Herter Brothers, the famous firm that would later design the lavish interiors of the W. K. Vanderbilt mansion.[33]

The Tribune Building and Post's Western Union Building—which were akin stylistically though differently detailed—had far-reaching effects on commercial design. The mode they helped initiate can be described as structurally expressive or rational: wall-bearing piers divide the facades into bays two or three windows wide, and the overall design is gridlike. Ornament is minimal, and is usually incised or low-relief, as on the Tribune Building. Often the secondary material (stone or terra-cotta) is light in color, intended to contrast with the red brick walls; and frequently this light-colored stone stripes the walls and functions as support at points of structural stress or as design emphasis, as across the tops of windows or at the base of the building. This bony, hard-edged, crisply detailed commercial mode flourished in New York and Boston in the 1870s and 1880s and quickly spread to Cincinnati, Chicago, and other cities.[34] One is tempted to call it the commercial Neo-Grec.

Wight attributes Hunt's urban style of the 1870s to the influence of Viollet-le-Duc, V.-M.-C. Ruprich-Robert, and Henri Labrouste; but perhaps more relevant to his commercial work are the designs of certain other architects. The details of such utilitarian buildings as C.-A. Questel's hospital at Gisors (1859–61), Gustave Auvray's public baths at Caen (ca. 1869), and especially Gabriel Davioud's stone-fronted Magasins Réunis (1865–66) in Paris—all of which Hunt could have seen either in situ or as illustrated in the *Revue générale de l'architecture*—closely approximate the segmental arches and flat, sharp-edged, incised motifs of the American Neo-Grec.[35] The two-story arcades, ironwork, and tripartite design for the Place de la République (formerly Place du Château-d'Eau) facade of the Magasins Réunis surely inspired Hunt (fig. 3.15).

Many New York buildings utilized features of the commercial Neo-Grec, among them Alfred H. Thorp's Racquet Club (1875–76; extant); Griffith Thomas's American News Company Building (1876–77); Edward H. Kendall's E. Oelbermann and Company Store (1876–77, extant); Stephen D. Hatch's Boreel building (1878–79); J. Morgan Slade's office building at 753 Broadway (1880); and W. Wheeler Smith's W. and J. Sloane Store (1881–82; extant; fig. 3.16). Chicago buildings that display similar characteristics include P. B. Wight's Cyrus Hawley and Stewart-Bentley buildings (both designed in 1872); Gambrill and Richardson's original design for the American Express Building (1872); William Le Baron Jenney's Portland Block (ca. 1872–75) and cage-like first Leiter Building (1879–80; fig. 3.17); several of Burnham and Root's

3.15 *Above:* Gabriel Davioud, Magasins Réunis, Paris, 1865–66. Elevation. Published in *Revue générale de l'architecture* 28 (1870), pl. 6.

3.16 *Above right:* W. Wheeler Smith, architect, W. and J. Sloane Store, New York City, 1881–82. Photograph by author.

3.17 William Le Baron Jenney, architect, first Leiter Building, Chicago, 1879–80, demolished. Photograph courtesy of the Art Institute of Chicago.

3.18 Preliminary perspective, Roosevelt (left) and Alexander Van Rensselaer buildings, 478–82 and 474–76 Broadway, New York City, drawing dated 3 November 1873.

early commercial buildings, e.g., the Grannis Block (1880–81); George H. Edbrooke's Hiram Sibley Warehouse (1882–83; extant); and the early work of Adler and Sullivan. Nearly as skeletal and almost as technically advanced as the first Leiter, James McLaughlin's remarkable Shillito Store (1877) in Cincinnati also belongs in this category. Predisposed by French training, ties to New York, or admiration for Viollet-le-Duc, these midwestern architects followed the lead of the New York school that Hunt had fathered.[36]

From the time they were completed, Hunt's adjoining commercial buildings on Broadway were admired for their exceptionally open, screenlike facades (fig. 3.18). The exotic Van Rensselaer Building (1871–72; first occupied by Rice, Goodwin, Walker and Company) and the Roosevelt Building were novel and functional expressions of the long-established cast-iron front, and embodied ideas Hunt had voiced back in 1858:

> Where land is exceedingly valuable, the whole lot is often built over for economy of space, and in the absence of interior courts and areas, it is necessary that the facade should become, as it were, one immense window for the sake of light . . . iron, requiring the protection of color, thus offers to us an opportunity of developing one of the greatest beauties of architecture.[37]

For the Van Rensselaer Building, which is not extant, Hunt devised a decorative Moorish-style facade with slender columns, lacelike cusped arches, and myriad colored surfaces painted to resemble tiles. The two Neo-Grec facades of the Roosevelt Building (the rear facade fronts on Crosby Street) are conspicuous for their extremely slender iron elements, designed to admit a maximum of natural light into the interior, and their pleasingly proportioned tripartite design.

The drawing reproduced here shows the Roosevelt Building in a preliminary study and the Van Rensselaer Building as completed. Although the styles of the buildings are quite different, Hunt's alignment of the horizontal divisions of the two fronts makes them compatible neighbors. As indicated by Bloor, the Roosevelt Building too was initially polychrome, but by 1876 both had been repainted. Apparently their innovative color schemes were not appreciated. Bloor, speaking with the bias of an admirer of Ruskin, associated Hunt with James Renwick, Jr., and Russell Sturgis in a common effort to express the nature of iron "without debasing their compositions, as usual, by sham construction in imitation of stone."[38]

Apartment Houses

It is not at all certain that the Stuyvesant (1869–70) was actually the first apartment house in America, as has so often been alleged; it may not even have been the first built in New York (fig. 3.19). However, it certainly launched the age of the apartment house. As early as 1857 Calvert Vaux had recommended "Parisian flats" as a solution to New York's already vexing middle-class housing problem, but only after the Stuyvesant succeeded in attracting a highly respectable tenantry was his recommendation taken seriously, for at the time many Americans associated multiple dwellings with the tenements of the poor. It should be noted, however, that, according to James Richardson, writing in 1874, a small apartment house had been built in Wooster Street and another in Hudson Street about 1855. (Richardson attributes the one in Wooster Street to Hunt.) There may have been an even earlier one: in 1902 a builder named Thomas Kilpatrick was credited with building in 1853 the first modern apartment house on Thirtieth Street near Lexington Avenue. Based on the "French etage or floor idea," it contained apartments for several families, "each with a bath and various other conveniences."[39]

Whether Kilpatrick's building or the other mysterious early examples can be accepted as apartment houses proper hinges on whether they met the accepted criteria for such dwellings: Did they have private toilets and hallways within

3.19 Stuyvesant Apartments, 142 East Eighteenth Street, New York City, 1869–70; demolished. Published in *Architectural Record* 11 (July 1901): 47.

each apartment (as tenements did not)? Did each apartment have its own kitchen? If there were no private kitchens and meals were served in a communal dining room, then these structures might better be classified as apartment hotels. Until it is proved otherwise, New York must credit Boston with the first apartment hotel in the Hotel Pelham (1856–57), designed by Alfred Stone of Arthur Gilman's firm. And, despite its name, Boston's Hotel St. Cloud (1869–70), designated by Nathaniel J. Bradlee, should probably be accepted as sharing with the Stuyvesant the distinction of being the "first American apartment house."[40] By 1874, about half of New York's nearly two hundred hotels were occupied by families and bachelors living there as long-term residents, but apparently not until the early 1870s did the city get its first apartment hotels.[41] The importance of the Stuyvesant Apartments, however, remains undiminished: it was probably the first American building to be called an apartment house, and was certainly the first to be recognized as such; and it did stimulate the building of "French flats" (the popular term in New York for the apartment house) in the 1870s.

The Stuyvesant was not modeled directly on the Parisian apartment house, though people apparently thought so. Rather, it represented a compromise between aspects of the New York row house and the concept of the *maison a loyer*. The peculiar styling of the facade seems contrived to suggest the mansarded, brick-fronted row houses then fashionable in New York as well as the mansarded French apartment house. As if to suggest the parlor floor of the New York row house, the second-story windows were longer than those of the other floors. But in fact the apartments on that floor had much higher ceilings, and rented at a higher rate than the other apartments because of their more desirable location.[42] Partition walls, visible on the roof, as well as the pattern of the fenestration of the floor immediately below the roofline contributed to the impression of a row of houses. Its unexpected Gothic details and polychromy were probably inspired by Viollet-le-Duc's block of flats at 28 rue de Liège (1846–48), and especially by the polychrome brick and stone-trimmed courtyard walls of that building. Surely Hunt's intention was to make this alien habitat appealing to a society accustomed to the privately owned, one-family row house. As in so much of his work, compromise produced electicism.

The layout of the apartments was equally a compromise (fig. 3.20). Each of the five floors accommodated four units, but each apartment above the lobby floor occupied approximately one-quarter of the total width of the building with its rooms arranged *en suite* between thick partition walls. It was as if each floor were a series of four one-story houses separated by party walls. The typical Parisian apartment house of the time consisted of two apartments per floor, but with one in the front and the other in the back, and *maisons de rapport* of the size and quality of Hunt's were normally planned around a central courtyard.[43] In fact, Hunt himself had lived in a large courtyard apartment house, 1 rue Jacob, while he was studying at the Ecole des Beaux-Arts.

Hunt contemplated using the courtyard plan. Among the drawings in the Hunt collection is an unidentified plan for an apartment house with a 36-foot by 28-foot light court in the center (fig. 3.21). Because it is designed for a lot of exactly the same dimensions as that of the Stuyvesant Apartments—112.9 feet by 92 feet—it must be an alternate plan for that building.[44] If one remembers the plan of the Studio Building, it comes as no surprise that Hunt was interested in the courtyard plan. In the case of the Stuyvesant, the plan actually

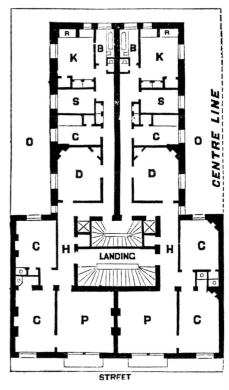

3.20 Plan of one-half of a typical floor, Stuyvesant Apartments. Published in *American Builder and Journal of Art* 1 (December 1869): 232. Key: **P**, parlor; **C**, chamber; **H**, hall; **D**, dining room; **S**, servant's room; **K**, kitchen; **B**, bathroom; **O**, open space.

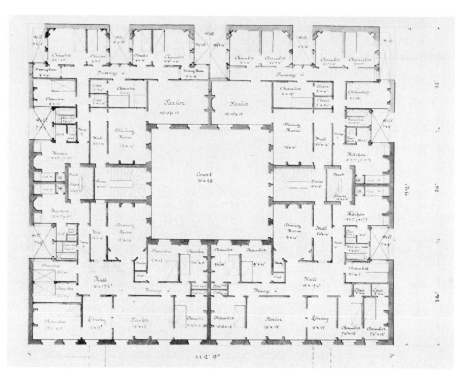

3.21 Alternate plan for the Stuyvesant Apartments, ca. 1869.

adopted was the better choice for the site, for in the alternative plan some outside rooms would have had only small air shafts for ventilation, and the parlors of the two back apartments would have looked out on the court. Vaux had warned against this feature of the courtyard plan, observing that "American ladies . . . think it far more lively and cheerful to look out on a busy thoroughfare than on a monotonous quadrangle, however elegantly it may be decorated." He also predicted that courtyard-oriented apartments would be harder to rent.[45] However, although Hunt himself was never to build a courtyard apartment house, his plan shows foresight. Almost immediately courtyards appeared on a modest scale in Detlef Lienau's Schermerhorn Apartments (1870–71), a row of four second-class apartment houses on Third Avenue at Seventy-first Street. These have two interior courts, really enlarged light shafts, the larger of which measured about twenty feet by thirty feet. Lienau's more exclusive Grosvenor House (1871–72), according to Ellen Kramer possibly the first building in the city constructed as an apartment hotel, was built in an L-shape around a forty-foot-square courtyard on lower Fifth Avenue.[46] Lienau, of course, may have been influenced by existing courtyard hotels such as New York's famous Astor Hotel (1834–36). The Van Corlear (1878–79) and the famous Dakota Apartments (1881–85), both designed by Lienau's pupil Henry J. Hardenbergh for Edward S. Clark, featured large central courtyards that functioned as carriage turnarounds. Other courtyard apartment houses followed these notable examples.[47]

The Stuyvesant has more than once been criticized as having been no better lighted or ventilated than contemporary tenements. Nothing could be further from the truth. In every respect the Stuyvesant provided its occupants with conveniences that clearly distinguished it from a tenement: each apartment had a bathroom, and not just one but *two* waterclosets; each had dumbwaiter service and a generous number (typically seven, counting the bathroom) of well-proportioned rooms, and every apartment had ample light and ventila-

3.22 Stevens House (later Victoria Hotel), south side of Twenty-seventh Street from Fifth Avenue to Broadway, New York City, 1870–72; demolished.

tion. In order to provide every room with a window, Hunt utilized three fifty-foot-deep courts, the one in the center twenty feet across and those at either end ten feet across. These opened onto the rear yard and admitted the strong south light, which was unimpeded by tall buildings, for throughout its existence there were only four-story row houses on the lots behind the Stuyvesant. Open courts were not legally mandated and were therefore rarely provided for tenements until the enactment of the 1901 tenement house law.[48] It is also important to realize that the width across the front of a typical apartment in Hunt's building was about twenty-eight feet, three feet wider than the generous front of a New York row house. All the amenities described above, as well as the spacious, tiled lobby and the four studio apartments on the top floor under the mansard, ensured the success of the Stuyvesant Apartments. By 1879 "several hundreds" of apartment houses existed in the city, at least forty-five of these in the "expensive" class.[49]

Only after 1880, when the economy had fully recovered from the financial depression of the mid 1870s and apartment living had gained a measure of social acceptance among the well-to-do, did the large luxury apartment house begin to appear in New York. But there were a few early ventures of this kind. One of the first, and the very earliest to be constructed as a wholly new building, was Hunt's elegantly Parisian Stevens House (1870–72), a pioneer elevator apartment house (fig. 3.22).[50] Built by the hotel entrepreneur Paran Stevens, who was the principal proprietor of the famous Fifth Avenue Hotel nearby, the irregularly shaped, eight-story block spanned the south side of Twenty-seventh Street for 254 feet from Fifth Avenue to Broadway and presented a front of about 105 feet on Broadway. Along Fifth Avenue Stevens House was initially only twenty-eight feet wide. Even its peculiar proportions and form, in part dictated by the pattern of the streets, recalled the buildings of Haussmann's Paris, where the new, radially planned streets had produced oddly shaped lots and strangely pointed buildings. But in 1873–74, Mrs. Paran Stevens, who had been widowed in 1872, enlarged the building by thirty-four feet on the Fifth Avenue side. Her architect was Arthur Gilman, the man whose firm had produced the first apartment hotel and who had bested Hunt in two important commercial competitions, those for the Equitable and Drexel Buildings.[51] (Hunt by then was attempting to collect fees owed him by Stevens and would file suit against the estate before the end of 1873.) Gilman's addition was styled to match the original building, perhaps even according to plans already made by Hunt.[52]

As originally constructed, Stevens House contained eighteen apartments, the larger ones laid out three to a floor. The servants for each household were to be accommodated in the attic. There are two unidentified plans in the Hunt Collection for a building smaller than Stevens House but one destined for a tract of strikingly similar shape and proportions. These plans show a large rear light court and a proportionately wider frontage than that actually built on the Fifth Avenue side. The ground floor incorporates several stores (there were five in Stevens House) and a restaurant (fig. 3.23). A dining room was almost certainly included in the building as initially completed, for even before Stevens House opened, its hotellike character was apparent.[53]

In 1874 James Richardson described Stevens House as "far more impressive to the beholder than profitable to the owner" and as having been "partially remodeled."[54] Gilman evidently remodeled the interior of the building at the

3.23 Unidentified plan of ground floor of a building similar in proportions and some details to Stevens House.

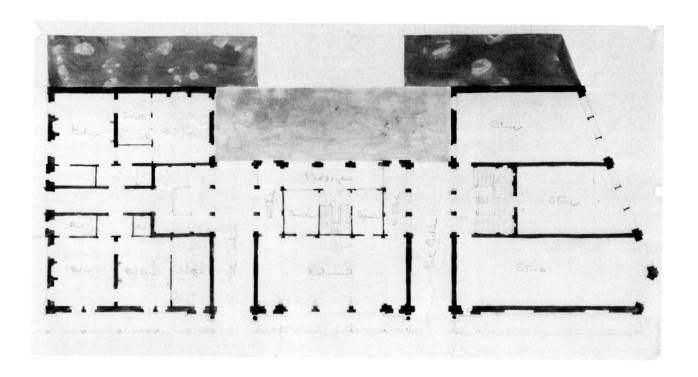

time he made the addition; the individual apartment kitchens were eliminated, and Stevens House became one of the city's first apartment hotels. By 1874 there were at least twelve men—all registered voters—living there, none apparently related, and by 1877 the building housed twenty-seven voters—all, of course, male. But some evidence suggests that these may represent only a small percentage of the actual number of residents.[55] Whether Stevens House was occupied as an eighteen-unit apartment house even for a short time is doubtful. The financial panic of 1873 as well as Mrs. Stevens's own financial problems with her husband's estate doubtless contributed to the failure of the initial enterprise. In 1879 the building was renovated as the Victoria Hotel, and opened to the traveling public. According to an advertisement of 1910, it was capable of housing five hundred guests.[56]

As originally planned, however, the facilities of Stevens House foreshadowed the luxury apartment houses of the 1880s, and its mansarded, block-long mass heralded the grand hotels of the 1890s. The iron balconies and long, stone-trimmed brick front of the Chelsea (1883–85), the mansard-roofed, Neo-Grec–influenced facades of the Van Corlear, and the amenities of the Dakota, where servants were quartered in the attic and communal dining facilities were available to the tenants, find parallels in the innovations planned for Stevens House. The Chelsea's duplexes and attic studios are other features that can be traced to the early leads of the Studio Building and the Stuyvesant Apartments.

It should be pointed out that in many ways Stevens House was European, for example in its combination of stores on the ground floor with apartments above. Given the large size of the apartments as first planned—some with five bedrooms—could it be that Paran Stevens intended to offer them on a cooperative basis, as was done in central Europe and Scotland? No evidence has yet been found to answer the question one way or the other.[57]

The Neo-Grec City House

More than any other architect, Hunt fostered the American Neo-Grec house front. His influence was felt in Boston, New York, and Chicago, and perhaps in other cities as well. The flat, sheared-off door and window enframements and low-relief ornament of his early Rossiter house in New York and his mansarded Dr. Williams houses (1859–60) in Boston presaged the domestic Neo-Grec that he developed in the late 1860s. These houses, his double house built for Martin Brimmer (1869–70) ten years later, as well as houses by the firm of his former pupils Ware and Van Brunt and also H. H. Richardson's Crowninshield house (1868–70), helped establish the Neo-Grec in Boston. Hunt's Marshall Field house (1871–73) in Chicago influenced the domestic work of P. B. Wight, Burnham and Root, and others there.[58] Hunt's twin houses with connecting studio built for the sculptor John Quincy Adams Ward (1868–1869; fig. 3.24), his two adjoining houses for William H. Osborne and Jonathan Sturgis (both 1869–70), and his Paran Stevens house (1870–71; see plate 7) launched the domestic Neo-Grec in New York.

The relatively simple facades of the Ward houses—exclusive of the reliefs, which were probably executed by the owner—and of the Stevens house dictated the distinctive New York variant of the style. Characteristically, the New York architects and builders who followed Hunt's lead picked up only the un-

3.26 Charles H. Lindsley, builder, house at 138 West Seventieth Street (detail of one house in a uniform row of four houses), New York City, 1881–83. Photograph by author.

3.24 *Above:* John Quincy Adams Ward houses, 7 and 9 West Forty-ninth Street, New York City, 1868–69; demolished.

3.25 *Above center:* Charles Badger, architect, *Maison de Paris,* 6 rue neuve des Capucines. Published in *Revue générale de l'architecture* 13 (1855), pl. 46.

molded lintels and stylized incised ornament rather than the more elaborate, gridlike articulation of his Osborne and Sturgis houses (which corresponds to the ornamental wood paneling of his contemporary Newport houses). Boston's so-called panel-brick style is related to this gridlike aspect of Hunt's urban style, and no doubt the Brimmer houses encouraged the fashion.[59]

The chief merits of the New York Neo-Grec house front were simplicity and modernity. The facade could be realized in either red brick trimmed in stone or as a full, unrelieved brownstone front. Its incised, mechanistic detail was far less expensive to carve than the heavily molded lintels and foliated brackets of the earlier Italianate mode, and could be executed quickly by relatively unskilled craftsmen. The mode was not based directly on any particular historic style, although its details were a mix of "Gothic" and "classical," with features such as the paneling that recall early Renaissance architecture in France. It is a style, moreover, indebted to Paris street fronts of the mid century. Compare, for example, Viollet-le-Duc's apartment house at 15 rue de Douai (1860–61) or an earlier house at 6 rue neuve des Capucines designed by Charles Badger (fig. 3.25) with Hunt's Ward houses. Hunt had surely noticed Badger's house in the *Revue générale de l'architecture,* for Van Brunt copied it while he was studying with Hunt.[60]

The relatively narrow widths of Hunt's row houses, only thirteen and a half feet in the case of the Ward houses, may have inadvertently encouraged a trend in the 1870s toward taller and narrower houses—the real-estate speculator's method of getting the most out of the least amount of property. But Hunt's innovative double-house unit, in which the facade is designed to suggest that the two houses are one, unfortunately did not start a trend in New York, although several such houses designed by McKim, Mead, and White were built in the city later on. After the panic of 1873 and its aftereffects had subsided, row after row of speculator-built Neo-Grec houses (fig. 3.26) and tenements were built in Manhattan and in Brooklyn, a practice that continued until nearly 1890 in Brooklyn.[61]

3.27 Lenox Library, Fifth Avenue (east side) between Seventieth and Seventy-first Streets, New York City, 1870–77; demolished.

The Lenox Library and the W. K. Vanderbilt Mansion

The two buildings that stand out most in Hunt's long career, although for different reasons, are the Lenox Library and the William Kissam Vanderbilt mansion (1879–82). Unfortunately, neither of these New York buildings is extant. The first is famous for the high quality of its design; the second for its overt, even blatant expression of the social aspirations of the client's wife, Alva Smith Vanderbilt, and also because it marked a turning point in Hunt's career: his emergence as the architect of the rich and the arbiter of luxurious taste.

The Lenox Library is widely recognized as Hunt's finest and most purely French-inspired design (fig. 3.27). Even Bloor, whose preferences in 1876 ran in the direction of the High Victorian Gothic, admired the "low horizontal lines, single subdued tint, the thoroughly expressed repose, and the quiet but elegant simplicity" of the Lenox Library. He contrasted those qualities with the "restless, aspiring vitality, the picturesque massing, and the bright double-tinted surface" of the Presbyterian Hospital.[62] Hunt was well aware of how effective the contrast would be; both were built with James Lenox's money on Lenox-owned land and were near enough to be seen simultaneously. Actually, Hunt's work of the early 1870s has more consistency than he is usually given credit for; though the effect is quite different, the tripartite scheme and tall, arch-framed windows of the library's center section correspond to several of Hunt's contemporary commercial designs.

68

It is striking that Hunt was permitted to build in so unfamiliar a style at a time when the High Victorian Gothic was preferred for libraries. The *New York Times* of 5 July 1871 "deplored" the predominance of classicism in the library as contrasted with the mixture of "pure neo-Grec" and Gothic in Stevens House and criticized elements of the design as stylistically discordant. In their choice of a modern, round-arched style, Hunt and Lenox may have intended to complement—or eclipse—the Astor Library downtown. Begun in 1849 by the German-born architect Alexander Saeltzer, and extended twice by additions in 1859 and 1881, the Astor Library is a *Rundbogenstil* palazzo. Until Lenox incorporated his library in 1870 with the intention of one day opening it to the public, the Astor was the only public library in the city.[63]

The French plan of the Lenox Library, with wings flanking a forecourt, was new to the city (fig. 3.28). Hunt's objective was to provide as much light as possible for the picture gallery at the center of the building and the reading room galleries in the wings.[64] The great height of these spaces is expressed in the facades by the tall second-story windows. A typically Parisian feature of the plan was the provision of an apartment for the superintendent or concierge, in this case on the half-level floor behind the vestibule and between the two staircases.

The Lenox Library, unique though it was among American buildings, was not without influence. Undoubtedly it inspired Post in the 1870s, although his Williamsburgh Savings Bank (1870–75) in Brooklyn, which has huge arches and other motifs similar to the library's, may have been designed earlier.[65] (More than once Post was able to realize Hunt's ideas before Hunt could.) It surely affected aspects of Post's Chickering Hall (1874–75; fig. 3.29) and Long Island Historical Society (1878–80); and its plan was probably a source of inspiration for the Villard Houses (1882–85) on Madison Avenue, which face in the same westerly direction and in which light was also a prime consideration. For the Criminal Courts Building (1891–93), architects Thom, Wilson, and

3.28 *Below:* Plan of second story, Lenox Library, ca. 1870.

3.29 *Below right:* George B. Post, architect, Chickering Hall, New York City, 1874–75, demolished. Photograph courtesy of The New-York Historical Society, New York City.

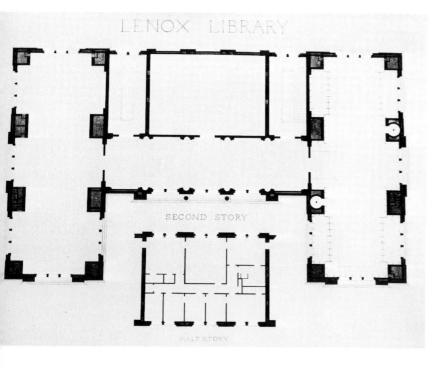

Schaarschmidt adapted the U-shaped plan and the wing facades of the library to a round-arched mode suggestive of German Romantic Classical architecture.[66] But by far the most prominent descendant of the library is the Fifth Avenue entrance wing of the Metropolitan Museum of Art (begun in 1897), Hunt's last major work and a fitting conclusion to a career begun in the service of artists and art collectors (fig. 3.30). Its triple-arched center section adjoined by lower, flanking portions—that is, the building as it appeared before McKim, Mead, and White added the north and south wings—appears in embryo in an alternative design for the library in brick with stone trim. Indeed, the several schemes for the library among the Hunt drawings foreshadow the American "Beaux-Arts" institutional buildings of the 1890s and later.

While the Lenox Library was under construction, Hunt was also at work enlarging the Newport house known as Château-sur-Mer for George Peabody Wetmore (fit. 3.31). Hunt's work on this mid-century house, done in two phases over a ten-year period (1870–73, 1874–80), transformed it from an "Italian villa" into a Second Empire château with Neo-Grec ornamental details. Not only did this ambitious enterprise usher in the palatial era of Newport—to which Hunt was to contribute so impressively—but it also heralded the chief specialty of Hunt's later career: the great house. By 1876 Hunt had received the commission for the W. K. Vanderbilt country house (1876–78) at Oakdale, Long Island: Idlehour was completed as a larger, shingled version of his earlier Newport villas. Soon afterward Hunt began work on Vanderbilt's Fifth Avenue mansion[67] (fig. 3.32) and Saint Mark's Episcopal Church (1879–80) in Islip, Long Island. Inspired by the Norwegian stave church, Saint Mark's was also built with W. K. Vanderbilt money. As the "Vanderbilt architect," Hunt's future was settled. As a result of this connection and its

3.30 Fifth Avenue entrance wing, Metropolitan Museum of Art, Fifth Avenue at Eighty-second Street, New York City, begun 1897; completed by Richard Howland Hunt in 1902.

3.31 *Above:* Château-sur-Mer, George Peabody Wetmore house, Bellevue Avenue, Newport, R.I. The original house was designed by Seth Bradford and built between 1851 and 1852; additions designed by Hunt were made between 1870 and 1880.

3.32 *Above right:* William K. Vanderbilt house, 660 Fifth Avenue, New York City, 1879–82; demolished.

aftermath, however, a small cloud settled over Hunt's reputation. Montgomery Schuyler alludes to the difficulty:

> While not one of his later houses can fairly be charged with making an effect of mere ostentation and prodigality, yet it is in the most conspicuous of them plain that the architect has not been hampered or compelled to curtail his design for want of money.[68]

Hunt nevertheless produced some magnificent houses. One of the finest was another Vanderbilt commission, the famous Newport mansion known as the Breakers (1892–95). For this seventy-room palace, the client, Cornelius Vanderbilt II, selected a Renaissance palazzo design from alternative schemes (another being for a French château) offered by the architect.[69]

The W. K. Vanderbilt mansion on Fifth Avenue resolved Hunt's struggles with his romantic, Gothic side. For this commission Hunt reinvented a legitimately composite style, one that combined Gothic forms with classically derived (Renaissance) details: the François I. Hunt's wood-banded villas and gridded urban facades reveal his preference for French late medieval and early Renaissance architecture, but previously he had rather freely combined motifs from various countries and periods. Perhaps Van Brunt's comments on the sixteenth-century Renaissance mode in his translator's introduction to Viollet-le-Duc's *Discourses* had steered Hunt toward the style. There Van Brunt refers to it as the first French national style and the "academic Paris style" and compares it to Ruskin's "English Renaissance," that is, the High Victorian Gothic.[70] As McClean realized, the style of Hunt's fantastic Fifth Avenue château attracted many followers. Among the most faithful was C. P. H. Gilbert, whose Isaac

Fletcher (1897–99) and Felix M. Warburg (1906–8) houses, now respectively the Ukrainian Institute of America and the Jewish Museum, are the only châteaux still standing on Fifth Avenue, where once there were no less than four by Hunt as well as several others.

By 1880 the struggle had ended for Hunt, and so had the most significant innovations of his career: the studio apartments, the apartment houses, the pioneering commercial buildings, and the vernacular domestic styles. This is not to say he suddenly ceased designing in his early modes. The Charles W. Shields house (1881–83) in Newport; the grander Levi P. Morton house (1886–87) in Rhinecliff, New York; and the neo–Louis XIII Belcourt, the O. H. P. Belmont mansion (1891–93) in Newport, repeat the picturesque forms of the early villas. Hunt's Fifth Avenue château for Mrs. William Astor and her son John Jacob Astor IV (1891–95), another double house, and one far grander than those of the late 1860s, confirms that the French Renaissance château remained a staple of Hunt's, though the details of his later houses varied from the François I. But the Guernsey Building (1881–82), another commercial Neo-Grec design, seems to have been the last of his office buildings; and although his firm produced several rows of tenements in the 1880s, there were no more apartment houses.

What followed were the palaces of the rich, some notable collegiate, public, and institutional buildings, and the great sculpture bases and tomb monuments—a fascinating aspect of Hunt's work that began in the 1860s and reached fulfillment in later years. Hunt also developed a rugged, Norman château manner for certain country houses, perhaps in response to the work of Richardson and McKim, Mead, and White; examples include the round-towered stone houses built for James Pinchot (1884–86) in Milford, Pennsylvania, for Archibald Rogers (1886–89) in Hyde Park, New York, and for Joseph R. Busk (1889–91) in Newport. Hunt's neoclassical work of the 1890s is also of interest. However, it was his early work, sometimes awkwardly designed but always brimming with new ideas, that opened the way to a more sophisticated American architecture. Hunt's greatest legacy may have been the American school he helped so much to create.

Notes

I am especially grateful to the Graham Foundation for Advanced Studies in the Fine Arts, whose grant awarded in 1979–80 enabled me to begin my study of Hunt's architecture. And I would like to thank Susan R. Stein for giving me the opportunity to write this chapter, as well as Sherry C. Birk, who assisted me on many matters related to the Hunt Collection. I am also indebted to Mosette Glaser Broderick, James T. Dillon, and Kenneth Cobb for information and sage advice.

1. *Proceedings of the Twenty-ninth Annual Convention of the American Institute of Architects* (1895), p. 87. And see also Henry Van Brunt, "Richard Morris Hunt," in *Proceedings*, pp. 71–84; P. B. Wight, "Richard Morris Hunt," *Inland Architect and News Record* 26 (August 1895); 2–4; *New York Times*, 1 August 1895, p. 13; Montgomery Schuyler, "The Works of the Late Richard Morris Hunt," *Architectural Record* 5 (October–December 1895): 97–180; Barr Ferree, "Richard Morris Hunt: His Art and Work," *Architecture and Building* 7 December 1895, pp. 271–75; and *New York Evening Post*, 31 July 1895, p. 2.

2. "Richard Morris Hunt," *New-York Daily Tribune*, 4 August 1895, p. 23. And see also "Influence de l'Art Français à l'Etranger," *La Construction Moderne* 7 (September 1895): 577ff.

3. Wight, "Hunt," p. 3; *Record and Guide* 56 (3 August 1895): 148; and Van Brunt, "Hunt," p. 81.

4. Van Brunt, "Hunt," p. 81 (and see "Hunt," *New-York Daily Tribune*, where the same thought is expressed by Cortissoz); and Bloor, letter to the editor, *New York Evening Post*, 3 August 1895 (Hunt scrapbook, HS M1, AIA Library).

5. Schuyler, "Works," pp. 109–10; and R. C. McClean, *Inland Architect and News Record* 26 (August 1895): 1.

6. *American Architect and Building News*, 13 June 1885, p. 282.

7. See, for example, Schuyler, "Works," p. 126; Wight, "Hunt," p. 4; and "Hunt," *New-York Daily Tribune*.

8. E.g., Wayne Andrews, *Architecture, Ambition, and Americans* (London, 1947), pp. 182–84; Antoinette F. Downing and Vincent J. Scully, Jr., *The Architectural Heritage of Newport Rhode Island, 1640–1915*, rev. ed. (New York, 1967), pp. 171–73. Henry-Russell Hitchcock, *Architecture: Nineteenth and Twentieth Centuries*, rev. ed. (Harmondsworth, 1977), does not even mention anything by Hunt after the W. K. Vanderbilt mansion.

9. For a full account of Hunt's career and the details of his personal and professional life, see Baker, *Richard Morris Hunt* (Cambridge, Mass., and London, 1980). The Newport mansions are analyzed appreciatively in considerable detail by Baker and also in William H. Jordy and Christopher P. Monkhouse, *Buildings on Paper: Rhode Island Architectural Drawings, 1825–1945* (Providence, 1982).

10. Schuyler, "Works," p. 104.

11. Brick buildings, brick ornament, and polychrome-patterned brick designs appear in César Daly's *Revue générale de l'architecture et des travaux publics* throughout the 1850s and in the French house books, e.g., Victor Petit, *Maisons de campagne des environs de Paris* (Paris, 185-?). Concurrently, the English, led by Butterfield, Ruskin, and Street, were also interested in brick. On the use of brick and architectural terra-cotta in late nineteenth-century New York, see *A History of Real Estate, Building and Architecture in New York City during the Last Quarter of a Century* (1898; reprint, New York, 1967), pp. 402–6 and 509–28. On the paneled *néo-grec* style, see Francis R. Kowsky, "The William Dorsheimer House: A Reflection of French Suburban Architecture in the Early Works of H. H. Richardson," *Art Bulletin* 62 (1980): 142–45.

12. I am indebted to Annette Blaugrund for allowing me to examine a full set of modern alteration plans of the Studio Building in her possession. Her article on the building's tenants reprints a description of the building published in *Crayon* (5 [January 1858]: 55) soon after it was completed: see A. Blaugrund, "The Tenth Street Studio Building: A Roster, 1858–1895," *American Art Journal* 14 (Spring 1982): 64. The dimensions of the original building are given as 95.5′ by 94.1′ in G. W. Bromley and Co., *Atlas of the City of New York: Manhattan Island*, 2d ed. (Philadelphia, 1894), pl. 11.

13. Others who have noticed the link between the Studio Building and the development of the apartment building include Richard Pommer, in his lecture on the early New York apartment house given at the Institute of Architecture and Urban Studies (March 1976), and Robert A. M. Stern, "With Rhetoric: The New York Apartment House," *Via* 4 (1980): 81.

14. On the competition, see my *P. B. Wight, Architect, Contractor, and Critic, 1838–1925* (Chicago, 1981), pp. 16–17.

15. Van Brunt, "Hunt," p. 77; Schuyler, "Works," p. 104.

16. Schuyler, "Works," p. 104 (Presbyterian Hospital); Hitchcock, *Architecture*, p. 272 (Yale Divinity School); and Baker, *Hunt*, p. 207 (Stuyvesant Apartments). Bloor, "Annual Address," p. 25, and others after him have noticed the mixture of *néo-grec* and Gothic in Hunt's work.

17. Neil Levine, "The Romantic Idea of Architectural Legibility: Henri Labrouste and the *Néo-Grec*," in *The Architecture of the Ecole des Beaux-Arts*, ed. Arthur Drexler (New York, 1977), p. 331; and see also David Van Zanten, "Architectural Composition at the Ecole des Beaux-Arts from Charles Percier to Charles Garnier," ibid., p. 208.

18. E.g., *Record and Guide* 11 (1872): 203 (Schulze and Schoen's Manufacturers and Builders Bank described as Renaissance style with "Neo-Greek flourishes"); *New York Times*, 26 April 1872, p. 1 (Paran Stevens obituary: term applied to Stevens House); and Bloor, "Annual Address," p. 25 (term applied to Post's Williamsburgh Bank).

19. E.-E. Viollet-le-Duc, *Dictionnaire raisonné de l'architecture française* (Paris, 1854), 1:34–35 (figs. 19 and 20).

20. Vincent J. Scully, Jr., *The Shingle Style and the Stick Style*, rev. ed. (New Haven and London, 1971), pp. xxiii–lix.

21. For a fuller discussion of this phenomenon see my "Richard Morris Hunt, the Continental Picturesque, and the 'Stick Style,'" *Journal of the Society of Architectural Historians* 42 (October 1983): 272–89.

22. Bloor, "Annual Address," pp. 28 and 29.

23. For a summary of opinions about the status of this building, see Winston Weisman, "A New View of Skyscraper History," *The Rise of an American Architecture*, ed. Edgar Kaufmann, jr. (New York, 1970), pp. 124–25.

24. Suggesting there is a common French prototype. Walter Cook, who had studied with J.-A.-E. Vaudremer in Paris in the mid 1870s, is likely to have designed the several arcaded buildings done by his firm. See my "The Tall Office Building Artistically Reconsidered: Arcaded Buildings of the New York School, c. 1870–1890," in *In Search of Modern Architecture: A Tribute to Henry-Russell Hitchcock*, ed. Helen Searing (New York, 1982), pp. 136–64.

25. Louis Sullivan, *The Autobiography of an Idea* (New York, 1922), pp. 190 and 213. On the question of Sullivan's early style and its relationship to Hunt's work of around 1870, see Paul E. Sprague, "Sullivan, Louis H.," *Macmillan Encyclopedia of Architects*, ed. Adolf K. Placzek (New York and London, 1982), 4:157. The Royal Phelps Building is noted in Baker, *Hunt*, pp. 504 n. 30 and 542.

26. A contemporary article on the new building relates that the supervising architect Edward E. Raht "drew all the plans and did all the work, Mr. Hunt being absent in Europe on account of sickness" and also mentions two elevator engines in the basement: see "The Coal and Iron Exchange," *New-York Daily Tribune*, 28 January 1876, p. 3. Plans in the Hunt Collection show two elevators, one on either side of the main staircase. Schuyler's statement, repeated by Baker, that the building was constructed without elevators, must be in error: see Schuyler, "Works," p. 107. Above the basement level, the building rose six stories on the main Cortlandt Street side and seven stories on the rear side.

27. Landau, "Arcaded Buildings," p. 161. The Tribune Building was only begun in June of 1873. A recent general history of American architecture that presents this trio as the earliest skyscrapers is Leland M. Roth, *A Concise History of American Architecture* (New York, 1979), pp. 161–62.

28. Bloor, "Annual Address," p. 24.

29. The letter, probably from Henry Chauncey, Hunt's brother-in-law, is in the Hunt Collection. According to Mrs. R. M. Hunt, the final drawings for the building were not made by Hunt (who was abroad from May 1874 to June 1875): see Alan Burnham, ed., "The Richard Morris Hunt Papers, 1828–1895," compiled by Catharine H. Hunt, p. 141 (Avery Library). For the penultimate design see "The New Tribune Building," *American Builder and Journal of Art* 9 (October 1873): 235; and *New-York Sketch-Book of Architecture* 1 (January 1874), pl. I. New Building Docket 465–1873 (24 June), New York City Municipal Archives, describes the height of the proposed Tribune Building as eight stories plus basement.

30. P. B. Wight, "Origin and History of Hollow Tile Fireproof Construction," *Brickbuilder* 6 (August–September 1897): 74. In the typescript of this article (Wight Collection, Burnham Library, Art Institute of Chicago), Wight credits Hunt with recommending the substitution of terra-cotta. That comment, as well as other personal remarks, were deleted from the article as published. In the *New-York Daily Tribune*'s detailed description of the Tribune Building at the time of its completion (10 April 1875, p. 12), the flat arches are said to be made of cement blocks; however, the *New-York Sketch-Book* (1 [January 1874], pl. I [text]) describes them as terra-cotta, as does Wight. The *Tribune*'s description of the arches is so detailed and promotional in tone that I suspect it was taken from printed material supplied by the manufacturer rather than by the architect's office. See also *A History of Real Estate*, pp. 398–402 and 476. For Hunt's role in the design of the New York Post Office, see Baker, *Hunt*, pp. 171–72.

31. *Record and Guide*, 24 April 1875, p. 296.

32. *A History of Real Estate*, pp. 398–99.

33. *New-York Daily Tribune*, 10 April 1875, p. 12.

34. However, the Noel and Saurel Building (1863–64) at 5–7 Crosby Street (also known as the French and Belgian Plate Glass Company Building), designed by the Paris-trained Detlef Lienau, may be the first example of the commercial Neo-Grec in New York: see Talbot

Hamlin, "The Rise of Eclecticism in New York," *Journal of the Society of Architectural Historians* 11 (1952): 7–8. *Néo-grec* decorative motifs of French or German origin appear early in Lienau's New York work: see Ellen W. Kramer, "The Domestic Architecture of Detlef Lienau, A Conservative Victorian," Ph.D. diss., New York University, 1958, pp. 163, 273.

35. Wight, "Hunt," p. 4. See *Revue générale* 19 (1861), pl. 56 (hospital), and 27 (1869), pls. 19, 20, and 25 (public baths).

36. Wight traced the new "rationalist" mode he saw developing in western architecture to the study of the Gothic and Viollet-le-Duc's writings: see "On the Present Condition of Architectural Art in the Western States," *American Art Review* 1 (1880): 128. See also Winston Weisman, "Commercial Places of New York: 1845–1875," *Art Bulletin* 36 (December 1954): 301 and figs. 120 and 127; Weisman, "The Commercial Architecture of George B. Post," *Journal of the Society of Architectural Historians* 31 (October 1972): 182–83; Landau, "Arcaded Buildings," p. 145; and Arnold Lewis and Keith Morgan, eds., *American Victorian Architecture* (1886; reprint New York, 1975), I-29 and I-40. (See pp. I-33–I-35 for similar work in Baltimore by Charles L. Carson). Other Chicago buildings that belong in this listing, all extant, are J. Speyer's Donohue Building (1883), the Richardson Building (1886; architect unknown), and the Conkey Building (ca. 1887; architect unknown): see *Process: Architecture* 35 (1983): 45–46. On Boston's commercial buildings of this type, many still standing, see Boston Landmarks Commission, "Central Business District Preservation Survey," 1980.

37. "Cast Iron in Decorative Architecture," *Crayon* 6 (1859): 24.

38. Bloor, "Annual Address," p. 27. Hunt's efforts to revitalize the cast-iron front in regard to color were anticipated in a modest way by the facade of a building by Renwick and Sands completed early in 1871 on Broadway between Spring and Prince Streets. There the basic neutral color was offset by gold- and red-painted details: *New York Evening Post*, 10 March 1871, p. 1; and *New York Illustrated* (New York, 1871), p. 16.

39. The substance of Vaux's address before the A.I.A. of 2 June 1857 is published in *Crayon* 4 (July 1857): 218, and as "Parisian Buildings for City Residents," *Harper's Weekly* 1 (19 December 1857): 809–10. See the last-mentioned source for Vaux's plans for an apartment house. See also James Richardson, "The New Homes of New York: A Study of Flats," *Scribner's Monthly* 8 (1874). 67. On Kilpatrick's apartment house, see *Record and Guide* 70 (29 November 1902): 808; and *New York Times*, 24 November 1902, p. 5.4. Other sources name pre-Stuyvesant New York apartment houses, e.g, the model houses built by Richard K. Haight at 256–58 West Thirty-seventh Street in 1852: see "French Flats and Apartment Houses," *Carpentry and Building* 3 (December 1881): 233. These, however, were built as working-class housing. The same builder was responsible for Haight House; see n. 50 below.

40. See Jean A. Follett, "The Hotel Pelham: A New Building Type for America," *The American Art Journal*, 15 (Autumn 1983): 58–73. Interestingly, though Follett credits Stone with the design of the Hotel Pelham on good evidence, Gilman took credit for it: see Arthur Gilman, "Family Hotels," *New York Times*, 19 November 1871, p. 5. There Gilman also claims that some thirty of these "family hotels" had been built in Boston by 1871.

41. Statistics on hotels from "Hotel Life, *New York Daily Graphic*, 16 January 1874, p. 507; and *New York Business Directory* (1874–75). The apartment hotel as distinct from the apartment house is defined in "Apartment Hotels," *Record and Guide*, 20 January 1877, p. 42; and Richardson, "New Homes," p. 68, distinguishes the apartment house proper from the apartment or "family" hotel. The apartment house is defined in *Appletons' Dictionary of New York and Vicinity*, 2d ed. (New York, 1879), p. 12.

42. Full description in "A Parisian House in New York," *The Sun* (New York), 4 November 1869, p. 3; and see David G. De Long, ed., *Historic American Buildings* (New York and London, 1979) 8:199 (first floor plan) and 204 (longitudinal section). For information about ceiling heights and rents, I am indebted to Jean-Louis Bourgeois; and see Amy Kallman Epstein, "Multifamily Dwellings and the Search for Respectability: Origins of the New York Apartment House," *Urbanism Past & Present*, 5 (Summer, 1980): 37.

43. See illustrations of two projects for small Parisian apartment houses in J.-N.-L. Durand, *Précis de leçons d'architecture données a l'école polytechnique* (Paris, 1805), vol. 2, pt. 3, pl. 26; and see the first-class *maisons à loyer* illustrated in César Daly, *L'Architecture privée au XIXme siècle sous Napoléon III* (Paris, 1864), vol. 1, and Victor Calliat, *Parallèle des maisons de Paris* (Paris, 1864), vol. 2. The Stuyvesant is described as containing "four complete houses" on each floor in "Houses on the European Plan," *Record and Guide* 4 (6 November 1869): 1.

44. The dimensions of the lot, indicated on the drawing, are specified in New Building Docket 562-1869 (Stuyvesant Apartments), New York City Municipal Archives.

45. Vaux, "Parisian Buildings," p. 810.

46. Kramer, "Domestic Architecture of Detlef Lienau," pp. 207–16.

47. In 1879 Hunt made known his preference for a single large court over several small courts for tenements in a critique of the prize-winning plans in the tenement house competition sponsored that year by the *Plumber and Sanitary Engineer*. Although his endorsement undoubtedly helped stimulate interest in this plan, his own firm's tenements, unfortunately, were not innovatively planned. It was not until the mid 1890s that the plan became popular for model tenements: see *New-York Tribune*, 7 March 1879, p. 1; and also cited in Anthony Jackson, *A Place Called Home: A History of Low-Cost Housing in Manhattan* (Cambridge, Mass., and London, 1976), p. 55. The 1879 competition initiated the infamous "dumbbell plan."

48. And the 1867 tenement law required only that every room either have a window or connect with a room that had a window—or, if less than one hundred square feet in area, be ventilated by a flue or an air shaft. The tenement laws are summarized and discussed in Jackson, *A Place Called Home*, chaps. 3 and 10; and see Epstein, "Multifamily Dwellings," p. 36, who points out other distinctions. *American Builder and Journal of Art* 1 (December 1869): 232, notes with approval that every room and hallway of the Stuyvesant had a window. P. B. Wight, in "Apartment Houses Practically Considered," *Putnam's Magazine* 16 (September 1870): 306, notices that, according to César Daly's standards, the Stuyvesant would be considered a first-class apartment house in France and also asserts its superiority in several respects to similar French buildings. Stern, "With Rhetoric," p. 80, states, "the Stuyvesant marked no advance over the working class tenements of its day." And in his *New York 1900* (New York, 1983; coauthors Gregory Gilmartin and John Montague Massengale), p. 280, Stern asserts, "the rooms were still poorly lit and badly ventilated."

49. *Appletons' Dictionary*, p. 12. Many of these were conversions, but most of the first-class apartment houses had been built as new constructions.

50. The contemporary Haight House, two houses converted into a luxury apartment house in 1870–71 by Richard K. Haight, also had an elevator and provided communal eating and laundry facilities. Haight's architect was Stephen D. Hatch, and I owe this information to Mosette Broderick.

51. Alteration Docket 714–1873, New York City Municipal Archives. In the Hunt Collection are drawings for the Drexel Building dated 1872. Gilman's Drexel Building, formerly at Wall and Broad Streets, was built in 1872–73.

52. A good photograph of the Fifth Avenue side as enlarged appears in *King's Photographic Views of New York*, ed. Moses King (Boston, 1895), p. 585. For the case of *Hunt v. Stevens*, see Baker, *Hunt*, pp. 210–13.

53. *New York World*, 8 October 1871, p. 3; and see also *New York Evening Post*, 10 March 1871, p. 1; *New York Times*, 16 April 1871, p. 3; and "Parisian Flats," *Appletons' Journal* 6 (18 November 1871): 562. The other unidentified plan in the Hunt Collection shows two-room suites (servants' quarters?) off a long corridor and double-piled at the ends of the building.

54. Richardson, "New Homes," p. 69.

55. "Apartment Hotels," p. 42; and John I. Davenport, *Registered Voters in the City of New York* (1874 ed.), p. 24 and (1877 ed.) p. 1103. A random check of the names listed in *Registered Voters* as living at Stevens House against city directories of the mid 1870s establishes that their occupations ranged from lawyer and editor to bank teller. *Registered Voters* gives room numbers opposite the names, the highest in 1874 being number 95 and the highest in 1877 being 192. It would appear that Gilman divided the original apartments into many small units at the time of his renovation and enlargement of the building, which suggests that Stevens House became a bachelor apartment hotel.

56. *Appletons' Dictionary*, p. 12; *Trow's New York City Directory* (1880–81); *Both Sides of Broadway*, compiled by R. M. De Leeuw in 1910 (New York, ca. 1911), p. 350. As late as 1895 the building was still owned by the Stevens family: see obituary of Mrs. Paran Stevens, *New York Times*, 4 April 1895, p. 1.

57. James T. Dillon of the New York City Landmarks Preservation Commission suggested this possibility to me. If this were so, it might explain the failure of the venture. On the history of cooperative apartments, see the prospectus for Hubert and Pirsson's Central Park

Apartments: American Banknote Co., *Central Park Apartments* . . . (1882), coll. New York Public Library. Hubert and Pirsson, architects of the Chelsea, introduced the cooperative system to New York about 1880: see Andrew Alpern, *Apartments for the Affluent* (New York, 1975), pp. 1 and 14–17.

58. P. B. Wight (unsigned), "Correspondence," *American Architect and Building News*, 1 April 1876, p. 110. And see Landau, *Wight*, pp. 35–36. Ware and Van Brunt's 117 Beacon Street, dated 1864 by Bunting, is an early example of their work in this mode: see Bunting, *Houses of Boston's Back Bay*, p. 126 (architect not identified). Bunting dates the first appearance in Boston of the type of decoration I am designating Neo-Grec to a Back Bay facade of 1861 (p. 124).

59. On the "panel-brick style," see Bunting, *Houses of Boston's Back Bay*, pp. 188–95.

60. Van Brunt Sketchbooks, Avery Library. On the Neo-Grec row house, see Charles Lockwood, *Bricks and Brownstone: The New York Row House, 1783–1929* (New York, 1972), pp. 227–28. Much of the incised, so-called Eastlake-style New York architectural ornament of the 1870s and 1880s, usually thought to have been inspired by Charles Locke Eastlake's furniture designs in his *Hints on Household Taste* (London, 1868), should probably be categorized as Neo-Grec. Under the heading "Brick and Stone Design," the English *Building News* (19 March 1869, p. 248) features window heads similar to those illustrated by Viollet-le-Duc (see n. 19 above) observing, "In these the brick [relieving] arch may be entirely omitted, substance of stone relieved by superficial treatment, or simple incising taking its place." Viollet-le-Duc's 15 rue de Douai is illustrated in Calliat, *Parallèle des maisons*, pls. 59–63, where Americans would have seen it.

61. See New York City Landmarks Preservation Commission, "Stuyvesant Heights Historic District Designation Report," (1971), pp. 30–40 (MacDonough Street).

62. Bloor, "Annual Address," p. 27. Although it is an early instance of the hospital "pavilion plan" in America, Hunt's plan for the Presbyterian Hospital is not discussed here because it was not the first. Samuel Sloan's Protestant Episcopal Hospital in Philadelphia, begun in 1860, and his Rhode Island Hospital in Providence, which opened in 1868 and on which Alpheus C. Morse collaborated, were earlier.

63. However, the Lenox Library was to be open only to scholars and students: see Baker, *Hunt*, pp. 181–82.

64. *New-York Sketch-Book* 3 (April 1876): 1 ff.

65. The competition for the Williamsburgh Savings Bank was held in 1869; however, Hunt may have already been working on the library design by that date.

66. It may be relevant that the architect in the firm of McKim, Mead, and White who seems to have been instrumental in the design of the Villard Houses, Joseph Morrill Wells, did some work for Hunt in the 1870s: see Mosette Glaser Broderick and William C. Shopsin, *The Villard Houses: Life Story of a Landmark* (New York, 1980), p. 37. The resemblance of the Criminal Courts Building (demolished) to the Lenox Library is also pointed out in Stern et al., *New York 1900*, p. 67.

67. For the dating of the Idlehour commission, see Broderick and Shopsin, *Villard Houses*, pp. 46–47. The intriguing question of which was designed first, Hunt's W. K. Vanderbilt mansion or Post's exactly contemporary, châteaulike mansion for Cornelius Vanderbilt II, has not been resolved. Post filed for a building permit several months ahead of Hunt, but Hunt had been working for the W. K. Vanderbilts for several years previously, which suggests that his design could have been on the boards earlier than Post's.

68. Schuyler, "Works," p. 126.

69. Jordy, *Buildings on Paper*, pp. 98–101.

70. E.-E. Viollet-le-Duc, *Discourses on Architecture* (Boston, 1875), 1:vii–viii.

4

The Central Park Gateways:
Harbingers of French Urbanism Confront
the American Landscape Tradition

Francis R. Kowsky

M ANHATTAN'S CENTRAL PARK is one of the outstanding artistic creations of nineteenth-century America. The park, which embodied notions of social as well as aesthetic progress, was the first large municipal pleasure ground in the United States, and had its origins in the conviction that nature could be a source of spiritual truth. Supported by native transcendentalist philosophy as well as British and American literature, this idea lay at the heart of much mid-nineteenth-century American art and thought. Indeed, one of the park's earliest and most constant advocates was poet William Cullen Bryant, who together with landscape painter Thomas Cole epitomized morally sensitive interpretation of the natural world. However, Richard Morris Hunt, who was twenty-two when Asher B. Durand painted his famous memorial to Bryant and Cole, *Kindred Spirits*, spent much of his youth in the orbit of French culture, first in Geneva and then in Paris. When he returned to the United States in 1855, he was less under the spell of Romantic naturalism than were many of his artistic and literary contemporaries. This fact, along with Hunt's apparent lack of regard for the democratic idealism that surrounded the creation of Central Park, provoked a serious conflict when he came to prepare designs for gateways to the park's principal entrances.

In 1860, when gates for the four Fifty-ninth Street accesses to Central Park were first discussed, the park was in its infancy.[1] It had come into being in 1856 when the city purchased a strip of undeveloped land 1.5 miles wide by 2.5 miles long, extending north from Fifty-ninth Street between Fifth and Eighth avenues. Two years later, a competition to determine a design for the new park was won by the entry submitted under the name "Greensward." It was the joint creation of Frederick Law Olmsted (1822–1903), a many-talented New Englander who at the time was superintendent of the park, and Calvert Vaux (1824–95), an English immigrant architect who had settled in New York City.

In part because of Vaux's role in the undertaking, Central Park and its remarkable plan evoked the memory of America's first landscape architect, Andrew Jackson Downing (1824–52). Through his writing, Downing had championed the cause of municipal parks. In his work, such as the pleasure grounds he laid out between the Capitol and the White House in 1851, he had popularized the English Romantic landscape tradition, adapted to American conditions. Vaux had come to America in 1850 to work with Downing at his office at Newburgh, New York. Before Downing's untimely death in 1852, Vaux collaborated with him on several projects, including the Washington grounds.

4.1 Proposed design for Central Park Gateway, Gate of Peace, Fifth Avenue and Fifty-ninth Street, New York City, 1863. From R. M. Hunt, *Designs for the Gateways of the Southern Entrances to the Central Park* (1866).

And although Olmsted knew Downing only slightly, he too shared his near pantheistic vision of natural beauty adapted to civic use. In an age of urban growth, Downing, Olmsted, and Vaux (who had moved to Manhattan by 1856) regarded nature as a remedy for the pernicious effects of city life. To them, the park embodied in physical form a deep-felt faith in the regenerative force of nature.

Grading and planting the desolate Central Park site began in the summer of 1858. Work was conducted under the supervision of Olmsted and Vaux, who were hired by the Central Park board of commissioners to oversee the implementation of their plan. When the Civil War broke out, however, Olmsted put aside his budding career as a landscape architect to become secretary of the United States Sanitary Commission, a civilian organization devoted to providing medical supplies to volunteer troops. Overdedicated and overworked, Olmsted found the job exhausting. In 1863, he resigned his post and went to California to manage the Mariposa gold mines. Vaux remained in New York, where, in partnership with Frederick Clarke Withers (1828–1901), a fellow Englishman who had joined him at Downing's, he developed a successful architectural practice.

Neither Olmsted nor Vaux was associated with the park in June 1863, when the board, apparently dissatisfied with the architects' gateway plans, empowered the Committee on Statuary, Fountains and Architectural Structures to conduct a competition for designs of the four southern entrances. Hunt, whose brother-in-law, Charles H. Russell, was a member of the committee, had already been consulted on the gateway issue.[2] He had, in fact, presented the committeemen with sketches. In September 1863, the board rejected all of the plans submitted by ten architects, presumably from New York, and voted to adopt Hunt's designs. In the spring of 1865, however, by which time Hunt's gateways had become controversial, the board deferred indefinitely all action on their construction.

Hunt's plans were made public in the summer of 1865, when he exhibited his five perspective views in the vestibule of the National Academy of Design. He also circulated photographs of his drawings, which were labeled "adopted by the Board of Commissioners of the Central Park." In the following year, Hunt published his proposals in an expensive little book.[3] William J. Hoppin, a friend who used the *nom de plume* "Civis," provided a long essay, originally printed in the *New York Evening Post*, discussing the merits of Hunt's designs. Accompanying the pictures, plans, and text, excerpts from the proceedings of the board of commissioners illuminated the history of the project.

Of the four gateways that Hunt envisioned, the one at Fifth Avenue was the most magnificent (fig. 4.1). It grandly announced the park to those who approached along the famous thoroughfare that led from the city's major commercial and residential districts. Hunt's plan consisted of four features: a four-hundred-square-foot plaza animated by a circular fountain base; a one-hundred-foot semicircular terrace overlooking the park on the west side of the plaza; two curving stepped cascades descending into the park on either side of the terrace; and, on the north, the actual entrances leading to the carriage roads and footpaths. Figurative sculpture decorated this architectural setting and wrapped the gateway in municipal meaning. The tall pedestals separating the central carriageways from the side paths sustained freestanding statues, the outer of which showed the ancient theme of horse tamers. In the center of the terrace, a fifty-foot column bore aloft the arms of the city, held by an Indian and a

4.2 *Above:* Proposed design for Central Park Gateway, Warrior's Gate, Eighth Avenue and Fifty-ninth Street, 1863. From R. M. Hunt, *Designs for the Gateways of the Southern Entrances to the Central Park* (1866).

4.3 *Above right:* Proposed design for Central Park Gateway, Artist's Gate, Seventh Avenue and Fifty-ninth Street, 1863. From R. M. Hunt, *Designs for the Gateways of the Southern Entrances to the Central Park* (1866).

sailor. At the base of the column, in a basin of water, were figures personifying the Hudson and East rivers, with Henry Hudson between them on the prow of a ship. Beneath the terrace, in a broad basin that collected water from the cascades, a large niche sheltered Neptune in his chariot.

The Eighth Avenue entrance was a broad open area from which radiated park roads and city thoroughfares (fig. 4.2). A large fountain marked the center of the space. This gate was designated the Warrior's Gate, in contrast to the Fifth Avenue entrance, the Gate of Peace, a disposition of sentiment that recalled the rooms at either end of the Galerie des Glaces at Versailles (and which departed from the names adopted by the board). A long curved stone bench surmounted by military statues extended between the park carriage roads that entered the square from the north and east. Equestrian statues on high bases stood in the middle of each roadway, dividing incoming from outgoing traffic. Pedestrians entered the park through gates at the sides of both carriage roads.

The pedestrian gates on Fifty-ninth Street opened directly into the park from the street. At the Artists' Gate at the head of Seventh Avenue, two imposing herms supported elaborate iron gate valves that guarded the central way (fig. 4.3). Just inside the park, a column rose to support the genius of the arts. Visitors could also enter on either side of the herms, where two semicircular stone benches, flanked by seated figures of painting, sculpture, music, and architecture, awaited them.

The Sixth Avenue gateway (fig. 4.4), which commemorated commerce, resembled the Artists' Gate. It too had stone exedras to either side of the swinging iron gates. Bronze rostral columns replaced the herms as gateposts and a flagpole stood in place of the column in the Artists' Gate. Statuary on the ends of the exedras dealt with themes appropriate to trade and prosperity.

All of Hunt's designs derived from the grand tradition of French civic planning. In the Paris of Hunt's day, this tradition was finding renewed expression under the leadership of Baron Georges Haussmann.[4] The plaza and fountain at the Fifth Avenue entrance especially evoked the Baroque perspectives of Haussmann's new boulevards and squares. Hunt, limited by a site embedded in

the prosaic gridiron of the Manhattan street pattern, had tried his best to create a long axial vista for his column that symbolized New York. To do this he had to utilize Sixtieth Street, an inconsequential thoroughfare, but the only one that afforded distant views, since the line of sight along Fifth Avenue bypassed the entrance. To underscore the importance of the prospect, Hunt included in his set of drawings a view down Sixtieth Street from the column (fig. 4.5). Similarly, the flagpole and column of the intermediate entrances were on an axis with Sixth and Seventh avenues. The entrance at Eighth Avenue was developed in the manner of a circle, a planning device common in Paris, where it was used to facilitate circulation at the juncture of major streets.

Hunt was even more specific in his references to French tradition in the sculpture that adorned the gateways. The horse tamers flanking the carriageways at the Fifth Avenue entrance were immediately recognized as not-too-distant adaptations of Guillaume Coustou's *Chevaux de Marly* of 1745. In Hunt's student days in Paris, these famous twin marble statues stood, as they still do, at the entrance to the Champs Elysées, where they had been moved in 1795. Bronze rostral columns like those at the Sixth Avenue gateway were nearby. The distinctive herms, with their air of mystery and guardianship, resembled those of the seventeenth-century *Grille des Hermes* (fig. 4.6) by Gilles Guerin at the entrance to the Cours des Offices at the Château de Fontainebleau.

Yet for all their French character, the gateway designs, except for sculptural details, imitated no particular French monument. Entrances to Parisian public parks, such as the Bois de Boulogne and the Bois de Vincennes, were much less imposing than those Hunt proposed for New York. An ornamental iron gate with a watchman's box to one side, or, in more important examples, a gatekeeper's lodge in the modern picturesque style, were typical of French park entranceways.[5] Fountains and monumental sculpture were placed in more urban surroundings, a fact of which Hunt was surely aware.

In his plans, Hunt addressed his gateways to the city rather than to the park. For this reason, he may have felt justified in making such a demonstration of monumental sculpture and classical formality. Aligned with the approaching streets and provided with benches, the gateways became objects demanding at-

4.4 *Above left:* Proposed design for Central Park Gateway, Gate of Commerce, Sixth Avenue and Fifty-ninth Street, 1863. From R. M. Hunt, *Designs for the Gateways of the Southern Entrances to the Central Park* (1866).

4.5 *Above:* Proposed design for Central Park Gateway, Gate of Peace, view looking toward Sixtieth Street.

4.6 *Grille des Hermes* published in Louis Dimier, *Fontainebleau* (Paris, 1908).

tention, works of art to be experienced against the backdrop of nature, but not intimately related to it. Furthermore, the iconography of the gateways extolled the city, the very reality that Olmsted and Vaux wished visitors to forget when they came to the park. These high-flown celebrations of the world of affairs ignored the populist and arcadian ideals that the park represented in the minds of its creators.

"The park typifies what we have been fighting for and the gates typify what we have been fighting against," wrote Vaux, who became the strongest opponent of Hunt's gateways. He saw them as "Napoleon III in disguise all over,"[6] and wrote to Olmsted in California in the spring of 1865 to inform him of his campaign to discredit them. Olmsted was receptive, for when he was still associated with the park he objected to Hunt's lack of sympathy for the values embodied in the landscape design.[7] In a letter to the board of commissioners, which was later published in the New York Evening Post, Vaux denounced the gateways as pompous and contrary to the spirit of the original park design. To his friend Clarence Cook, he wrote that the best gateways were the simplest; there should be no transition between the city and the park. "The first need of the visitor when he leaves the city sidewalk," said Vaux, "is a perfectly free and unencumbered draught of 'Park'—The success we have aimed for is to make the change from city to country instantaneous and complete and in accordance with our theory that the change cannot be too abrupt."[8] Vaux thought seating especially inappropriate at the entrances, which he argued should not be crowded "with people merely waiting, etc. etc—The imperial style presumes that people wait, wait, hang around and provision is made for clients, courtiers, subordinates, lacqueys."[9]

The question of "imperial" character was the most troublesome one for Vaux and other critics of Hunt's schemes. With the country embroiled in a civil war, a conflict that many in the North saw as a crusade against despotism, imagery associated with Europe's grandest monarchy was likely to provoke reaction. Furthermore, Napoleon III's attempt to establish a French emperor in Mexico had recently strained Franco-American relations. For Vaux, the park was a thoroughly American institution, a translation of democratic "ideas into trees and dirt."[10] Both he and Olmsted subscribed to Downing's injunction to "place spacious parks in your cities and unloose their gates as wide as the gates of morning to the whole people."[11] To Olmsted, Vaux declared that the park was "the big art work of the Republic."[12]

In addition to his pride in this great democratic undertaking, Vaux had personal reasons for disliking Hunt's schemes. Indeed, in his own work, Vaux frequently showed the influence of modern French design. The triumphal arch he developed with Downing for the White House grounds, the mansard-roofed house on Fifth Avenue he planned for John A. C. Gray, and the new streets he and Olmsted created called parkways, all bore the stamp of Paris. Yet, his own respect for French architecture in other situations aside, Vaux, as one of the creators of the original park plan, might have been expected to be protective of his role as park architect and of the work he and Olmsted had already done. "My objections are to the conception of the works with reference to their situations," he stated, "—no feeling for the landscape [is] exhibited."[13] This was especially true, in Vaux's mind, of the Fifth Avenue entrance, where Hunt's proposal would have required the alteration of the surface and the destruction of many trees.[14] The result would have been a disturbing gap in the perimeter wall of green that was one of the chief features of the Greensward plan. Not only did Vaux wish to see his own gateway schemes preserved, but, moreover, he did not want anything built that would diminish the terrace he had designed inside the park. He confided to Clarence Cook that it was "the only thing that gives me much encouragement that I have in me the germ of an architect that might with good chance and proper culture be developed."[15] Hunt's gateways—the drawings for which, Vaux conceded privately, were "splendidly got up and very striking"[16]—might, he feared, "spoil the whole design of the terrace by weakening the emphasis."[17] Furthermore, he asked Cook why money should be diverted from the as yet unfinished terrace to pay for costly and unnecessary gates.[18]

Cook, the influential art critic of the *New York Daily Tribune*, echoed many of Vaux's objections to the gateways in the essay he published on Hunt's proposals in August 1865. To Cook, who had been an assistant to Downing, Hunt's designs were as "un-American as it would be possible to make them" and unsympathetic to the rural character of the park. "We don't like to be reminded of the existence of such riff-raff as the French emperor," he wrote, "when we are in our Park." Likewise, he pleaded that "we want the most beautiful trees, the loveliest flowers in profusion . . . we want to forget the city utterly while we are in the Park."[19]

Joining Vaux and Cook in the attack on Hunt was the architect Russell Sturgis. Writing in *The Nation* in 1865 and 1866, Sturgis complained that Hunt's imagery was too intellectual for American taste.[20] Furthermore, Hunt's designs were faulty on a number of technical points. He also doubted that sculptors good enough to execute the statuary properly could be found in America.

Hunt, the first American to know modern French architecture intimately, gave his countrymen in his gateway designs their first true glimpse of continental classicism. This came at a time when the late phase of the Gothic revival, closely identified with the moralism and naturalism of John Ruskin, was ascendant in American architecture. The New York architectural profession in particular was dominated by men, many of whom, like Vaux, were English-trained and devoted to the ideals expounded in *The Seven Lamps of Architecture* and *The Stones of Venice*. Sturgis and Cook were both members of the Ruskin-oriented Society for the Advancement of Truth in Art and wrote for its magazine, *The New Path*. The argument advanced most strongly by Cook, that in Hunt's designs "nothing springs out of the needs of the place, nor is dictated by conditions that exist and ought to be respected," condemned them by implication for not meeting the criteria of "truth" as it applied to artistic creation.[21] Commenting on Hunt's Eighth Avenue entrance, Vaux stated that his own design, which employed a wide and a narrow opening for ways of different width, was "the true statement of the public's need." "Why falsify the facts," he asked, "at great expense . . . because Mr. Hunt is unable to solve the problem of wide and narrow except by making it into two *wide* [entrances] regardless of TRUTH."[22] And although left unsaid, it was understood that the critics would have preferred designs in a medieval style, with its opportunities for naturalistic carving and freedom of expression. "We in America," stated Cook, "desire ideas, and are not satisfied with tasteless 'refroidées'—to coin a word—of classical conventionalities."[23] The neo-Baroque fanfare of Hunt's gateways must have seemed anathema to men instructed by Ruskin to despise as decadent the architecture of the Renaissance and Counter-Reformation.

By reason of his worldly background, Hunt shared neither the devotion to ideology nor the prejudice against classicism that characterized so many of his colleagues. Because of this he either ignored or misunderstood the ethical mood that prevailed in New York architectural circles. Montgomery Schuyler, writing at the end of Hunt's life, recognized his uniqueness for the mid 1860s. He even expressed the opinion that, had Hunt stayed in America instead of going to Paris, he would have become one of the outstanding proponents of the Gothic revival.[24] As it was, Hunt's early domestic architecture in the French picturesque style supported Schuyler's claim. Such works as the Griswold house at Newport were even appreciated by the staunchest critic of Hunt's gates, Vaux.

Although Vaux was not vindictive toward Hunt—he even hoped that Hunt might be commissioned for other work in the park—he labored diligently behind the scenes to see that the gateway proposals were put to rest.[25] Through his friendship with Andrew H. Green, the penurious comptroller of the Central Park board, Vaux sought to prevent the implementation of the designs. His efforts, which he described to Olmsted in long letters that also pleaded for Olmsted to return to New York and resume his career as a landscape architect, resulted in success. In May 1865, he wrote to Olmsted: "I met Green today in the street, he told me, as if it were a matter of course, that all further proceedings in regard to the gateways had been stopped. He was painfully mild, and I expect there have been some unpleasant scenes."[26] In July, the board voted to rehire Olmsted and Vaux as landscape architects to the park, a move that in effect sealed the fate of Hunt's proposals.

By the time the 1865 annual report appeared early the following year, even the names Hunt had chosen for his gateways had been superseded. The question of enlarging the entrances, however, continued to be discussed. By 1870, the Eighth Avenue entrance had been greatly expanded over the design suggested in the Greensward plan. The new scheme was developed by Vaux and Jacob Wrey Mould (1825–86), another architect from England (fig. 4.7).[27] On the park side of a large circle that received traffic from Broadway, Fifty-ninth Street, and Eighth Avenue, a curved symmetrical grouping of plantings, stone

4.7 Calvert Vaux and Jacob W. Mould's design for the Eighth Avenue Gateway to Central Park. Published in the *Annual Report of the Central Park Commissioner* (1869).

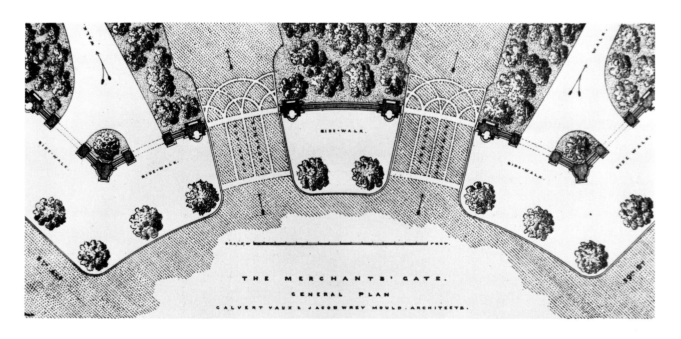

THE MERCHANTS' GATE.
GENERAL PLAN
CALVERT VAUX & JACOB WREY MOULD, ARCHITECTS.

posts, and iron gates gave access to the carriageways and paths. The general conception of the design may have been influenced by Hunt's plan for the area.

Olmsted and Vaux also proposed that the Fifth Avenue entrance, named the Scholar's Gate, be made more spacious. The entrance itself was to retain the continuous line of trees and foreground plaza, but another open space was to be created on the west side of Fifth Avenue between Fifty-eighth and Fifty-ninth streets. The board never fully carried out their idea.

In 1869, Olmsted and Vaux suggested enlarging the pedestrian entrances at Sixth Avenue, called the Artists' Gate, and at Seventh Avenue, designated the Artisans' Gate. In March they wrote to the president of the board of commissioners outlining their plans to rebuild these entrances and to develop each avenue between Fifty-eighth and Fifty-ninth streets into "public place[s] of liberal dimensions." Reversing the stand Vaux had taken earlier on the virtues of plain park entrances, Olmsted and Vaux argued: "The main fact we have to deal with is a gateway situated at the point where a broad city avenue is abruptly terminated by the wall of a great park, evidently a salient conjunction of circumstances, and a conspicuous architectural opportunity." A drawing of "an arcade or shelter erected for the convenience of the public, over the wide sidewalk, in front of the Park entrance" accompanied the letter but failed to appear in the annual report.[28] A design for a park gateway fitting this description and the Fifty-ninth Street location, however, was exhibited in the summer of 1869 at the National Academy of Design by Vaux and Withers (fig. 4.8). At the time, Withers was professionally associated with Olmsted and Vaux and often did architectural work for the firm. The picturesque Gothic design (which would have been duplicated at both the Sixth and Seventh avenue entrances) was surely Withers's conception, for Withers was a leading High Victorian Gothic architect. It underscored the Ruskianian preferences of the park designers and staunchly rebuked Hunt's classicism. Yet the partners' attempt to gain support for their proposal by showing a handsome watercolor rendering at the National Academy of Design met with no more success than had Hunt's resort to that same forum. The arcade remained only on paper, and even its identity was later forgotten.[29]

The Central Park gateways were one of several projects with which both Hunt and Olmsted became involved during their nearly contemporary careers. As in the case of the gateways, they were adversaries in the mid 1870s in the widely publicized dispute surrounding the construction of the state capitol at Albany. Called in to advise his friend William Dorsheimer (1832–88), the lieutenant governor, on whether or not the original capitol design (prepared by the architect Thomas S. Fuller with Arthur Gilman) should be carried to completion or scrapped, Olmsted suggested the latter course. With Henry Hobson Richardson (1838–86), who was another Olmsted friend and frequent collaborator, and Leopold Eidlitz (1823–1908), a man whom Olmsted had long held in high regard, he and Dorsheimer waged what became a heated battle to depose Fuller and put Richardson and Eidlitz in his place. Hunt, as the outspoken president of the New York chapter of the American Institute of Architects, led the opposition to this challenge, which he regarded as an affront to the ideals of professionalism that the fledgling organization had been created to promote. Despite his articulate argument for retaining the original architect, Hunt found himself once again on the losing side in a contest with Olmsted; the capitol eventually grew to its present form above Fuller's ground story according to the plans of Richardson and Eidlitz.

4.8 Calvert Vaux and Frederick Withers's design for a park entrance. Courtesy of Withers Collection, Avery Architectural and Fine Arts Library, Columbia University.

Ironically, it was Dorsheimer who first brought Hunt and Olmsted together on a commission. In 1885–86, he asked Olmsted to landscape a tract of land he had purchased on Telegraph Hill at Newport, Rhode Island. At the same time, he commissioned Hunt to prepare plans for a house to be erected on the site. Possessing "one of the most sightly locations on the island and one that can hardly be compared for beauty the world over," Hunt's dwelling was constructed only after Dorsheimer's death.[30] In 1891, the Busk family, who had acquired the landscaped grounds, erected Indian Spring, the rambling shingle and stone house that Hunt had initially intended for Dorsheimer.

The Cornelius Vanderbilt mausoleum on Staten Island (1886) was another collaborative effort. Hunt's French Romanesque tomb embedded in a rocky hillside was surrounded by an appropriate landscape scheme developed for the site by Olmsted. Two years later, at the request of Cornelius Vanderbilt's grandson, Hunt and Olmsted embarked on their most significant joint venture, the house and grounds of George Washington Vanderbilt's estate, Biltmore, at Asheville, North Carolina. The quintessence of the American artistic country house, a type given first expression by A. J. Downing in the 1840s, Biltmore allowed Hunt and Olmsted to exercise the full range of their creative talents. And despite differing temperaments, backgrounds, and philosophies, they worked together to produce an enduring marriage of architecture and nature, elements that they had been unable to reconcile in Central Park.

Hunt never again planned such monumental gateways as those he had envisioned and fought for in Central Park. Yet his designs were not forgotten by those who found merit in them. At the time of Hunt's death, a committee of the Architectural League of New York suggested that a fitting memorial to the architect would be the erection of the park gates he had designed thirty years earlier. Criteria of aesthetic judgment had changed greatly in those intervening decades, and Hunt's designs would have been appreciated by Belle Epoque sensibilities for the very qualities for which they were criticized in the 1860s.

This revolution in taste had seen continental standards overthrow the moralistic medievalism of the Gothic revival that had held sway in American architecture during the 1860s and 1870s. The shift away from English to French examples had grown steadily after the Civil War. Olmsted himself had imitated

Parisian features of city planning in his 1868 parkway scheme for Buffalo, which included a triumphal arch, squares and circles, and domesticated versions of the Place de l'Etoile and the Avenue de l'Impératrice. His friendship with Frédéric-Auguste Bartholdi had resulted in the acquisition of the sculptor's cast-iron nereid fountain for the U.S. Capitol grounds, which Olmsted landscaped in the 1870s. And at Biltmore, Olmsted had laid out a formal esplanade in front of Hunt's château. But most of all, America's attention in matters of design turned toward France because of the large number of young Americans who followed Hunt's lead after the war and went to study architecture in Paris. These men, who came from many American cities, firmly established in New York and elsewhere the ideals taught at the Ecole des Beaux-Arts.

By the time that Olmsted retired from practice in the mid 1890s, the success of Hunt, McKim, Mead, and White, Carrère and Hastings, and Ernest Flagg, to name a few, had directed the mainstream of American architectural theory and practice along the course of monumental classicism. During the early years of the decade, Olmsted and Hunt worked with many of the leaders of this movement on the World's Columbian Exposition held at Chicago to commemorate four hundred years of American history. By then, architects had gained allies among the new class of art-conscious, civic-minded industrialists who found architectural imagery derived from ancient Rome and Renaissance and Baroque Europe congenial to their perception of New World wealth and power. Conceived broadly as a definitive statement of modern material progress, the Chicago exposition became an event that marked the ascendancy of the architecture of grandeur fostered by repatriated students of the Ecole des Beaux-Arts. The "city beautiful" phenomenon that in the wake of the Exposition's popularity affected virtually every major American city, emphasized classical tradition, compelling vistas, and architecture over nature. Hunt's Central Park gateways, which had confronted American audiences of the 1860s with a new language of urban design, had been prophetic.

Notes

1. The literature on Central Park, already substantial, continues to grow. A selected bibliography includes Charles Beveridge and David Schuyler, eds., *Creating Central Park, 1857–1861*, vol. 3 of *The Papers of Frederick Law Olmsted* (Baltimore, 1983); Mary Ellen Hearn, ed., *Art of the Olmsted Landscape* (New York, 1981); Jeffry Simpson, *Art of the Olmsted Landscape: His Works in New York City*, (New York, 1981); Elizabeth Barlow, *Frederick Law Olmsted's New York* (New York, 1972); Albert Fein, *Frederick Law Olmsted and the American Environmental Tradition* (New York, 1972); Albert Fein, ed., *Landscape into Cityscape: Frederick Law Olmsted's Plans for a Greater New York City* (Ithaca, 1968); Henry Hope Reed and Sophia Duckworth, *Central Park: A History and Guide* (New York, 1967); Frederick Law Olmsted, Jr., and Theodora Kimball, *Frederick Law Olmsted, Landscape Architect, 1822–1903* (New York, 1922, 1928); and Clarence C. Cook, *A Description of the New York Central Park* (New York, 1869).

2. For a full account of the history of Hunt's gateway designs, see Paul R. Baker, *Richard Morris Hunt* (Cambridge, Mass., 1980), pp. 146–56.

3. Richard Morris Hunt, *Designs for the Gateways of the Southern Entrances to the Central Park* (New York, 1866).

4. For background on the transformation of Paris in Hunt's time, see David Pinkney, *Napoleon III and the Rebuilding of Paris* (Princeton, N.J., 1968), and Adolphe Alphand *Les Promenades de Paris* (Paris, 1867–73).

5. For a discussion of the European picturesque tradition in domestic architecture, see Sarah Landau, "Richard Morris Hunt, the Continental Picturesque, and the 'Stick Style,'" *Journal of the Society of Architectural Historians* 42 (1983): 272–89.

6. Letter from Calvert Vaux to Clarence Cook, 6 June 1865. In the Frederick Law Olmsted Papers, Manuscript Division, Library of Congress.

7. Letter from Frederick Law Olmsted to James T. Field, 21 October 1860. Reprinted in Beveridge and Schuyler, *Creating Central Park*, pp. 269–70. In n. 12, p. 271, Beveridge and Schuyler discuss Hunt's gateways.

8. Vaux to Cook, 6 June 1865.

9. Ibid.

10. Ibid.

11. Frederika Bremer, *The Homes of the New World* (London, 1853), 3:438.

12. Letter from Calvert Vaux to Frederick Law Olmsted, 3 June 1865. In the Frederick Law Olmsted Papers, Manuscript Division, Library of Congress.

13. Vaux to Cook, 6 June 1865.

14. For other opinions pro and con concerning the gateways, see Baker, *Richard Morris Hunt.*

15. Vaux to Cook, 6 June 1865.

16. Vaux to Olmsted, 10 May 1865. In the Frederick Law Olmsted Papers, Manuscript Division, Library of Congress.

17. Vaux to Cook, 6 June 1865.

18. Ibid.

19. Clarence Cook, "Mr. Hunt's Designs for the Gates of the Central Park," *New York Daily Tribune*, 2 August 1865, p. 8.

20. Unsigned articles by Sturgis appeared in *The Nation* 1 (1865): 186–88, and 410–12; and 3:255–56. Sturgis's authorship is attested to in *The Nation, Index of Contributors*, p. 467.

21. Vaux to Cook, 6 June 1865.

22. Ibid.

23. Ibid.

24. Montgomery Schuyler, "The Works of the Late Richard Morris Hunt," *The Architectural Record* 5 (1895): 104.

25. Vaux to Olmsted, 30 May 1865. In the Frederick Law Olmsted Papers, Manuscript Division, Library of Congress.

26. Vaux to Olmsted, 12 May 1865. In the Frederick Law Olmsted Papers, Manuscript Division, Library of Congress.

27. The plan first appeared in the *Ninth Annual Report of the Board of Commissioners of the Central Park for the Year Ending December 31, 1865* (New York, 1866). The general plan for the gateways appeared in the *Thirteenth Annual Report* (1869). The earlier version showed two entrances of unequal width. The later plan indicated gateway openings of the same width.

28. *Thirteenth Annual Report* (1869), pp. 151–52.

29. See my *The Architecture of Frederick Clarke Withers and the Progress of the Gothic Revival in America after 1850* (Middletown, Conn., 1980), pp. 95, 180 n. 98, 204. A reproduction of the rendering is preserved in the Withers file box at the Avery Library, Columbia University.

30. *The Newport Daily News*, 13 October 1885.

5.1 *Top:* Lenox Library, east along
Fifth Avenue between Seventieth
and Seventy-first streets, New
York City, 1870–77; demolished.

5.2 *Left:* Detail of facade of the
Lenox Library.

5

The Lenox Library: What Hunt Did and Did Not Learn in France

David Van Zanten
In memory of Ann

THE LENOX LIBRARY in New York, designed and erected by Richard Morris Hunt in 1870–75, seems a profoundly French Beaux-Arts design (figs. 3.28, 5.1–5.2).[1] Its facade, for example, is strikingly similar to that of the municipal Musée-Bibliothèque in Grenoble designed by Charles Questel in 1862–64 and erected from then to 1875 (fig. 5.3).[2] Both buildings were to house a library and an art collection. Both are monumental public structures facing broad public gardens. In both the compressed mass is articulated at the front by advancing wings enframing a shallow forecourt with a formal entrance facade of three arched bays. Their masses are measured but not veiled by a layer of pilasters and string courses through which the actual arched construction freely emerges. These Renaissance classical details have been reconstituted to become more responsive to each other, more expressive, larger in scale, and often harsher. There are even exact correspondences such as the peculiar tall, narrow pediments breaking the rooflines of both structures.

Hunt was in France in 1867. While he did not visit Grenoble, he would have seen a series of impressive wash drawings of Questel's design in the Exposition Universelle (for which he was a juror on the Committee of the Fine Arts). Furthermore, Questel's paradigm was the most appropriate one available in France and its author's reputation was very high in the Parisian profession.[3] It is interesting that in December 1867, the program of the *rendue* for the *premier classe* proposed at the Ecole des Beaux-Arts was that of a similar *musée-bibliothèque* and that the premiated project reiterated the Questel-Hunt facade scheme yet again.[4]

Everything would seem very simple were it not for the fact that in the mass of preliminary sketches and drawings Hunt made for the Lenox Library we can see him evolving his scheme from basic principles and from arrangements quite distinct from those of Questel's building (figs. 5.4–5.7). This forces one to admit that the resemblance of Hunt's and Questel's designs might be coincidental, a case of similar conclusions being reached by two artists thinking in the same manner.

Reinforcing this implication of Hunt's preliminary sketches, namely, that he evolved the scheme independently, are several important distinctions between his and Questel's designs. The resemblances are no deeper than the facades: the plans are totally different. Questel's building has at its center two long top-lit spaces side by side (the museum gallery and the library reading room) surrounded by a ring of lower service chambers. It thus stretches far back from the

5.3 Charles Questel, architect, Musée-Bibliothèque, Grenoble, France.

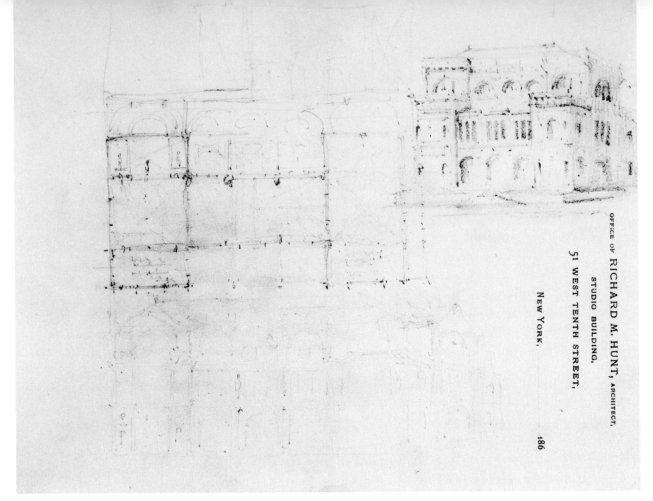

92

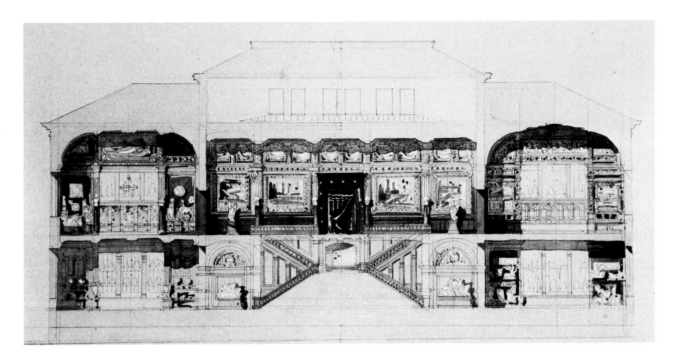

5.4 *Opposite, top:* Preliminary
sketch of the plan and facade
of the Lenox Library, ca. 1870.

5.5 *Left:* Proposed elevation of
the Lenox Library, ca. 1871.

5.6 *Top:* Proposed section of the
Lenox Library showing galleries
and reading rooms.

5.7 *Bottom:* Proposed Lenox
Library elevation in brick.

public facade and has only a row of square windows on its unaccented side elevations. Hunt's structure, on the contrary, is shallow with a central three-story mass containing the galleries and stairhalls flanked by two lower wings rotated at right angles to it and containing four vaulted library spaces, two superimposed in each wing (see fig. 3.28). The placement of the major spaces along Hunt's side elevations results in a very different and more original treatment there than at Grenoble. To support the loads and thrusts of the vaults, Hunt has defined each wing by eight tall, broad piers expressed externally up to the cornice. Between them Hunt stretches broad-arched screen walls, projecting in front of the piers below and receding behind them above. To give monumental emphasis and to unify his three major elevations, Hunt sets pediments supported by pilasters emerging out of the piers at the center of each face of the wing masses. This is a clear, logical, and profoundly satisfying piece of architectural thinking. It has no direct model either at Grenoble or elsewhere in French mid-nineteenth-century architecture. It is also something that we can see Hunt evolving and perfecting by agonizing degrees in the numerous sketches and studies that survive. He is clearly not copying Questel. He has learned to think architecturally, and the parallel with Questel's design only demonstrates how well he has done so.

The Lenox Library, then, is not a copy, but an independent, parallel creation. Yet the problem of understanding it only starts here. Hunt designed it fifteen years after he had left the Ecole and settled in New York. His French parallels are not with buildings of the late 1840s and early 1850s when he was in Paris, but rather with those of the late 1860s, most particularly Questel's Musée-Bibliothèque. In grasping the Lenox Library, one must thus proceed with a number of possibilities in mind. First, that the gap between the building's conception in 1870 and Hunt's departure from the Ecole in 1853 might be explained by the fact that he was still figuring out how to apply concretely and on a large scale what he had learned. Second, since the library's French style is not that of the 1840s and 1850s, but rather that of the 1860s, that Hunt must have been following the evolution of French architecture after his return to America, even if all the direct contact he had was two trips of 1861–62 and 1867. Third, that what must have prepared Hunt to take advantage of his later visits to Paris must have been his experience as a practical architect in New York between 1855 and 1870. By the end of the 1860s he had learned just how to evaluate and apply the suggestions of his French contemporaries. Fourth and last, that Hunt's very acquaintance with practical architecture in New York must make one ponder the degree to which—in spite of superficial appearances—the Lenox Library must have been, in the end, an American building after all.

The primary evidence that Hunt might not have been ready to produce a mature Beaux-Arts design before 1870 is a series of projects he produced during the decade and a half after 1853 in which it is clear that he is still struggling to achieve real facility in design. In 1861 he produced an unsuccessful competition design for the National Academy of Design (see fig. 7.3); in 1865 two more for the Brooklyn Mercantile Library and the New York Historical Society; in 1866 a project for the Academy of Music and the American Institute; and in 1868 one for the Union Theological Seminary.[5] These were all projects at least as large as the Lenox Library and similar in scale to Ecole designs. Yet they are an unimpressive lot, many in the contemporary American Ruskinian vocabulary and the others conventional Italianate (American Institute) or "Second Empire" (New York Historical Society).

More telling, however, are several designs of this period that are more modest in scale but also more unequivocally French: that of the Rossiter House of 1853–55 (fig. 5.8), that of the Williams Houses erected in Boston in 1859–1860 (fig. 5.9), and that of the Union League Club for New York of 1867 (see fig. 6.19). In each case Hunt was dealing with similar problems of composition and ornamental emphasis and it is clear that he as yet lacks the mature touch displayed in the Lenox Library.

The Rossiter House design (crudely executed in brownstone with an extra story) reproduces the Parisian *maison particulière* in the French Renaissance style of which there are many examples from the 1840s in the seventh and eighth arrondissements.[6] What is remarkable is the thinness of Hunt's membering (emphasized by his mixing of brick and limestone) and the slightness of the relief. This emphatic reticence had characterized his student work at the Ecole. The Williams Houses display the same compressed surfaces, but now with much more going on. Arches over the first floor windows are unornamented and beveled back into the wall. The pediments of the third-story windows are just triangular blocks with decorative incisions on their surfaces. The spandrels of the first and third floors are brought out with a strange continuous fluting. Hunt is obviously trying to make his moldings read as a parturition of the architectural mass: he is trying to push them back into it so as to give them the weight of raw material and he is trying to inflect their geometry to express the materials in which they are executed. This effort has carried him away from the reproduction of a historical style toward an abstraction of classicism, Renaissance in its use of the round arch but Greek in the simplicity of its surfaces and moldings. This reconstitution of the classical style was precisely what was being ex-

5.8 Thomas P. Rossiter house, 11 West Thirty-eighth Street, New York City, 1855–57; demolished. (Cf. fig. 6.8.)

5.9 Dr. H. H. Williams and Dr. Morland houses (*right*), 13, 14, and 15 Arlington Street, Boston, 1859–60; demolished. Courtesy of the Boston Public Library.

plored at the Ecole des Beaux-Arts in the late 1840s and early 1850s and what later (in the 1860s) came to be called the "Modern Greek" or *néo-grec*.

This intriguingly named fashion had emerged among the Parisian students as a consequence of the completion of the Bibliothèque Ste.-Geneviève by Henri Labrouste in 1850.[7] Here they were confronted by a building in the Renaissance arched system, but so skeletalized that it began to seem a mere cage of piers, like a Greek temple, and clothed with simple, emphatic moldings that could only be archaic Greek. In 1861 there had appeared the first theoretical exposition of the *néo-Grec* in English by Hunt's student Henry Van Brunt, in an essay entitled "Greek Lines" that appeared in the *Atlantic Monthly*. Van Brunt distinguished between copying the forms of former styles and taking inspiration from the "lines" of Attic building. Labrouste, he says, was the first to perceive the freedom of Greek architecture, which "gave it a life and refinement which his appreciative eye sought in vain among the approved works of the Academy." The younger architects were following in his footsteps in creating a modern architecture embued with intricately expressive poetry in its moldings and silhouettes.

> If a designer had a thought to express, his Greek lines enabled him to put it in architectural forms just as a poet attunes *his* thought to the harmony and rhythm of verse. . . . Laymen, accustomed to the cold architectural proprieties of the old renaissance, and habituated to the formalities of the five orders, the prudish decorum of Italian window-dressings and pediments and pilasters and scrolls, were surprised to see ideas at once so clearly set forth in architectural forms and the intention of the building in which they occurred was at once patent to the most casual oberver, and the story of its destination told with the eloquence of a poetical and monumental language. . . . Like the gestures of pantomime, which constitute a distinctive and universal language, these abstract lines, coming out of our humanity and rendered elegant by the idealization of study, are, it is hoped, restoring to architecture its highest capacity of conveying thought in a monumental manner.

What this meant in practice was the reduction of architectural mass to a functionally expressive skeleton and then the dressing of that skeleton in freely imagined profiles that in their simplicity admitted the weight of the masonry and in their expressive curves became highly modulated and lyrical. The Bibliothèque Ste.-Geneviève, of course, was the first and purest declaration of this "Modern Greek"; Questel's Musée-Bibliothèque at Grenoble was a later, softer reflection of it.

This is not the place to rehearse the history of Hunt's adherence to the *néo-grec* during his student years in Paris and early years in America.[8] Suffice it to note that many of his student projects had been unqualifiedly *néo-grec*; that in 1860 the *Boston Almanac* had already described the Williams houses as "designed in the extreme modern French style"; that Van Brunt knew French architecture only through his friend and teacher Hunt; and finally that contemporary critics—most particularly Montgomery Schuyler—agreed that the term should be applied to his early work. I hurry past Hunt's flirtation with the mode because already in his Union League Club design of 1867 it is obvious that he himself is trying to get beyond it. Lefuel, his master, had not been a *néo-grec*: his accomplishment in the New Louvre had been to introduce a new richness of massing and modeling into French architecture that, however, might still recognize consistency of surface and materials in the spirit of the *néo-grec.*[9] This is the synthesis that one sees Hunt trying to make in the Union League project twelve years after his apprenticeship under Lefuel at the New Louvre. Here Hunt spreads his moldings evenly over the surface as at the Williams Houses (using reliefs and niches to place emphases between windows balancing the voids). He mixes this now with the French Baroque vocabulary of the New Louvre and opens the bays to broad arches defined by deep embrasures. But he gets all his accents wrong: this is surely the worst-scaled design Hunt ever produced. The ground floor is too low and the attic too high. The three middle stories are equal in height while only the second floor should dominate because of its function as the *piano nobile,* a problem Hunt makes worse by emphasizing the second and third stories while making no effective distinction between them. The relationship of the central pediment to the dormers is positively agonizing.

Hunt, here at the end of the 1860s (about to leave for his second visit to Paris since his return to the United States) is obviously only beginning to mature his style, and had we not the Lenox Library of three years later to document his eventual success, we might give him up for lost.

Hunt had spent six years as a student at the Ecole des Beaux-Arts. Subsequently he had been employed as an *inspecteur de la 5ème classe* in the drafting office at Lefuel's New Louvre during the months of June to December 1854. (He was one of some twenty *inspecteurs* of that lowest class, earning 2,000 francs per annum, part of a total architectural staff there of forty-five, as is recorded in the pay records in the Archives Nationales, 64 Aj 65.) Nonetheless, the projects from the first decade and a half of his practice in New York make one pause and consider whether he had been, in fact, completely prepared to commence independent practice in 1853. Certainly a first-rate French government architect in the mid nineteenth century would not have been considered to be ready so quickly. The Service des Bâtiments Civils in France established an office or *agence* for each building project with a strict hierarchy of posts: *dessinateur* (draftsman), *sous-inspecteur* (scribe and draftsman), *inspecteur* (superintendent of construction), *architecte-en-chef* (architect-designer).[10] Several boards of *inspecteurs généraux* approved designs and visited sites. This system not only enforced the efficient division of labor but also created a system of extended apprenticeship as young architects were promoted up the ladder. Among Hunt's contemporaries at the Ecole were Léon Ginain (1825–98, Grand Prix of 1852 and a personal friend), Charles Garnier (1825–98, Grand Prix of 1848), and Honoré Daumet (1826–1911, Grand Prix of 1855).[11] (Hunt had been born in 1827.) Ginain had returned from Rome early in 1858 and had been named *inspecteur* in Lefuel's Louvre *agence* and *auditeur* with the Conseil des Bâtiments Civils. In 1861 he was named *Architecte de la Ville de Paris* for the sixth and seventh arrondissements, a chiefly supervisory position in which he received the opportunity to erect two small schools, one on the rue de Poissy and the other on the rue St.-Bénoit. It was only in 1867 that he had a chance to produce a major design, that of the church of Notre-Dame-des-Champs. Garnier, before the opportunity suddenly thrust upon him by his victory in the Opéra competition in 1861, had similarly worked as *Architecte de la Ville de Paris* during the 1850s and had felt himself lucky to have private commissions for an apartment building on the boulevard de Sebastapol and for a funerary chapel for the duc de Luynes in the parish church at Dampierre. Daumet had extended his years in Italy by joining Léon Heuzey's archeological expedition to Macedonia. Returning to Paris in 1862 he was named *inspecteur* to Emile Gilbert and then to Questel (who became his father-in-law) at the Asile Ste.-Anne. In 1867 he received his first great opportunity, that to divide the design and direction of the work at the Palais de Justice with the aging *architecte-en-chef*, Louis Duc.

Between the time they entered the Ecole and the time they received their first major commissions, twenty-four years elapsed in the case of Ginain, eighteen in that of Garnier (who was considered lucky), and twenty-one in that of Daumet. Twenty-two years separated Hunt's entry into the Ecole in 1848 and his commencement of the Lenox Library project in 1870.

Ginain, Garnier, and Daumet, however, were the leaders of their profession and all Grand Prix winners (which provided them with five extra years of schooling in Rome). They had been too elaborately trained in design to be held back in subordinate posts. A French architect who had merely studied six or eight years at the Ecole, like Hunt, might have a drabber career. For example, Hunt's friend Adolphe Crépinet (1827–92) started as an *inspecteur* under Lefuel at the New Louvre and rose to be architect for the maintenance of the Hôtel des Invalides in 1862.[12] And Crépinet was a particularly respected and lucky non–Grand Prix winner: he held a high post in the Louvre *agence*, placed among the top five in the first Opéra competition (1860), received the opportunity to design Jerome Napoleon's tomb in the Dome des Invalides, and had a private practice (for which he designed the Compagnie Générale du Crédit Espagnole in Madrid in 1858).

When a government architect of the first rank did receive a major commission, what a huge volume of space he was asked to enclose, what a mammoth budget he was accorded, and what an army of assistants he was given to direct! Garnier's *agence* at the Opéra was supervised by V.-L. Louvet, a Grand Prix winner himself (1850) and *inspecteur principal* from 1861 to 1870.[13] He was supported by a *premier inspecteur*, Jourdain, who succeeded him as *inspecteur principal* in 1870. Jourdain was aided by a *second inspecteur*, Edmond Le Deschault, who succeeded to Jourdain's post upon the latter's elevation. Below them came a mass of simple *inspecteurs*, *dessinateurs*, and *sous-inspecteurs*, at least eighteen of whom are known by name. Fifteen of these were students at the Ecole des Beaux-Arts and six were to win the Grand Prix de Rome while several others were *en loge*. This was a very distinguished drafting force and Garnier later was justly proud of it.

I have made reference to the unusual number of studies that survive for the Lenox Library. The sketches seem to be from Hunt's own hand but the many carefully laid-out perspective studies must have been executed by well-trained assistants. We know that at least one early American Ecole product was in Hunt's office at the time, Sidney Stratton, who in 1873 showed Louis Sullivan around and advised him to seek employment in Philadelphia with Hunt's student Frank Furness.[14] The mysterious and faithful Maurice Fornachon was signing most of the correspondence at this time.[15] Would Eugène Létang, the first French Ecole product to arrive, and who had been teaching at MIT since 1869, have also been touched for help? The year 1870 was a moment of tremendous activity for Hunt and he had clearly developed a large and smoothly running office. It is frustrating that we do not know more about its organization and personnel.

Balancing this evidence that Hunt needed more time and experience during the 1850s and 1860s is the fact that in his sketchbooks he was continuing to study French architecture and was trying to grasp it as it evolved during the frenetic Second Empire. Besides keeping up with the latest French publications he visited Paris twice, in 1861–62 and in 1867.[16] Hunt's sketchbooks from these two trips contain lists of names and addresses as well as, in 1867, an account of some of his exact activities. During the earlier trip we find mention of Lefuel (whom he visited at the Louvre and subsequently had to dinner) as well as the architects Félix Duban, Ginain, Crépinet, Marcellin Varcollier, Théodore Ballu, and Alphonse Girard. In 1867 he noted the addresses of Duban, Ginain, and Ballu again plus those of Viollet-le-Duc, Albert Lenoir, Louis Duc, and Edouard Guillaume, as well as those of several delegates to the Exposition Universelle, the Austrian Friedrich von Schmidt and the Englishmen James Fergusson and Lieutenant Colonel Scott. He also recorded his activities during one week. On Tuesday, he met Schmidt and went to call on Viollet-le-Duc, seeing Ballu's church of La Trinité on the way. From there they proceeded to the Musée de Cluny, the church of the Sorbonne, St.-Etienne-du-Mont, the Luxembourg Palace, Notre-Dame on the Ile de la Cité, the Hôtel de Ville, the Tour St.-Jacques, and St.-Germain-l'Auxerrois (all near each other in the center of Paris). After that busy but essentially touristic day Hunt spent Wednesday shopping on the boulevards, visiting Lefuel at the Louvre, and going to the Odéon in the evening. Thursday he devoted to his duties as a juror at the Exposition Universelle. Friday Hunt called on Ballu and with Schmidt visited La Trinité at length. Then he proceeded to the Opéra (still not out from its scaffolding then) where he was shown around by Garnier. Finally he visited Ballu's new church of St.-Amboise, and then again the Hôtel de Ville. Saturday was devoted to shopping and a state dinner; Sunday to service at the American Episcopal church and to visits with American friends.

Hunt's trips were chiefly for pleasure. His stays in Paris were only a month or so at a stretch and most of his time was spent traveling. In spite of this brevity, there is method in what he did in Paris. First, he visited his contemporaries at the Ecole—Crépinet, Varcollier, Ginain, and Guillaume. Second, he kept up with work at the Louvre (where construction continued all through the Second Empire) and with his old friends in the *agence*. Crépinet was the head of the Louvre *agence* and Girard an important *inspecteur*.[17] Duban was responsible with Lefuel for parts of the building and Hunt's visit to him in 1860 was to see his newly restored Galérie d'Apollon. Third, Hunt informed himself about the principal buildings just going up: Ballu's restored Tour St.-Jacques and his churches of La Trinité and St.-Amboise; Garnier's Opéra; Duc's Palais de Justice; and the restoration of the Ste.-Chapelle and the Musée de Cluny, overseen by Viollet-le-Duc and Albert Lenoir respectively. Several of these projects Hunt visited in both 1861 and 1867 (the Louvre and the Palais de Justice) and several of the architects he visited both times (Lefuel, Duban, Ginain, Ballu). These were not therefore just random visits or quick rounds of the high spots. Hunt was keeping track of certain people and of specific projects.

I speculated above that what so confuses Hunt's Union League Club design is an attempt to translate a *néo-grec* sense of surface and solid mass into the richer three-dimensional style of Lefuel's New Louvre. Significantly, this was the problem being addressed in several of the Parisian projects Hunt was following during the 1860s: Lefuel's continuing work at the Louvre; Duban's work there and at the Ecole des Beaux-Arts just across the Seine; Duc's at the Palais de Justice; Ballu's at La Trinité; and finally Ginain and Crépinet's in their premiated projects for the Opéra as well as Garnier's in his executed design.

Interspersed with Hunt's notes in his 1867 sketchbooks are the first thoughts for his competition project for the Equitable Building in New York.[18] These show that if he was not actually making the first efforts to design it during his visit he was at least going back over these pages upon his return to freshen certain memories. The building was to be a rental office building on lower Broadway of especially palatial character. In Hunt's designs we see him trying to draw his composition together at one point of intense monumental emphasis in the center. This he accomplishes by opening the facade in its central two bays on the second and third floors in a broad glass-filled void and then enframing the opening with projecting brackets, colonnettes, and arches. The vocabulary is that of the French Baroque and the layering that demonstrated by Lefuel (in imitation of Lemercier) at the Louvre (fig. 5.10), but the context is new and the relief reduced. That Hunt was thinking of the Louvre is nonetheless clear not only in the placement of one of the Equitable sketches across from a watercolor of the Parisian model in his sketchbooks (fig. 5.11) but also by the explicit reproduction of Lescot's Louvre facade in one of the alternative projects Hunt drew up for submission.

The Equitable designs, however, are just a prelude to the Lenox Library. Here Hunt magisterially solved the problem of mass composition by pushing his central volume back behind a forecourt and raising it a story over flanking wings. He has solved the problem of unifying the wing elevations by defining broad piers at each corner and repeating the form twice in the center of each side elevation. Between these Hunt has thrown the broad arched windows of the library spaces and in front of them, in the central bays, set pilaster-borne pediments. His mass composition is not new; it was a basic *parti* in Beaux-Arts student projects. But his side elevations are less familiar. Questel proceeded differently at Grenoble: a French architect hesitated to break the wall plane so brutally. At best what are broad piers in Hunt's design would be pilasters or wall spurs as in Duban's Ecole des Beaux-Arts facade of 1858–62 or Labrouste's cele-

5.10 Hector Martin Lefuel, New Louvre, Paris. Courtesy of Giraudon, Paris.

5.11 Equitable Life Assurance Society Building, project, New York City, ca. 1867, with watercolor of the New Louvre and Tuileries, Paris (on facing pages in Hunt's travel book).

5.12 Henri Labrouste, Bibliothèque Ste.-Geneviève, Paris. Courtesy of James Austin, Cambridge.

brated Bibliothèque Ste.-Geneviève, opened in Paris in 1851 while Hunt was still there (fig. 5.12). This last structure, like Hunt's library wings, is but a skeleton of piers joined by arches with screen walls between. Yet in naming these other modern sources for Hunt's design, one again realizes how differently he has applied Duban's and Labrouste's models and one must admit that Hunt is thinking, not copying. Duban's and Labrouste's buildings are very long, unaccented at their center, and reticent in their relief. They embody the very *neogrec* that Hunt had spent all the 1860s trying to escape through the study of Lefuel and the Louvre. Thus Hunt broadens Labrouste's subsidiary piers to match his corner masses; he divides the library space into two three-bay units and rotates them to enframe a dominant central mass; he makes the relief deeper, the moldings starker, and the masses heavier. He has achieved Lefuel's ends by Labrouste's means.

I have compared the massiveness and deep ornamental relief of the Lenox Library to similar qualities in Lefuel's Louvre and spoken of further parallels in Ballu's La Trinité, Garnier's Opéra, and Duc's Palais de Justice. All of these designs share the Baroque three-dimensionality of the Second Empire. Nonetheless, one would not confuse Hunt's broad, angular moldings with Lefuel's and Ballu's lush surfacing or with Garnier's inventive and varied profiles, or even with Duc's archaizing detailing. A blindman running his hand over the surfaces of these buildings would have been able to distinguish them immediately. It is nowhere clearer that Hunt is merely moving parallel to his Parisian contemporaries than in his *ravalement*—in his treatment of ornamental surface carving.

Nonetheless, the particular quality of molding and relief is familiar in another context. A New Yorker in the early 1870s would have found it also in the powerful Ruskinian Gothic designs of Hunt's contemporaries Russell Sturgis and William Appleton Potter (Chancellor Green Library at Princeton of 1873 especially; fig. 5.13).[19] (Hunt was working at both Yale and Princeton in 1870.)

Indeed, immediately after designing the Lenox Library Hunt suddenly transformed himself into a Ruskinian Gothicist in his Presbyterian Hospital (1869), Yale Divinity School (1870), Stuyvesant Apartments (1870), Tribune Building (1876), and Delaware and Hudson Canal Building (1876)—not to mention his Brimmer House in Boston and Osborne-Sturgis House in New York (both of 1870). During his visits to Europe, in fact, his interest in Gothic architecture—both original and revived—was as great as that in modern designs. In 1860 in Paris, besides the Louvre and the Palais de Justice, Hunt visited the Ste.-Chapelle and the Tour St.-Jacques, magnificent Gothic structures then under restoration. In 1867 Hunt went out with Schmidt, a celebrated Gothicist trained in the "lodge" at Cologne Cathedral, and visited Viollet-le-Duc and the Gothic and Renaissance monuments of the center of Paris. At that time he contemplated visiting Viollet-le-Duc's restoration of the château at Pierrefonds and in a subsequent visit in 1874 he did so, making a series of watercolor sketches of it. His travels in the countryside, which occupied the greater part of his trips, were principally from one medieval monument to another (as were most tourist voyages of the time).

Montgomery Schuyler said of Hunt's work during the 1870s that it was "a persistent but unsuccessful attempt to avoid Gothic architecture." One might reverse this, with the Lenox Library in mind, and say that in 1867–70 Hunt's designs were a persistent but unsuccessful attempt to avoid classical architecture. I have mentioned that in 1861 Hunt's student and friend Henry Van Brunt had published the first exposition of the *néo-grec*. Soon afterward, however, Van Brunt commenced a more monumental scholarly enterprise, the translation of Viollet-le-Duc's *Entretiens sur l'architecture*, publishing the first volume in 1875 and the second in 1881. Clearly, around 1870 the rationalist *néo-grec* in New York was transforming itself into rationalistic Gothicism. In a sense this should not have been surprising. In France, the most radical strand of the *néo-grec*—that emanating from Labrouste—had already thus transformed itself during the 1850s when Labrouste, who closed his atelier in 1856, sent his best students on to Viollet-le-Duc. Anatole de Baudot and Eugène Millet, two of the most prominent French Gothic rationalists around 1870, had been part of this migration. Thus the explanation for Hunt's metamorphosis might seem very simple: he was following the French lead again. But Hunt's Gothic—in its symptoms at the Lenox Library and in its outbreak in the Yale Divinity School—is as distinct in its brutality and bigness from these French models as was his *néo-grec*. One could make the same comparison between his Yale Divinity School and Viollet-le-Duc's Pierrefonds that was made earlier between the Lenox Library and the Louvre and Opéra. Hunt's work suggests New York Ruskinian Gothic, not French medievalism. One must ask once again how European ideas entered his mind and how they were transformed by his experience.

It has been observed of religious doctrines brought to America in the nineteenth century that they were transformed by contact with the local tradition of puritan Congregational Calvinism.[20] That is, as the details of these doctrines and philosophies were dimmed or lost by their translation to the United States, the doctrines became one or another expression of a general conception of austere piety—something that was often quite against their original spirit. This pattern would seem to have been repeated in mid-century architecture. Ruskinian, *néo-grec*, and French Gothic rationalism all became starker, more moralistic, and more puritanical upon crossing the ocean. They all lost their decorative, sentimental qualities. Sturgis's work is as distinct from Butterfield's as Hunt's is from Lefuel's or Viollet-le-Duc's. Nor should this be surprising. American architectural doctrine was as moralizing as that of the contemporaneous social and religious movements and the profession was dominated by churchmen and ministers' sons (almost exclusively Calvinist or Episcopalian). Ecclesiology was in large part an architectural doctrine; Ruskinianism a moral one. James Lenox was not only Hunt's client for the library bearing his name but also for the Presbyterian Hospital, a great philanthropic establishment "for the poor of New York . . . without regard to Race, Creed or Color. . . ."

It is enlightening to see American moralizing architectural doctrine paralleling contemporaneous social and religious theory in becoming more puritanical, but there remains the problem of the expression of such abstract puritanism in actual architectural forms. It is tempting to see the heaviness, angularity, and starkness of Hunt's articulation of the Lenox Library or that of Sturgis's Farnum Hall and Potter's Chancellor Green Library as directly symbolic of the Congregationalist and Presbyterian Calvinism that dominated all three institutions. Yet one cannot, for to do so would be to acknowledge no intermediate stage between the idea and the form, no place where there might be a reservoir of motifs and forms to be selected and reconstituted to produce the final design. That intermediary stage in European architecture existed in the study of historical architecture. Through years of daily acquaintance and intimate study, English Ruskinian and French *néo-grec* or Gothicist designers worked out precisely how a rational, moral society would appear to have gone about building. In Ruskin's *Stones of Venice* (1851–53) one reads how a medieval wall was built or arch spanned, stone by stone. The revolution represented by Labrouste's first work, his *envoi* restoring the temples at Paestum, was one to establish just how the ancient Greeks built. The matter and beauty of Viollet-le-Duc's *Entretiens* and *Dictionnaire raisonnée* (1854–68) consist in the revelation of the infinite complexity and ingenuity of Gothic construction.

But one thing totally missing from Hunt's training—as well as from the training of all his American contemporaries—is just these years of quiet mental exercise on historic monuments. Nor did he (or they) make good this lack in any way. Hunt visited Europe as a tourist, not as an archaeologist. He passed by many medieval sites in 1861–62, 1867, and later, but all he ever recorded in his sketchbooks were quick picturesque perspectives. There are no studies of construction or planning. There is not a single *relevé* in all the piles of the Hunt papers in Washington. This whole lobe of his architectural brain did not exist.

Where, then, could Hunt have worked out his ideas about rationalism? The answer is obvious: in actual building. A large building in New York in 1870 was an assemblage of massive pieces of stone backed and often interspersed with thick brickwork (fig. 5.14). American quarries, like those at Quincy, Massachusetts, could produce and ship huge bulks of stone, and the bigger the pieces, the solider the construction. It was this practical technology of stone piling that the American architect was called upon to render expressive in 1870 and many in New York chose to do so in the scale and majesty of the work itself. To have been living then in New York amid the Babylonian construction sites like that shown in figure 5.16 as city construction raced pell-mell past Midtown up along Central Park must have left one vividly conscious of just how and on what scale building was done. (One might extrapolate the sense from the more recent experience of skyscraper construction, especially in the 1920s and 1930s.) This had a reality to the man of 1870 that the stones of Venice or the vaults of the Ile de France completely lacked. It would be in this daily converse with actual construction that it would seem most logical to place the formulation of Hunt's, Sturgis's, and Potter's "moral" architecture. Again, it is in the work of one of Hunt's students that this becomes most unmistakable. In the 1870s, the Unitarian minister's son Frank Furness raised a series of constructions in Philadelphia in which one can read and enjoy every massive piece and jointing as if they were huge Chinese apples (fig. 5.15). Furness felt no need to visit Europe at all.[21]

5.14 New York Tribune Building under construction, 1875.

5.15 Frank Furness, Provident Trust Company, Philadelphia, 1876–79. Courtesy of the Art Institute of Chicago.

I have attempted to make three points in this essay: that Hunt was not ready until 1870 to produce a mature design; that this long delay forced him to respond to the contemporaneous evolution of French architecture and thus to change his ideas at the same time that he was maturing them; and that during that fifteen-year hiatus he had become an American architect and thus could not but speak what was, in the end, a profoundly American language. For all the simplicity of my tripartite division of Hunt's experience, this is a very complex evolution to follow and one needing far more space than this chapter permits. Exactly what *did* Hunt do at the New Louvre in 1854? Just how did he organize his office for the big jobs of 1870? Who were his assistants and how much did he owe to them? Just what were his ideas about architecture in these years and what did he feel he had in common with James Lenox, President Woolsey of Yale, and President McCosh of Princeton? What did it really feel like to live amid the tumultuous construction projects in New York in 1870? How did this—combined with a strong moral consciousness, a French artistic training, and an opportunity to make something very big and very fine—move the sensitive architect's hand across the sheet on his drawing board?

Notes

This chapter, unfortunately, is only a sketch. The research was truncated prematurely by my wife's tragic death while we were working at the Archives Nationales in Paris in August, 1982. The thinking and writing were made very difficult by the aftermath of that event. I would have wished to pursue a number of points much further and hope eventually to do so.

1. Paul Baker, *Richard Morris Hunt* (Cambridge, Mass., 1980), pp. 181–86. The building was erected and administered under a state charter (granted in 1870) with funds donated by James Lenox. Annual reports were published beginning in 1871. They trace the construction, starting with the "maturing" of the plans in the winter of 1870–71 and culminating in the "gradual occupation" of the building in 1875. See also *American Architect and Building News*, 1 September 1877.

2. Published in *Encyclopédie d'architecture* (1875), pp. 9–18.

3. See C. Daly, Charles-Auguste Questel," *Revue générale de l'architecture et des travaux publics* 44 (1888), cols. 246–54; G. Raulin et al., "Charles Questel," *L'Architecture* 1 (1888): 49–51.

4. The project, by Henard, is reproduced in *Intime Club; Croquis d'architecture* 2, no. 9 (January 1868), pl. 2

5. Baker, *Richard Morris Hunt*, pp. 538–39.

6. Many are reproduced in C. Normand, *Paris moderne*, especially vols. 3 (1843) and 4 (1849).

7. On the *néo-grec*, see Neil Levine, "The Romantic Idea of Architectural Legibility: Henri Labrouste and the Neo-Grec," in *The Architecture of the Ecole des Beaux-Arts*, ed. Arthur Drexler, (Cambridge, Mass., 1977), pp. 325–416. On the *néo-grec* in the United States, see the same author's M.A. thesis at Yale University, *The Idea of Frank Furness's Buildings* (1967).

8. Montgomery Schuyler explores this in his lengthy review of Hunt's work, "The Works of the Late Richard Morris Hunt," *Architectural Record* 5, no. 2 (October–December 1895): 97–180.

9. See my discussion of Lefuel's transformation of the Louvre design in *The Second Empire: Art in France under Napoleon III* (Philadelphia, 1978), pp. 59–61 and 73. See also L. Vitet, "Le nouvel Louvre," *Revue des deux Mondes*, 1 July 1866, pp. 57–93; J.-L. Pascal, "Hector Lefuel," *Revue générale de l'architecture et des travaux publics* (1881), cols. 259–65; H. Delaborde, "Hector Lefuel, architecte: sa vie et ses oeuvres," *Encyclopédie d'architecture* (1882), pp. 83–88.

10. This was all specified in a law of 22 July 1832, later much amended and clarified. See Charles Gourlier, *Notice historique sur le service des bâtiments civils à Paris et dans les departements* (Paris, 1848; later, expanded editions 1886 and 1893).

11. Garnier: Monika Steinhauser, *Die Architektur der Pariser Oper* (Munich, 1969; with full bibliography); Ginain: J. Gaudet, "Notice sur la vie et les oeuvres de Léon Ginian," *L'Architecture* (1898): 317–24; Charles de Randerode, "Nos Architectes contemporaines . . . Léon Ginain," *Semaine des constructeurs* 22, no. 26 (25 September 1897): 306–8; Daumet: Charles Girault, "Pierre-Jérome-Honoré Daumet," *L'Architecture* (1911): 425–26; "Honoré Daumet," *L'Architecture* (1914): 49–55.

12. E. Delaire, *Les architectes élèves de l'Ecole des Beaux-Arts* (Paris, 1907), s.v. "Crépinet."

13. This profile of the Opéra *agence* has been pieced together by Professor Christopher Mead at the University of New Mexico, who has completed a doctoral dissertation at the University of Pennsylvania on the subject of Garnier and the Opéra. I am indebted to him for his sharing this material with me.

14. Louis Sullivan, *The Autobiography of an Idea* (New York, 1956), p. 190.

15. A scattering of letters about the construction of the building survives at the New York Public Library (the successor institution), all signed by Fornachon. The letterhead reads: "The Office of Richard Morris Hunt."

16. Baker, *Richard Morris Hunt*, pp. 127–33 and 156–61.

17. Delaire, *Les architectes élèves*, s.v. "Girard."

18. On the Equitable competition, see Winston Wiseman, "The Commercial Architecture of George B. Post," *Journal of the Society of Architectural Historians* 21, no. 3 (October 1972): 176–203, esp. 178–79.

19. L. Woodhouse, "William Appleton Potter, Principal Pasticheur of Henry Hobson Richardson," *Journal of the Society of Architectural Historians* 32, no. 1 (May 1973): 175–92; Sarah Bradford Landau, *Edward T. and William A. Potter, American Victorian Architects* (New York and London, 1979). Roger Stein, *John Ruskin and Aesthetic Thought in America, 1840–1900* (Cambridge, Mass., 1967).

20. Timothy Smith, "Religion and Ethnicity in America," *American Historical Review* 83, no. 5 (December 1978): 1155–85; and idem., *Revivalism and Social Reform in Mid-Nineteenth Century America* (Nashville, 1957).

21. James O'Gorman, *The Architecture of Frank Furness* (Philadelphia, 1973). There is a single reference to Furness's having visited Europe late in his career and finding it uninformative: see Levine, *The Idea of Frank Furness's Buildings*, p. 92n.4.

Role and Reputation:
The Architectural Practice of
Richard Morris Hunt

Susan R. Stein

ARCHITECTS' REPUTATIONS rest mainly on the buildings they have designed. In this Richard Morris Hunt is no exception. Hunt's popular and professional reputation has been based almost entirely on the Beaux-Arts-style works executed in the last years of his career: the Administration Building of the World's Columbian Exposition (fig. 6.1), the Fifth Avenue wing of the Metropolitan Museum of Art, and most of all, the grand country estates for America's elite. These celebrated works, however, were certainly not Hunt's only important products. His long and complex career has often been misinterpreted by those who are unaware of the breadth of his endeavors. In many ways Hunt's last and most famous works are less characteristic of his style than designs bearing the distinctive imprint of the early and middle years of his architectural practice.

The recent accessibility of Hunt's drawings has made possible a reassessment of his overall achievement based upon a critical analysis of his surviving records. This chapter examines some of the evidence from Hunt's records in order to assess the basis of his reputation for the famous later works and to place the remainder of his career—indeed, the bulk of it—in perspective. There are two sources of information. The first is the drawings from his days as the first American to study at the Ecole des Beaux-Arts in Paris. Here he received his formal training and his style began to develop. The second source of evidence is reflected in the drawings he did once he returned to this country and began a practice. We can obtain considerable insight into Hunt's role in designing the later works by analyzing the role he played in his own office, especially in design, throughout most of his career. Through the knowledge gained by close examination of Hunt's drawings, his own style, as distinct from that of others who worked in his office, can be isolated, and the design role he played at various points in his career can be assessed. The drawings themselves provide a worthwhile commentary on the artistic qualities of the dean of nineteenth-century American architecture.

The Period Abroad

It should come as no surprise that Hunt, who arrived in Europe in 1843, underwent a considerable transformation before he returned home more than a decade later. Among the drawings that survive from Hunt's study with Samuel Darier in Geneva is a rather routine copying of a series of antique columns (fig.

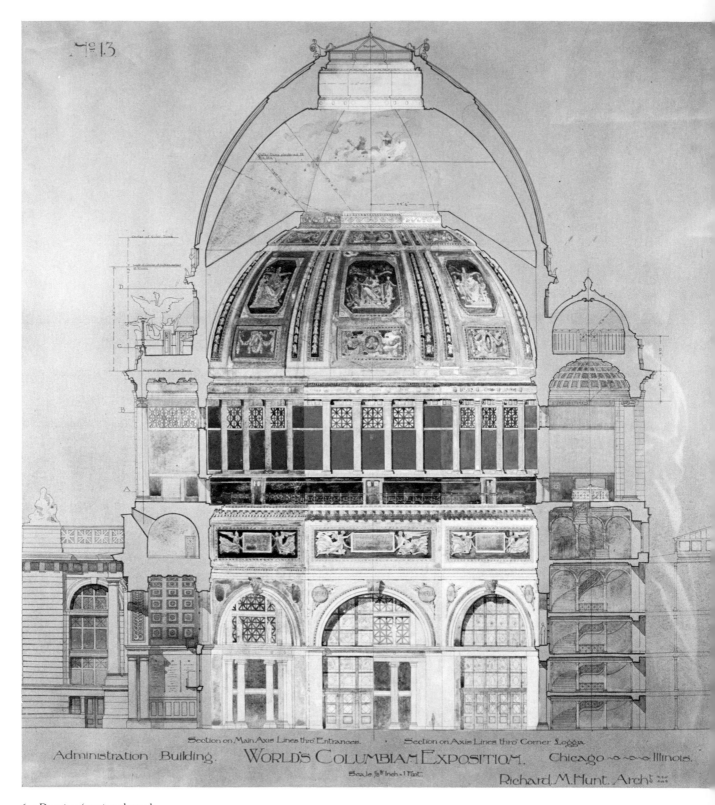

6.1 Drawing (section through
main axis) of the Administration
Building of the World's Columbian Exposition, Chicago, 1892.

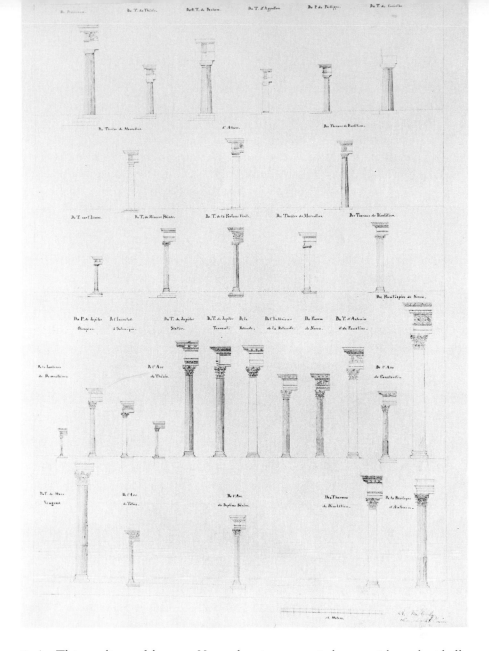

6.2 Columns drawn between May 1844 and August 1845 when Hunt was studying architecture in the atelier of Lefuel.

6.2). This earliest of known Hunt drawings, carried out with a decidedly wooden touch, dates about 1844. Each column is exactly rendered. The drawing is notable only insofar as it fails to reveal any suggestion that its author might later prove to be a capable artist.

Drawings executed during the subsequent years Hunt spent at the Ecole des Beaux-Arts begin to demonstrate versatility and considerable talent. Clearly, it was his training at the Ecole that produced the rational architect. The many projects, described in detail in chapter 2, vary measurably in the skill of their execution. The earliest drawings, as one might suspect, are the most plodding. Fastidiously drawn, they are timid and have a noticeable lack of confidence, typical of the beginner. Hunt's drawing for a public square is characteristic of these early works.

As he tackled complicated *projets* and *esquisses* at the Ecole, his assurance grew. The *projets* do, of course, reflect the rigors of the Ecole's method, which demanded that drawings conform to a defined aesthetic. Each drawing was an analytical response to a well-described program.[1] In no case did the drawing overpower the idea it embodied. Technique was a carefully defined means to achieve an equally well-defined end, a measured model of restraint. By 1854

Hunt seems to have discovered both himself and the "style" he later pursued, but that proves to be more the result of his travels than of the training he received at the Ecole.

Examination of Hunt's forty-eight travel sketchbooks reveals that Hunt's drawing technique was somewhat bifurcated. The thousands of drawings contained in his sketchbooks diverged entirely, in style and technique, from those completed for *esquisses* and *projets*. The Ecole drawings were tight, whereas the sketches were loose and free. The sketchbook style eventually prevailed.

Hunt was an indefatigable traveler. He carried small notebooks with him as he journeyed throughout Europe and the Middle East, recording his impressions of well-known monuments as well as of indigenous architecture. When he sketched turbaned Egyptians, he did so with the fluidity of Delacroix. In Egypt, he was evidently as entranced with the people he saw as he was with architecture. Veiled women, belly dancers, merchants, and servants captured his attention and were noted in watercolor (figs. 6.3 and 6.4). In his sketches, photography, and collecting of books and objects, Hunt expanded his vision. When traveling in Egypt, he even carried his own camera—this was in 1853—and assembled wonderful salt prints of Karnak and the Pasha's Palace at Thebes. The sheer number of these different kinds of images (there are thousands) suggests how determined he must have been to learn what he could and to share that learning when he returned to the United States.

Undoubtedly the buildings that Hunt visited and studied while he was abroad had a hand in shaping his style during the early part of his career back in the United States.[2] Our concern here, however, is how he recorded what he saw. The sketches of Pesaro and Fontainebleau (figs. 6.5 and 6.6) for example, effectively record their salient features in a quick shorthand. The hastily drawn line is soft, vaguely blurred, and strong. This was the work of a student who knew that he would be dependent on his own documentation for later study.

Before returning to the United States, Hunt won an exceptional honor for an American. Hector Martin Lefuel, in whose atelier Hunt had trained, invited Hunt to participate in the design of the Pavillon de la Bibliothèque at the Louvre (fig. 6.7). He served as an assistant to Lefuel and experienced the excitement of working on the most important building in Paris in the great era of Napoleon III and Haussmann's rebuilding of Paris. The surviving drawings, executed by Hunt on drafting paper, demonstrate a kinship with Hunt's sketches. The ideas are fresh, and Hunt infused Lefuel's concept with his own vitality.

The refined presentation drawing of the Rossiter house of 1855, completed in Paris, is handled in a very different manner (fig. 6.8). A watercolor, it shows all of the still polish of the Ecole method. The complexity of the facade was rendered with great care to accentuate engaged columns and sculpture. The effect upon Hunt's prospective clients must have been astutely considered. Hunt, through his drawing, persuaded the Rossiters to accept an unusual design. With its active facade, the house was quite avant garde for the New York City of the 1850s. The conservative drawing technique, however, resembled a miniature and, with its familiar quality, was intended perhaps to mask the character of the house.

The design of the Rossiter House marks the end of Hunt's time in Paris and the period of his transition from student to professional architect. In 1855 he departed from Paris—though he would return many times—and set off for New York and the career that awaited him.

6.3 *Top:* An Egyptian with a rifle, drawn by Hunt in 1853.

6.4 *Opposite, top, left:* An Egyptian carrying a table, sketched during Hunt's visit to Egypt in 1853.

6.5 *Opposite, top, center:* Pesaro, ca. 1853.

6.6 *Opposite, top, right:* Fontainebleau, sketched in the 1840s or 1850s.

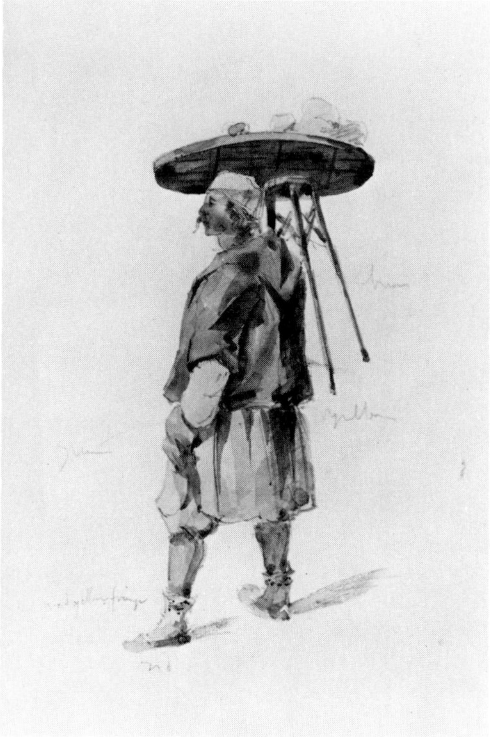

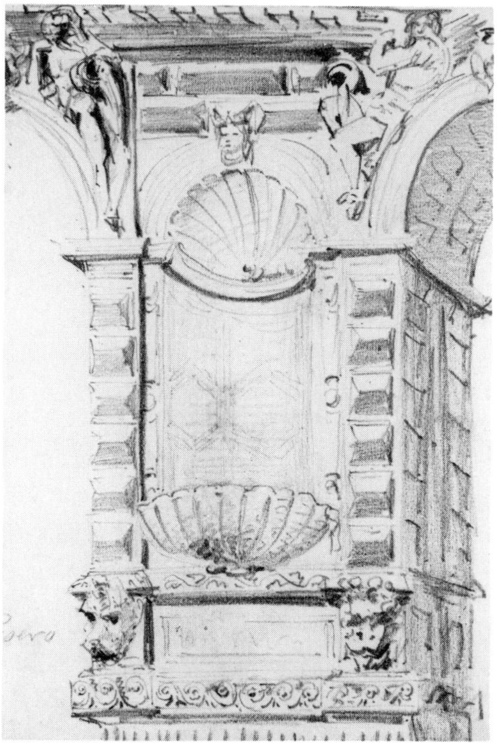

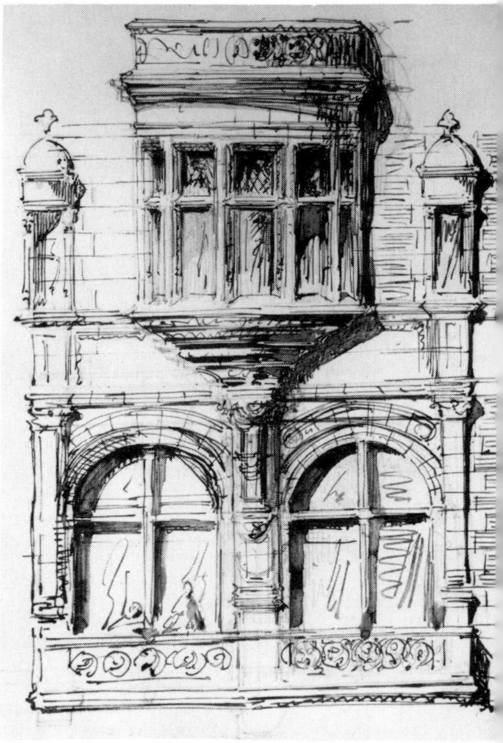

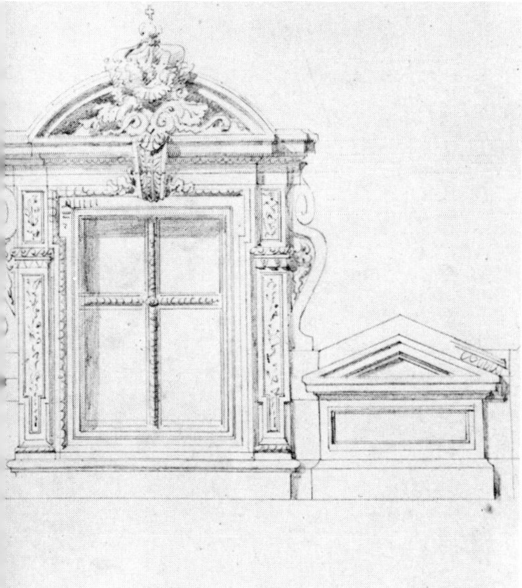

6.7 *Above:* Dormer drawn for the Pavillon de la Bibliothèque, pencil on tracing paper, 1854.

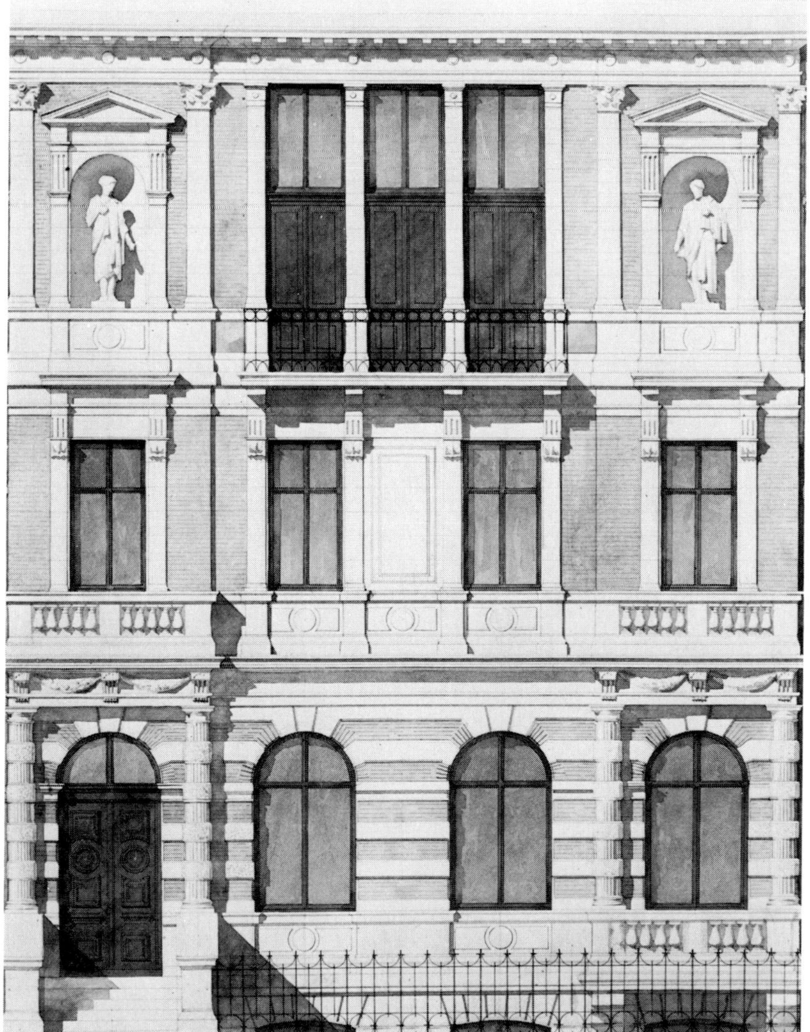

6.8 *Right:* Thomas P. Rossiter House, 11 West Thirty-eighth Street, New York City, 1855.

Hunt's Office and Practice

The office Hunt established was small, and stayed small. It never fit the image conjured by descriptions of the eighty or so draftsmen at the office of McKim, Mead, and White. Four or five draftsmen were usually on hand, and much later Hunt's son, Richard Howland Hunt, joined him. The practice spanned forty years. Just over 240 different projects are known and about thirty of these were never executed.

The way in which the office functioned certainly was modeled after what Hunt knew in France. It was much like the atelier of Lefuel, although much smaller. Here Hunt was the master. With his great collections of architectural books, prints, photographs and drawings, he readily attracted several of the most able young students (fig. 6.9). Henry Van Brunt, his pupil and later a distinguished architect and critic, wrote in 1895 that Hunt's library was then "by far the richest, most comprehensive, and most curious collection of books on architecture and other fine arts which at that time had been brought together in the new world."[3] The studio was lined with paintings, plaster casts of moldings, photographs and antique relics. This unique atmosphere attracted Frank Furness, Charles D. Gambrill, William R. Ware, and George B. Post as students.

6.9 Hunt's office, lined with books, prints, casts, and photographs, functioned as an atelier.

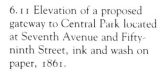

6.10 Proposed elevation of the painter Frederic E. Church's house (Olana, designed later by Calvert Vaux) near Hudson, N.Y., ca. 1867.

6.11 Elevation of a proposed gateway to Central Park located at Seventh Avenue and Fifty-ninth Street, ink and wash on paper, 1861.

The early projects were chiefly residential and differed from the public buildings Hunt had been trained to design. Yet in these projects his style blossomed. In a scheme for Frederic Edwin Church's Olana, the flamboyant, free style of his sketchbooks merged with the rigorous, tight style of the Ecole. The Moorish-style house with its tiled arch was rendered confidently. Hunt's own hand is evident in both sketches and presentation drawings, which were elevations (fig. 6.10). It is a fair surmise that much of the concept was supplied by Church, since Hunt's drawings are similar to the scheme later pursued by Calvert Vaux, whom Church finally selected to design the house.

The Central Park gateways drawings of roughly the same period illustrate another approach to drawing that Hunt was forced to develop, the perspective rendering (fig. 6.11). At the Ecole, drawings were either plans incorporating the site or elevations. In America, potential clients, unschooled in architecture, required a drawing that was capable of revealing the finished building as it would look in its surroundings. The perspective presentation was meant to lure the prospective client. Before the Central Park gateways of 1863, Hunt had had no experience with this kind of drawing. He realized, however, that his gateways drawings must expand the usual Ecole presentation renderings. In some he included people, an altogether revolutionary step in architectural

drawing. Hunt tried to convey to the Board of Commissioners the liveliness that he thought his scheme would encourage. Nevertheless, the continental classicism of the gateways proved too much for the commissioners and they instead hired Vaux and Olmsted.

Hunt's complete mastery of drawing technique as he entered the middle period of his career is revealed in the picturesque villas that Vincent Scully calls the "stick-style" houses of the late 1860s and early 1870s.[4] The Hitchcock-Travers (1869) and Thomas Appleton houses share a certain fluidity, a style of drawing that is comparatively free of restraint (fig. 6.12). Hunt prepared elevations of each house that united the bold, enthusiastic line of his sketches with the prescribed idiom of the elevation. Hunt realized that the formality of the Ecole's method was not persuasive with American residential clients. Apparently they were more apt to be wooed by an appealing image than the precision of a formal, flat elevation. This manner of drawing, however, was not limited to "stick-style" houses. The William Osborne house in New York City (fig. 6.13) is drawn using a similar technique.

The designs for the Appleton and Travers houses display Hunt's remarkable cleverness in linking European and American forms and also proved innovative in their distinctive techniques. Several other sketches preserved in Hunt's records of this middle period are also worth noting, for they epitomize Hunt's style. A hasty sketch in black ink on French blue paper for the Appleton house (1870; fig. 6.14) demonstrates Hunt's deftness. Apparently a beginning sketch, the finished house was much as it was drawn and reveals that Hunt's solution was reached relatively early in the design process. The same holds true for the renovations and additions to Château-sur-Mer (1872) that Hunt did for George Peabody Wetmore. Hunt's ethereal watercolor sketch for the new tower captures his early vision (fig. 6.15).

6.12 *Above left:* Preliminary alteration study for the Hitchcock-Travers house, Narragansett and Ochre Point avenues, Newport, R.I., 1869. This drawing typifies Hunt's fluid drawing technique.

6.13 *Above:* Perspective elevation of the William H. Osborne house and studio, 32 Park Avenue, New York City, 1869.

6.14 *Below left:* Sketch of the Thomas G. Appleton house, Catherine Street, Newport, R.I., 1870.

6.15 *Below:* Proposed tower addition to the George Peabody Wetmore house, Château-sur-Mer, Newport, R.I., ca. 1869.

6.16 Proposed elevation of the Drexel Morgan Company, Broad at White Street, New York City, watercolor and pencil on paper, 1872.

6.17 Elevation proposed for the New York Stock Exchange, watercolor, pencil, and ink on paper, 1880.

Although Hunt's own techniques had thus advanced beyond what he had been taught at the Ecole, he did employ the Ecole's drawing method in a variety of projects. These were chiefly competitions by invitation for commercial structures. Most were drawn by draftsmen, since Hunt apparently was too busy with other projects to devote much time to them. Hunt's office submitted drawings for the Equitable Life Assurance Society (1868), Drexel Bank (1872; fig. 6.16), Western Union Telegraph Company (1872), and the New York Stock Exchange (1880) buildings, and all were rejected. With the exception of the Stock Exchange proposal (fig. 6.17), the submitted drawings were rendered, to Hunt's detriment, rather flatly. The architectural history of the period would have been quite different had these buildings been erected. The conceptually innovative Equitable Life and Western Union headquarters were skyscrapers, or at least early versions of them, and had they been built, they would have changed Hunt's career and been the commanding force in office design.

As it was, Hunt designed two buildings that contributed substantially to the evolution that led from the office building to the skyscraper. Hunt himself drew the conceptual sketches and even several presentation drawings for the New York Tribune and the Delaware and Hudson Canal Company. He experimented with the Tribune's organization to orient it to the corner and to Nassau Street (fig. 6.18). The proposal, oriented to the corner, showed a sculpture of a seated Horace Greeley above the entry, definitely an early application of sculpture to building in America. In both buildings the drawing technique was surprisingly loose and closer to that of residential presentation drawings than to stiff competition drawings.

6.18 Elevation of the New York Tribune Building, pencil on paper, 1873.

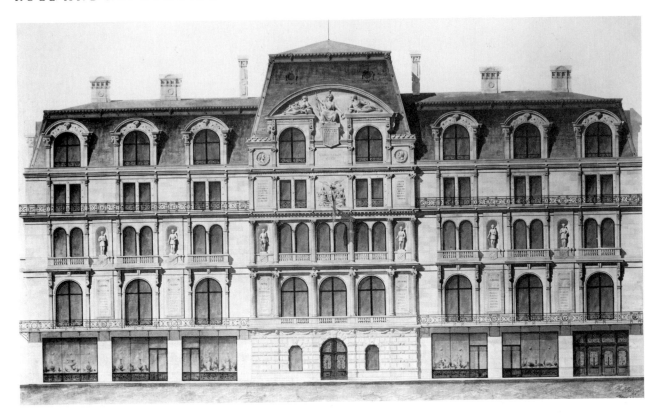

Several projects are the obvious descendants of the full-blown, colorful Ecole treatment. A drawing rendered by Hunt for the proposed Union League Club (1869; fig. 6.19) is as fine a finished drawing as Hunt ever made. It is light, highly ornamented, and enriched by a sculpted facade. Nonetheless, the building was not realized. Only drawings for the Lenox Library (1870–77; fig. 6.20) approached the mature finesse of the Union League Club. More than forty were drawn by Hunt and his subordinates, and were put together in a variety of ways. Two presentation drawings, one with brick and the other with stone, were prepared by Hunt and approximate the technique used on the Tribune elevations. Sections (see fig. 5.6) through the interior resemble the fine, lively detail of the Union League presentation drawing.

As Hunt's career advanced, evidence of his involvement in particular projects diminished. He was involved to a high degree, however, in some important projects of the 1880s. These include the Yorktown Monument (fig. 6.21), the Statue of Liberty, various pedestals for sculpture, and several houses. The Statue of Liberty stands alone among them in demonstrating Hunt's development of a concept. Hunt drew only conceptual sketches illustrating each of the possible schemes (1883–84; fig. 6.22) and left the more elaborate presentation drawings to his staff. The latest presentation drawing from Hunt's own hand was the Yorktown Monument (1880), on which he collaborated with sculptor John Quincy Adams Ward and his former pupil, Henry Van Brunt.[5] Only two houses of the period show evidence of Hunt's hand, Grey Towers, for James Pinchot, and Crumwold Hall, for Archibald Rogers. The surviving drawings for the Henry G. Marquand and Odgen Mills houses in New York City, and Levi P. Morton's Ellerslie (fig. 6.23) in Rhinebeck, New York, show the hands of Hunt's various draftsmen. Presumably Hunt sketched or described his ideas

6.19 Elevation proposed for the Union League Club, New York City, watercolor, pencil, and ink on paper, 1879.

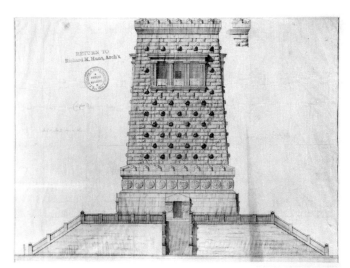

6.20 *Top:* Elevation of the Lenox
Library, watercolor and pencil on
paper, 1871.

6.21 *Left:* Perspective elevation
of the Yorktown Monument,
watercolor and pencil on paper,
ca. 1880.

6.22 *Above:* Preliminary study of
the Pharos I scheme for the pedestal of the Statue of Liberty, ink
and wash on tracing paper.

and then turned the project over to his draftsmen. Relatively few of these sketches were saved.

After 1887 Hunt's involvement in his office lessened. His son, Richard Howland Hunt (1861–1931), fresh from Paris and the Ecole des Beaux-Arts, entered the practice and apparently assumed a major role quickly. He played a part in designing Ellerslie (1886–87), the New York Free Circulating Library branch on Thirteenth Street (1887–88), the Maturin Livingston House on Sixty-ninth Street (1887–88), Beechwood (1888–90), for William Astor, in Newport, and others. Richard Howland Hunt's style was distinctive, too, from that of his office colleagues; his hand was longer and leaner, the line stretched. The younger Hunt was also schooled in the latest trends in French architecture. He was familiar, as was his father, with the new Parisian hotels designed by architects Esnault-Pelterie, Mewes, Cochet, and Magne.[6]

It is worth recognizing, therefore, that at this point Hunt's involvement in the life of his office had become less intense. He was in all likelihood senior adviser, luminary, and if not merely a figurehead, less often at the cutting edge of design decisions than when he had been at the peak of his energies. By the late 1880s evidence of his hand in the drawings produced by his office, so much a reflection of his central role in certain projects during most of his career, had all but disappeared. Works completed during the last decade of Hunt's life had a quite different character from those of the earlier decades. Country estates for various Vanderbilts (Marble House [1888–92] for William K. Vanderbilt, the Breakers [1892–95] for George W. Vanderbilt), Ochre Court (1888–92) for Ogden Goelet, and Belcourt (1892–94) for Oliver H. P. Belmont, seemed to dominate. Hunt's reputation as the learned dean of American architecture suddenly was overtaken by his association with these visible scions of American industry and the realization of their opulent lifestyle. In later years Hunt was remembered for these works alone.

It is ironic, then, to discover that these buildings, with which Hunt's reputation is so intimately connected, bear so little of his imprint. The Metropolitan

6.23 Proposed elevations of the Levi P. Morton house, Ellerslie, Rhinebeck, N.Y., ca. 1886. The drawing is attributed to Richard Howland Hunt.

6.24 Preliminary study for the Fifth Avenue wing of the Metropolitan Museum of Art, pencil on tracing paper, 1894.

Museum of Art is a notable exception, however, as Hunt's early sketch for the elevation asserts that he originated the design (fig. 6.24). No sketches or drawings by Hunt himself are known to exist for the Breakers, Ochre Court, Marble House, Belcourt, or Beechwood. Based on this evidence, at least, it is highly likely that Hunt played a larger role in securing and carrying out these later commissions than in the design process associated with them. Probably his son Richard Howland Hunt should be given far more credit for these works than has been done previously. As notable as Hunt's career became for the design of these later projects, it is to his earlier work that one should look for evidence of his essential style and significance as an architect.

Notes

1. Seventy of these written programs saved by Hunt are held in the Hunt Collection and have been described by Richard Chafee on pp. 37–42.

2. See Sarah Bradford Landau's excellent article "Richard Morris Hunt, the Continental Picturesque and the 'Stick Style,'" *Journal of the Society of Architectural Historians* 42 (October 1983): 272–89. Professor Landau discusses picturesque imagery and the European sources of American wood or stick-style houses.

3. Henry Van Brunt, "Richard Morris Hunt," *Proceedings of the Twenty-ninth Annual Convention of The American Institute of Architects* (Providence, R.I., 1895), pp. 75–76.

4. Vincent Scully, *The Shingle Style: Architectural Theory and Design from Richardson to the Origins of Wright* (New Haven: Yale University Press, 1955).

5. For an account of the Yorktown Monument's design and construction, see Lewis I. Sharp, *John Quincy Adams Ward: Dean of American Sculpture* (Newark: University of Delaware Press, 1985), pp. 202–4.

6. Some of these hotels were published in P. Gelis-Didot, *Hotels et Maisons de Paris: Facades et Détails* (Paris: Libraires-Imprimeries Reunies, 1893).

7.1 R. M. Hunt, a funerary monument for three families, a *project
rendu* that won a *première mention*
on 5 October 1849.

7

Richard Morris Hunt and His Influence on American Beaux-Arts Sculpture

Lewis I. Sharp

RICHARD MORRIS HUNT, America's first architect trained in Paris at the Ecole des Beaux-Arts, exerted a profound influence on American sculpture during the second half of the nineteenth century. As the spokesman of the new style in America, one of the tenets he championed was the collaboration of the arts and especially the integration of architecture and sculpture. Hunt's commitment to this Beaux-Arts principle was evident in his revolutionary designs for the gateways to Central Park, developed in the 1860s, and in his first collaborations with the sculptor John Quincy Adams Ward in the late 1860s and 1870s. In the 1880s Ward and Hunt continued to work together to create some of America's finest Beaux-Arts public monuments. During the same decade, Hunt designed the monumental base for probably the nineteenth century's most famous public monument, Frédéric-Auguste Bartholdi's Statue of Liberty. In the 1890s Hunt joined forces with the Austrian-born sculptor Karl Bitter to produce a number of highly ambitious architectural projects that were richly decorated with sculpture. While all of these collaborations are documented, the pivotal role Hunt played in the field of American Beaux-Arts sculpture has not previously been acknowledged.

Hunt's involvement with the Beaux-Arts treatment of sculpture had its origins, naturally enough, in his student days at the Ecole. The importance of competitions or *concours* in architectural design at the Ecole has been noted in chapter 2. *Concours* were of two types, *projets rendus*, finished drawings done over a two-month period, and *esquisse* competitions executed in a single twelve-hour period.[1] Some of Hunt's Ecole drawings, preserved at the American Institute of Architects Foundation, reveal the Academy's concern with incorporating sculpture into the proposed architectural programs. In a set of drawings dated 8 August 1849 for a funerary memorial to three families, the building is not only decorated with sculpture, but the three phallic columns that surmount the monument and the building itself also have a definite sculptural quality (fig. 7.1). A drawing by Hunt, awarded a mention in 1851, has a large sculpture relief on the facade of the building (see fig. 2.13). Another set of drawings, dated 6 September through 11 November 1853, for a Ministry of Justice includes a grand public space adorned with an equestrian statue and a monumental seated statue of Napoleon (see figs. 2.28–30).

While Hunt's training at the Ecole was thorough, his success was limited. During his lower class tenure he was awarded a number of mentions in his competitions; as a first student, however, he was completely unsuccessful. Paul R.

Baker, in his biography of the architect, states that his "official record suggests that Hunt's work at the Ecole des Beaux-Arts was rather undistinguished."[2] In contrast to his status at the Ecole was his position in Lefuel's atelier, where he became an important part of the architect's studio. Paris during the 1840s and 1850s was undergoing a radical change from a medieval town to an imperial-style city with a vast building program and grand public spaces decorated with public monuments and fountains. Much of the new building was done in the new Second Empire style, an architecture of elegance, with a plasticity that lent itself to a richness of sculptural ornamentation. In 1854, Lefuel was appointed architect to Napoleon III and director of the new structures being built to connect the Tuileries and the Louvre.[3] Lefuel, Baker asserts, had "long appreciated his American pupil's talents" and invited Hunt to join his staff as *inspecteur des travaux* at an annual salary of two thousand francs.[4] Lefuel continued to utilize the High Renaissance style developed for the Louvre extensions by the architect Louis Visconti before his death in 1853; however, Lefuel dressed the facade with more sculptured ornamentation. Hunt took an active part in the designing and overseeing of the construction of this work. Baker writes of Hunt's involvement in the building:

> Richard's own work on the Louvre extensions under Lefuel obviously gave him excellent practical experience. . . . Hunt reputedly drew the working plans and designed many details for the Pavillon de la Bibliothèque opposite the Palais Royal [see figs. 1.31 and 6.7], including the façades and the archway leading from Rue de Rivoli to the inner courtyard. Three full stories in height, with an uppermost mansard story, and with elaboration of balconies, columns, caryatids, antifixae, pedimental sculpture, and acroteria, the Pavillon presents a surfeit of decoration to the modern eye but was welcomed as most suitable to the new Paris of the Second Empire.[5]

The influence of Lefuel's rich use of sculptured ornamentation combined with Hunt's observations of the city planning of Paris with its great boulevards and vistas of monuments to become part of the American's architectural vocabulary. Throughout his long career Hunt cultivated close relationships with sculptors and his collaborations with them became an important part of the American Beaux-Arts movement.

Beyond his collaborative projects, Hunt also made a significant contribution to the field of American sculpture through his rich and abundant use of sculptural decoration in the buildings he designed. His use of sculptural decoration ranged from simple statues placed in the two niches on the facade of the Rossiter house, erected between 1855 and 1857, to the elaborate use of sculptural decoration incorporated into the design of the New-York Historical Society (fig. 7.2) ten years later. Other buildings in which Hunt incorporated sculptural decoration without the collaborative assistance of a sculptor include the designs for the National Academy of Design (1861; fig. 7.3); the American Institute (1866; fig. 7.4); the Union League Club (1867; see fig. 6.19); the Equitable Life Assurance Society Building (1867; see fig. 3.8); the Lenox Library (1870; see fig. 3.27); the Western Union Telegraph Company Building (1872; see fig. 3.10); and the New York Stock Exchange Building (1880; see fig. 6.17). Hunt's use of sculptural decoration in these buildings and in his collaborative projects was bold and innovative and reflects both his Beaux-Arts training and his understanding of contemporary French urban planning and de-

7.2 *Opposite:* R. M. Hunt, proposed New-York Historical Society, 16 January 1866.

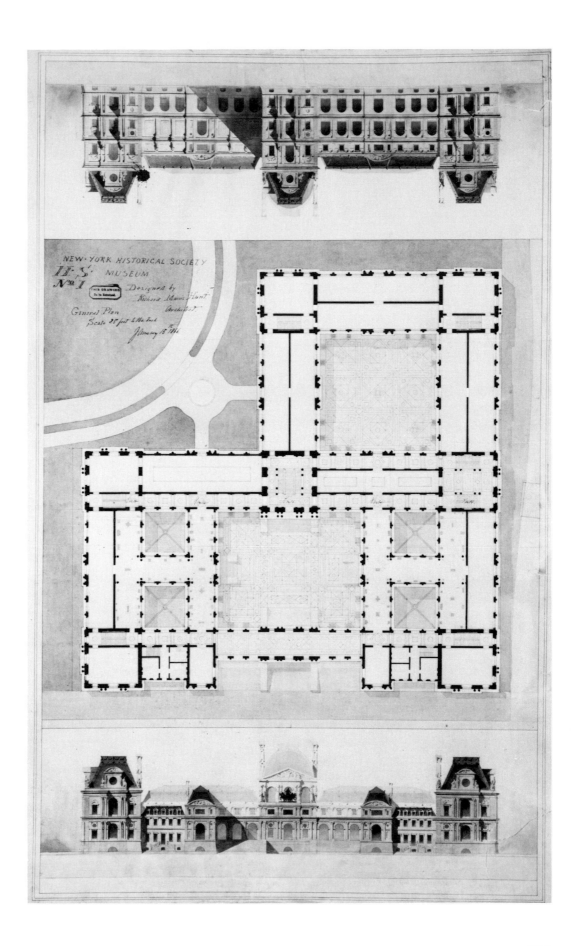

7.3 R. M. Hunt, proposed National Academy of Design, to be located at Fourth Avenue and Twenty-third Street, New York City, 1861.

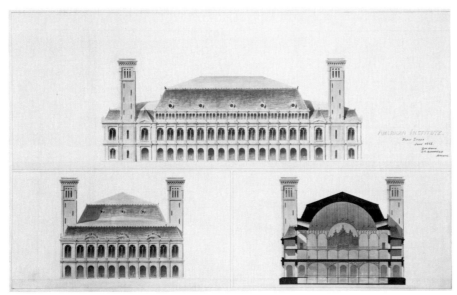

7.4 R. M. Hunt and R. C. Hatfield, first study for the proposed American Institute, June 1866.

sign. While there is scant information relating to Hunt's own feelings about the integration of architecture and sculpture, and there is no manuscript material documenting his artistic relationship with the collaborating sculptors, it seems clear from his drawings and surviving projects that sculpture was an integral part of his architectural vocabulary and that he was the dominant artistic personality in his collaborative relationships.

Hunt returned to the United States in 1855 and set up a studio in New York City. With a training and experience that far exceeded any of his contemporary American architects, Hunt set about designing a number of public and private buildings. In the early 1860s he was awarded a large and important commission: the southern entrances to New York City's Central Park.[6] (For a complete discussion of the subject, see chapter 4.) Although Hunt's designs were formally accepted in the summer of 1863, by 1865 they had become the subject of heated controversy. The underlying factor in the conflict was the grandiose

7.5 R. M. Hunt and H. K. Brown, Abraham Lincoln Monument, Union Square, New York City, 1868.

7.6 R. M. Hunt and H. K. Brown, proposed monument for Robert Fulton; unexecuted.

character of Hunt's architectural gateways. French in inspiration and populated with statues and fountains, the gateways were designed as entrances to the park along Fifty-ninth Street: at Fifth Avenue the Gate of Peace; at Sixth Avenue the Gate of Commerce; at Seventh Avenue the Artist's Gate; and at Eighth Avenue the Warrior's Gate. As Baker points out, Hunt's gateways were compatible with his own concept of the park as a pleasure garden of manifold uses,[7] but Olmsted and Vaux considered them aristocratic, pompous, and foreign. Opposed to any intrusion into the park of nonlandscape, architectural elements, Olmsted and Vaux "were determined that the area should remain rural, an oasis of greenery and 'natural' land contours in the center of the island city."[8] In the end, Hunt's designs were rejected, though a special committee paid him ten thousand dollars in 1868 for the work he had done.[9] Yet despite their rejection, Hunt's thoroughly French designs for the gateways exerted a profound influence on American architects and sculptors. The gateways clearly articulated the collaborative relationship of architecture and sculpture in urban design. This revolutionary concept became a major tenet of the Beaux-Arts movement that was not realized until the 1890s in the "City Beautiful" movement, the Columbian Exposition, and Stanford White's entrances to Brooklyn's Prospect Park.

While Hunt's gateways were under attack, the Civil War came to an end in the spring of 1865, only for the nation to plunge into new despair with the assassination of Lincoln. The Union League Club, under Hunt's direction, took charge of the funeral arrangements in New York. Union Square was decorated and a temporary monument was set up—a white marble pedestal standing on a black dais surmounted by a bust of the late president. A permanent monument to Lincoln, consisting of a granite pedestal and a standing bronze statue by the sculptor Henry Kirke Brown, was dedicated in 1868.[10] While there is no documentation that Hunt designed the base of Brown's Lincoln, a scale drawing by Hunt of the monument exists (fig. 7.5).[11] Hunt and Brown were on good terms and the two men collaborated on a proposed monumental tomb to Robert Fulton (fig. 7.6), the versatile engineer, artist, and inventor. The am-

bitious concept for the tomb was an immense cube, punctured on all four sides by vaulted openings through which Fulton's sarcophagus would be clearly visible. Crowning the cube was to be a semicircular dome surmounted by Brown's figure of the seated Fulton, cast in bronze and holding a model of his ship, the *Claremont*. Below the dome, on each of the four corners of the cube's top surface, were to be placed a prow of the ship in which Brown's seated allegorical figures, representing the four continents, were also to be cast in bronze. The spaces on the four edges of the cube between the prows were to be occupied by reclining male figures in stone, probably intended as allegories of the sciences.

Late in 1865, shortly after the end of the Civil War, Hunt executed his first public monument, a memorial in New York City's Trinity Church to the naval hero Captain Percival Drayton who died on 4 August 1864. The memorial was commissioned by Alexander Hamilton, Jr., and John Jacob Astor, Jr., and was done in collaboration with the sculptor L. Larmande.[12] Completed in May 1867, the memorial, constructed of bluish gray stone and standing fourteen feet high, was placed against the rear wall of the interior of the church. Hunt also prepared drawings for two Civil War memorials that were never executed. The first, a watercolor on bluish paper, was a simple monument consisting of a fluted shaft surmounted by a cannonball and with small cannons on each of the four corners of the base of the monument (fig. 7.7). The second, a more complex monument, was a massive octagon-shaped base topped by a seated female figure (fig. 7.8). Below her on four corresponding sides were perched bronze eagles that flanked reliefs of battle scenes, and below the eagles were placed groups of soldiers and sailors. Between these groups there was space for the listing of the names of the men killed in action. The entire monument was situated in a basin fed by fountains at the base of the pedestal.

The following year Hunt completed his first public monument with the sculptor John Quincy Adams Ward, the statue of Commodore Matthew Calbraith Perry (fig. 7.9) for Newport, Rhode Island. One of the greatest naval heroes of the nineteenth century, the memorial was commissioned by Perry's son-in-law, the wealthy New York banker August Belmont, in 1865. The statue, which began Ward's long and illustrious career as a sculptor of public monuments, was unveiled in Touro Park on 1 October 1868 on a cylindrical pedestal designed by Hunt. Ward later encircled the base with a bronze bas-relief frieze that portrayed the major events in Perry's naval career.[13]

During the next quarter-century Hunt and Ward collaborated on fifteen public monuments and were associates in numerous civic and artistic organizations.[14] Of their collaboration, Hunt's wife reported that "R—— planned out the general idea of the monument, Ward did the sculpture and R—— furnished drawings for the pedestal and studied up the inscriptions."[15] How much of that is fact and how much is wifely devotion is a matter of conjecture, but there is the ring of truth about it. Hunt also designed for Ward a house with a studio in New York City in 1868, a studio and stable in Urbana, Ohio, in 1881, and a combination house and studio in New York in 1882 (see fig. 3.24).[16] The working relationship between the two men was a primary influence on Ward's sculpture and their artistic collaboration was responsible for a major chapter in the history of the Beaux-Arts movement in America.

In 1866, the City of New York invited "all the principal sculptors" to submit a model for a proposed statue of William Shakespeare, in celebration of the

7.10 *Above:* R. M. Hunt, proposed pedestal of the William Shakespeare monument, Central Park, New York, 1866. J. Q. A. Ward sculpted the statue, and Jacob Wrey Mould was later awarded the commission for the pedestal.

7.11 *Opposite, bottom, left:* R. M. Hunt and J. Q. A. Ward, Seventh Regiment Memorial, Central Park, New York, 1874.

7.7 *Opposite, top:* R. M. Hunt, proposed Civil War Memorial, ca. 1867; unexecuted.

7.8 *Far left:* R. M. Hunt, proposed Civil War Memorial, ca. 1867; unexecuted.

7.9 *Near left:* R. M. Hunt and J. Q. A. Ward, Commodore Matthew Calbraith Perry Monument, Newport, R.I., 1868.

7.12 *Above, center:* R. M. Hunt and J. Q. A. Ward, proposal for the Seventh Regiment Monument, showing a circular scheme, Central Park, New York, 1868–74.

7.13 *Above, right:* R. M. Hunt and J. Q. A. Ward, alternate proposal for the Seventh Regiment Monument, Central Park, New York, 1868–74.

tricentennial of the poet's birth.[17] Ward was awarded the commission for the statue, while Hunt must have anticipated collaborating on the monument since he developed a number of drawings and watercolor schemes for the base (fig. 7.10). Probably the lingering bad feeling between the principals of the park and Hunt over the gateway controversy resulted in the monument's pedestal, which was finally unveiled on 23 May 1872, being designed by Jacob Wrey Mould, one of the park architects.[18]

In the late 1860s the country was caught up in a fever to erect bronze monuments to the military heroes of the Civil War, and Ward and Hunt once again worked together, this time on memorials to the Seventh Regiment (figs. 7.11– 7.13) for New York City, and to Major General John F. Reynolds (fig. 7.14) for

Gettysburg, Pennsylvania. Fifty-eight men from New York's Seventh Regiment had died in the Civil War, and soon after the war ended the regiment formed a Monument Association to see to the erection of an appropriate memorial to their fallen brothers.[19] In May 1868, members of the group approached Ward to execute a statue ten feet in height. The completed statue was inscribed "1869," but was not unveiled until 22 June 1874, a delay that seems to have resulted from problems concerning the choice of its site and the treatment of its pedestal. From the large number of Hunt drawings that survive, it is clear that Hunt and Ward envisioned a fully developed Beaux-Arts-style monument, which would have predated by twelve years the monument to Admiral David Farragut created by Stanford White and Augustus Saint-Gaudens for Madison Square Park in New York. One of Hunt's drawings reveals a complex circular scheme (fig. 7.12) that skillfully combines architecture and sculpture in a monument carefully sited in the park's landscape. Three sets of stairs—one at the front, one on either side, each flanked at the bottom by bronze eagles—provide access to a circular walk at the memorial's base. Surrounding the walk and leading up each stairway is a richly decorated balustrade. At the center of the monument is a graduated pedestal surmounted by Ward's Seventh Regiment soldier standing in eternal vigilance. Probably in an effort to placate the park architects and commissioners, Hunt and Ward abandoned this opulent Beaux-Arts plan and developed a less complex, nonarchitectural one. That monument (fig. 7.13) was to have been flanked by two sculptural groups: at the left, two soldiers relaxing in camp; at the right, a soldier caring for a wounded comrade. The second version was developed far enough that Ward actually made models of the two groups, but again the monument's design and its placement in the park could not be resolved. The final statue—the soldier that was to have stood atop the pedestal in the original scheme—was ultimately placed not at its intended location, the Warrior's Gate at One-hundred-tenth Street and Seventh Avenue, but on the West Walk, opposite Sixty-ninth Street. The pedestal was reduced to a simple base that Hunt had designed for the monument to Major General Reynolds that had been unveiled two years earlier on 31 August 1872.[20] Although Hunt's and Ward's efforts were thwarted, the drawings for the Seventh Regiment Memorial reveal that the two men were working successfully in a fully developed Beaux-Arts style by the early 1870s.

The decade of the 1870s was a productive period for both Hunt and Ward, and yet following the completion of the Shakespeare statue they did not collaborate on another project for almost ten years. The celebration of the nation's centennial in 1876 generated great patriotic excitement, causing a large number of public monuments to be erected across the country. While Hunt and Ward had a number of centennial commissions, Hunt's most notable collaboration at this time was done with the sculptor Frédéric-Auguste Bartholdi: the statue of Liberty Enlightening the World on Bedloe's Island in New York harbor (fig. 7.15). A gift from the people of France to the people of the United States, the monumental sculpture was inaugurated on 28 October 1886.[21]

Hunt became involved in the Statue of Liberty project in 1881. The idea for the monument, however, had originated in France in 1865. Bartholdi credited the concept of the monument to Edouard-René-Lefebvre de Laboulaye, a distinguished legal scholar who specialized in American political history. An ardent republican, Laboulaye believed the celebration of the Franco-American alliance during the American war of independence would rekindle democratic

7.14 R. M. Hunt and J. Q. A. Ward, Major General John F. Reynolds Monument, Gettysburg, Pa., 1872.

principles in Second Empire France. At a dinner party on his estate on the outskirts of Versailles in 1865, Laboulaye suggested the idea of public monument as a gift to the United States. Bartholdi, who was among the guests, was encouraged to undertake the monument. The Alsatian sculptor, however, became preoccupied with a plan to make a gigantic statue of a female figure holding a light at the entrance to the Suez Canal, which opened in the fall of 1869. When this commission did not materialize, Bartholdi in 1871 sailed to the United States to promote Laboulaye's monument—a statue strikingly similar to his Suez Canal figure. During his visit, Bartholdi selected Bedloe's Island as the site for the monument and gained the necessary support to obtain the financial backing needed in France. By 1875, and with the ascension of the moderate republicans in the government, the $400,000 needed for the monument was realized.

During the next year Bartholdi developed the final model for the 151-foot-high sculpture. He was assisted on technical problems first by the archeologist-architect Viollet-le-Duc and then by Gustave Eiffel, who actually designed the armature for the statue. The right hand and torch were exhibited at the Centennial Exposition in Philadelphia in 1876 and were shown again with the head at the 1878 Exposition Universelle in Paris. By 1883 all of the sheets of copper, 3/32 of an inch thick, had been hammered into wooden patterns and were ready for assemblage.[22]

While work progressed rapidly on the statue, construction of the pedestal was plagued by financial problems. Finally in 1885 Joseph Pulitzer, the owner and editor of the New York World, came to the rescue, and through a well-publicized campaign in his paper raised the necessary $100,000 to complete the pedestal.[23] From the outset, Hunt, who had been named architect in chief of the pedestal in 1881, based his plan on preliminary determinations made by Bartholdi (fig. 7.16) and the French Committee regarding the size, shape, and decoration of the pedestal. The foundation of the pedestal was ingeniously set into the walls of Fort Wood—an eleven-point star. Hunt's designs, developed between 1882 and 1884 in elaborate models known as Pharos I and II (fig. 7.17), were reduced from 114 feet high to 89 feet because of a concern regarding its proportions and a shortage of funds.[24] The final design (fig. 7.18) for the executed pedestal was one of Hunt's finest collaborations in the sphere of public sculpture. The height and mass of the pedestal—the major architectural considerations—are perfect. The monument commands a dominant position in New York's busy harbor, yet the pedestal does not overwhelm or in any way lessen the significance of Bartholdi's statue. The use of the star-shaped fort as the base of the monument, with its radiant points, was both a structurally and a visually sound foundation, as well as an appropriate form for the monument to rise from. The openings into the pedestal and the panels, the pilasters, the shields, and all the other architectural decorations are all effectively articulated to enliven visually the mass of the pedestal—but it is the solidity and vertical thrust of the pedestal that makes Hunt's contribution such an important part of the success of the Statue of Liberty.

In the 1880s Hunt and Ward entered into four collaborative ventures. Two were centennial statues—the Lafayette, in Burlington, Vermont, and the Washington, in New York City. The Lafayette statue portrays the sixty-four-year-old marquis on his second American tour in 1824–25.[25] The memorial was unveiled on 26 June 1883, in a small park in front of the proposed site of

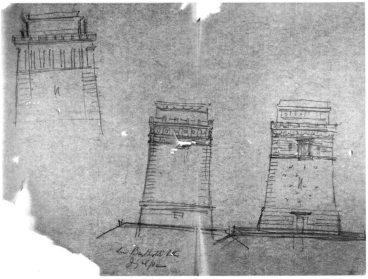

7.15 *Top:* R. M. Hunt and
Frédéric-Auguste Bartholdi,
Statue of Liberty, Bedloe's Island,
New York, 1886.

7.16 *Above:* Early studies of the
pedestal for the Statue of Liberty
attributed to Bartholdi, ca. 1882.

7.17 *Right:* R. M. Hunt, the
Pharos I scheme for the pedestal,
Statue of Liberty, May 1884.

7.18 *Opposite:* R. M. Hunt, the
final scheme for the pedestal,
Statue of Liberty, August 1884.

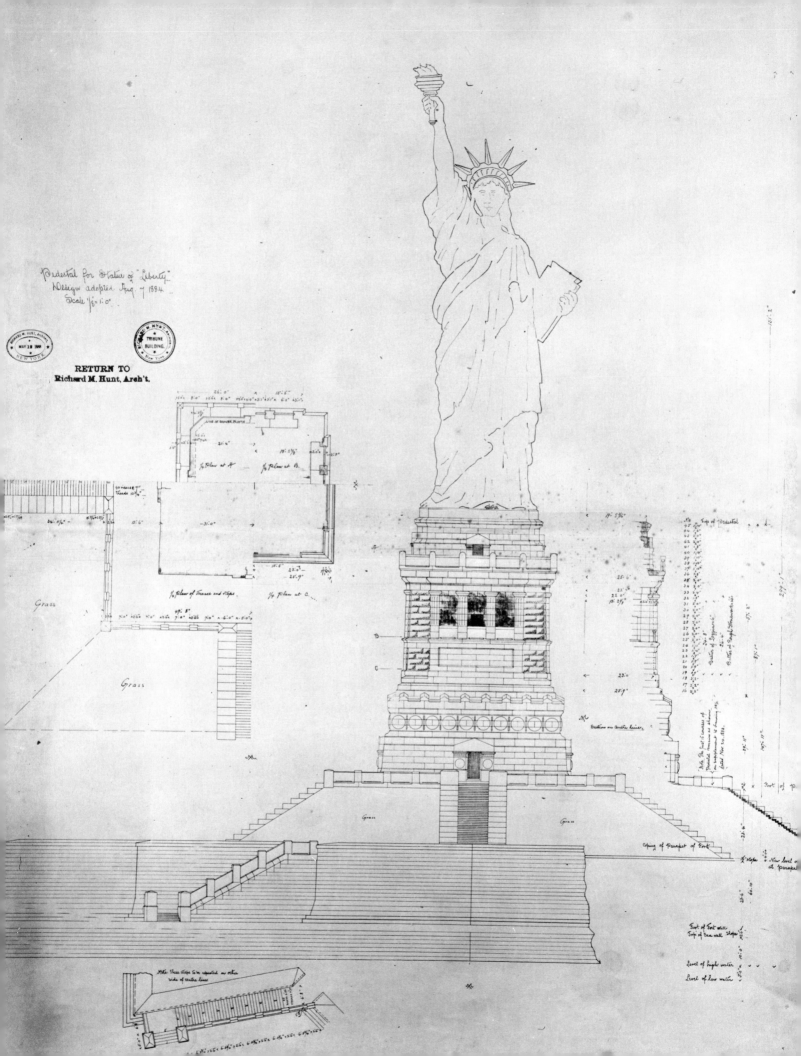

Pedestal for Statue of "Liberty"
Design adopted Aug. 7 1884.
Scale 1/8" = 1' 0"

Grass

Grass

Grass

Grass

Grass

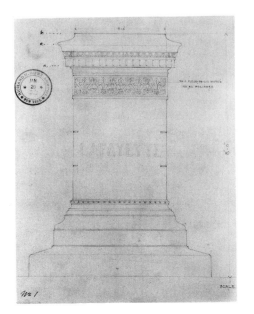

the Billings Library, designed by Henry Hobson Richardson for the University of Vermont. For the statue Hunt designed a stately but simple granite pedestal decorated with a band of palmettes (fig. 7.19). The Washington statue (fig. 7.20), in contrast, is one of the masterpieces of the two artists' collaborative relationship.[26] Situated high on the steps of the old Sub-Treasury Building (now Federal Hall), Hunt sited the statue so that it dominates the plaza formed by the junction of Wall and Broad Streets—the spot where Washington took his oath of office as first president of the United States. He is portrayed by Ward as he lifts his hand from the Bible at the end of the swearing-in ceremony. In his dramatic rendering of the historical event Ward has produced a statue of complete creative integrity and Hunt has sited the monument with a nobility fitting the momentous occasion. The dedication of the Washington statue took place on 26 November 1883—the centennial anniversary of the evacuation of British troops from New York. The popularity of these unveiling ceremonies is attested by the crowd of six thousand people, including Chester A. Arthur, then president, and Grover Cleveland, governor of New York, that attended the event, even though the day was cold and rainy.

The following year Hunt was approached, probably at Ward's suggestion, to execute a granite memorial to Simon Kenton, the "celebrated Ohio backwoodsman."[27] Ward had prepared a model for a statue of Kenton in the 1850s. However, his hopes that the Ohio legislature would commission a statue of Kenton were dashed when the first shot was fired on Fort Sumter, since the state was obliged to contribute a million dollars to the expenses of the war. Ward's wish that the plaster model be executed in bronze or marble and placed in the rotunda of the capitol was never realized. After the war there was a renewed effort to erect a memorial to Kenton. In 1865 the remains of the old pioneer were brought from Zanesfield, Ohio, and interred in the Oak Dale Cemetery in Urbana, Ohio. A modest appropriation was finally secured in 1884, but it was not sufficient to permit the enlargement of Ward's figure. Hunt was commissioned to design a pedestal to mark Kenton's grave site in the cemetery (fig. 7.21). On the south side of the memorial is the head of an Indian and the inscription "1775–1836 / SIMON KENTON"; on the north side is the head of

7.19 *Above left:* R. M. Hunt and J. Q. A. Ward, pedestal for the marquis de Lafayette Monument, Burlington, Vt., 1883.

7.20 *Above center:* R. M. Hunt and J. Q. A. Ward, George Washington Monument, Sub-Treasury Building (now Federal Hall), Nassau and Wall streets, New York City, 1883.

7.21 *Above right:* R. M. Hunt, Simon Kenton tomb, Oakdale Cemetery, Urbana, Ohio, 1884. Photograph by Elizabeth Macy.

a wolf and the inscription "ERECTED BY THE STATE / OF OHIO 1884"; on the west side is the head of a bear; and on the east side, the head of a panther. The top was left in a rough, unfinished condition, reportedly at Ward's suggestion that there might at a future time be sufficient public interest to sponsor a worthy capital for the memorial. The necessary funds were never secured, however, and the uncompleted memorial stands today in the Oak Dale Cemetery only a short distance from the replica of the Indian Hunter that marks the sculptor's burial site.

In the 1880s Hunt and Ward also collaborated on three victory monuments: the Alliance and Victory Monument for Yorktown, Virginia; and the proposed soldiers' and sailors' monuments for Brooklyn, New York, and Indianapolis, Indiana. The Yorktown Monument (fig. 7.22) was an elaborate column recalling Cornwallis's surrender of the British forces on 19 October 1781.[28] The monument was done in a collaboration between Ward, Hunt, and the architect Henry van Brunt, who adapted their design from one French architects had submitted just previously for a Constitutional Assembly Memorial to be built at Versailles (fig. 7.23).[29] The monument consisted of three parts: a base thirty-seven feet high and thirty-eight feet square, on which a narrative of the Alliance and Victory would be inscribed; a sculptured podium twenty-five and half feet high and thirteen feet in diameter; and a column sixty feet high. The sculpture designed by Ward included the emblems for the base, the thirteen classical maidens that encircle the sculpture podium at the base of the shaft of

7.22 *Below left:* R. M. Hunt, J. Q. A. Ward, and H. Van Brunt, Yorktown Monument, Yorktown, Va., 1880–84.

7.23 *Below right:* Constitutional Assembly Memorial, Versailles, France. Published in the *American Architect and Building News* (15 October 1881).

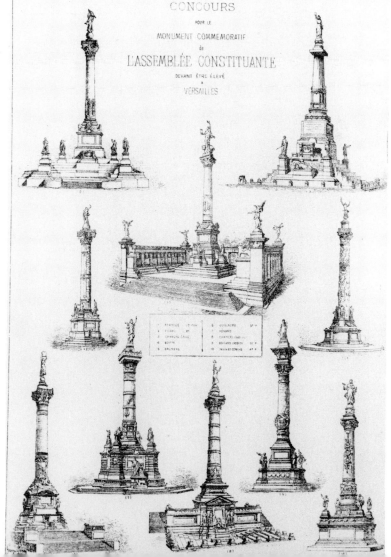

7.24 R. M. Hunt and J. Q. A. Ward, Soldiers' and Sailors' Monument, Brooklyn, New York, 1885–86; unexecuted.

7.25 R. M. Hunt and J. Q. A. Ward, Soldiers' and Sailors' Monument, Indianapolis, Ind., 1887–88; unexecuted.

7.26 R. M. Hunt and J. Q. A. Ward, the Pilgrim, Central Park, New York, 1885.

the column, and the figure of Liberty that surmounts the Composite order of the column. The work was well received when it was completed in 1885, but it did not arouse the enthusiasm the artists anticipated because of its somewhat remote location.

In 1885–86 Hunt and Ward worked on the proposed Soldiers' and Sailors' Monument for Brooklyn (fig. 7.24).[30] The subcommittee in charge of planning the project had set its goal high, with a suggested budget of $250,000. With their encouragement, Hunt and Ward devised what would have been the most grandiose public monument in the country. The design they submitted in February 1886 was for a work that would have stood seventy feet in height, the central shaft crowned with a twenty-four-foot-high sculpture entitled *Peace*. The shaft was to be encircled by two sets of reliefs: the first, nine feet high and over forty-nine in circumference, in stone on the upper drum of the shaft; the second, five feet high and a hundred and twenty feet in circumference, in bronze at the base. On the platform of the monument were to be four bronze seated figures, each eight feet high, representing the four services: infantry, cavalry, artillery, and navy; and four fifteen-foot-high bronze equestrian statues of Washington, Jackson, Scott, and Grant. The magnitude of the project seemed to set everyone on edge (Hunt was even piqued with Ward because his name and photograph had been omitted in newspaper reports on the proposed monument). With a revised estimate of $500,000, the proposal proved too costly for Brooklyn, and the project was abandoned in 1887.

That same year Hunt and Ward also submitted a proposal for a Soldiers' and Sailors' Monument for Circle Park in Indianapolis (fig. 7.25).[31] A commission, appointed by the Indiana legislature, solicited designs from ten American architects and placed an advertisement in newspapers in the major cities of the United States, Canada, England, France, Germany, and Italy.[32] Seventy archi-

7.27 R. M. Hunt and J. Q. A. Ward, William Earl Dodge Statue, Herald Square, New York City, 1885.

7.28 R. M. Hunt and J. Q. A. Ward, James A. Garfield Monument, Maryland Avenue and First Street, S.W., Washington, D.C., 1887.

tects responded. Hunt's monument called for a series of thirteen reliefs, each eight feet high and twelve feet long, to decorate the circular base of the monument; and three statues eight feet high representing the army, navy, and the Sanitary Commission. The tall shaft of the monument was surmounted by a twenty-foot-high crowning statue of Indiana. In the end the commission was awarded to a German architect, Bruno Schmitz. While Hunt and Ward had not been successful in gaining the commissions for the latter two projects, their three victory monuments once more proclaim the mastery of the Beaux-Arts style that they, its leading American practitioners in the 1880s, had come to exercise.

Soon after Ward moved into his studio/residence in 1882, he and Hunt began to work on two monuments for New York City: the Pilgrim and the Dodge. The Pilgrim (fig. 7.26), set up at the intersection of the East Drive and the Seventy-second Street entrance to Central Park, was unveiled on 6 June 1885.[33] Ward intended the Pilgrim to be both symbolic of the principles of the New England Society, which had commissioned the statue, and a quintessential portrait of "one of the Company of the Mayflower." For the monument Hunt designed a rusticated base made of three large granite blocks superimposed on each other, which Baker contends "recalled Plymouth Rock."[34] For each side Ward modeled bronze relief friezes that were flanked by Doric triglyphs. On the front the emblem of the New England Society is represented by a Bible lying closed on a rock with a sword between the pages. On the back, the *Mayflower* under full sail is shown, while on the side panels are represented an allegory of industry and education and a representation of American Indian artifacts.

In executing the standing portrait of William Earl Dodge (fig. 7.27), a wealthy New York merchant and philanthropist, Ward returned once more to the straightforward realistic portraiture that was his forte.[35] The statue was commissioned by the Chamber of Commerce of the State of New York, which raised the necessary funds through public subscription. The finished statue was unveiled on 22 October 1885, where Thirty-fourth Street, Broadway, and Sixth Avenue meet at Herald Square. The monument's black granite pedestal included a circular bench behind the pedestal, at the foot of which a stream of water flowed from the head of a lion into a drinking fountain (a symbol of Dodge's lifelong devotion to the cause of temperance). When the statue was moved in 1939 to Bryant Park, behind the New York Public Library, the Hunt pedestal did not accompany it—a great artistic loss.

In 1883 the Society of the Army of the Cumberland commissioned Ward to execute a memorial to President James A. Garfield (fig. 7.28).[36] The president had been assassinated two years earlier by a deranged office seeker whose government appointment had been blocked by Garfield's reform policies. Almost immediately Hunt began preparing a series of sketches for the base, but it was not until 1885 that he and Ward were commissioned to execute the pedestal and base sculpture to represent, in Ward's words, the "three important phases in Garfield's life: the Student, the Warrior and the Statesman."[37] To complement Ward's sculpture, Hunt designed an ornate neo-Baroque pedestal that bears a striking similarity to Jean-Baptiste Pigalle's 1765 monument to Louis XV (fig. 7.29), in Rheims. The Garfield pedestal is composed of a tapered cylinder superimposed on a triangular base whose corners form rectangular seats for the three figures. The cylinder is divided by decorative moldings into horizontal sections, a series of graduated architectural masses and lines. A rich movement of receding and projecting elements with attendant play of light and shadow is thus created, transporting the viewer's eye to the dramatic figure of Garfield, who is shown as he pauses in an address, holding the text of his speech against his chest and looking emphatically out at his audience. The Garfield statue was unveiled in Washington on 12 May 1887, at the foot of the Capitol, in a ceremony attended by President Grover Cleveland, justices of the Supreme Court, members of Congress, officers of the Society of the Army of the Cumberland, and both Ward and Hunt. This splendidly conceived and finely crafted monument, one of the outstanding achievements of the American Beaux-Arts movement, is the result of Ward's successful use of allegorical figures to personify the different stages of Garfield's life, the animated poses and vibrant realism with which he presents them, and finally, the remarkable collaboration between him and Hunt.

Far less ambitious was the monument to Lincoln Goodale that the two men executed for Columbus, Ohio.[38] Goodale, a wealthy Ohio merchant and physician, had given Columbus a large tract of land for a park that still bears his name. The bronze portrait bust, on a tall granite pedestal inscribed with the donor's name, rises from a spreading volute-decorated base, which forms the back, to a basin and terminates with a carved eclectic order, and was unveiled on 26 September 1888.

In the early 1890s Hunt and Ward worked on their last two and perhaps finest public statues, those of Horace Greeley and Henry Ward Beecher, both for New York City. The statue of Greeley (fig. 7.30), the founder of the *New York Tribune* and one of America's greatest (if most controversial) editors, was unveiled on 20 September 1890.[39] In the Greeley statue, Hunt and Ward were confronted at the outset with difficult problems. Shortly after Greeley's death

7.29 Jean-Baptiste Pigalle, monument to Louis XV, 1765.

7.30 *Below:* R. M. Hunt and J. Q. A. Ward, Horace Greeley Statue, Nassau and Spruce streets, New York City.

7.31 *Right:* R. M. Hunt, detail of the proposed Greeley sculpture incorporated into the facade of the New York Tribune Building, ca. 1873.

in 1872, Hunt was commissioned to build a new Tribune Building on the corner of Nassau and Spruce Streets.[40] Approximately ten years later a narrow wing was added to the building from designs prepared by Hunt.[41] It was probably during this second building program that Whitelaw Reid, Greeley's business partner and a subsequent editor of the *Tribune*, engaged Ward and Hunt to execute a monument of Greeley for the building. Drawings by Hunt of the Tribune Building reveal that the architect experimented with various sitings of the statue on the facade of the building (fig. 7.31). In the end, however, he settled on a sidewalk niche in front of the newspaper building. Ward was confronted with two basic problems: he had to create an imposing portrait statue even though his subject was an eccentric-looking man with a small, round head, a face somewhat absurdly framed by unkempt throat whiskers, and whose figure had to be seated in order to fit into its destined sidewalk niche. The informally posed portrait of Greeley, its challenges met and conquered, has a realism and a psychological presence that make it one of Ward's finest portrait statues. The Greeley statue remained at the Tribune Building site until 1916, after which it was moved to City Hall Park, where it still stands on Hunt's original pedestal.

Hunt's and Ward's work on the Beecher Monument (fig. 7.32) began during the popular preacher's last days.[42] As Beecher's life began to ebb, arrangements

7.32 R. M. Hunt and J. Q. A. Ward, Henry Ward Beecher Monument, Borough Hall Park, Brooklyn, New York, 1891.

were made for Ward to take a death mask. On 8 March 1887, Ward received a telegram: "Beecher died nine-thirty. Dr. Seele says mask should be taken within four hours."[43] Having taken the death mask, Ward was the logical choice to execute the statue. On 6 April 1888, he signed a contract for $35,000 with the Beecher Statue Fund Committee to "design, model, execute and complete in fine bronze a statue . . . eight feet in height" as well as two or three figures "representing some phase of . . . Beecher's character of public career."[44] Public interest in the Beecher statue was enormous and its progress was reported regularly in the press, and when it was cast on 10 May 1890, the event was attended by two hundred elegantly dressed men and women. When the finished monument was unveiled a year later on 24 June 1891, it was a major civic event, attracting over fifteen thousand people to Borough Hall Park in Brooklyn. The Beecher Monument, on a black pedestal designed by Hunt, is the epitome of the best nineteenth-century American public statuary. In it can be seen Ward's method of dealing with problems of both portraiture and fundamental sculpture. The statue is one of prodigious monumentality, yet Ward has modeled a convincing, realistic image of Beecher the man, who stands before the crowd he is about to address. The statue is a massive triangular shape and its volumes are broadly treated, but Ward has simplified the surface details by clothing the figure in a knee-length Inverness cape. In contrast to the almost austere quality of the work are the small, intimately represented genre of figures on its base. On the right, a small boy supports a young girl who reaches up to place a wreath at Beecher's feet—an expression of Beecher's love for children. On the left, a young black woman places a palm leaf before him—a gesture of gratitude for the role he played in the abolitionist movement.

Although they were at the very pinnacle of their collaborative relationship, Hunt and Ward ceased to work together after the unveiling of the Beecher. There is no indication that the two artists had a falling out. Ward's output after 1890 greatly diminished as he gave greater time to public and private organizations that promoted the commissioning of public art projects and policed their progress, and failing health also began to sap his energy increasingly during the last twenty years of his life.

While the majority of Hunt's monuments were done in collaboration with a sculptor, in 1887 he alone was commissioned to do the Wadsworth Memorial Fountain for Geneseo, New York (fig. 7.33). The fountain was commissioned by two brothers, William Austin and Herbert Wadsworth, in honor of their mother. The fountain, Baker points out, was modeled on a street fountain Hunt had seen and had sketched in Bern, Switzerland, on one of his visits to that city in 1844 or 1845.[45] The large basin of the fountain is cut from a single piece of Bay of Fundy red granite. A shaft rises out of the basin. At the base of the shaft are four arms that extend outward over the basin and deliver a steady supply of fresh water; at the top of the shaft a small bronze bear sits on his haunches and holds a lamp standard in his forepaws. Besides the Wadsworth Memorial Fountain Hunt also designed alone a large number of private cemetery memorials. However, with the exception of the classical Greek-inspired tomb for August Belmont in Island Cemetery, Newport, Rhode Island, which includes two caryatids, Hunt's funerary memorials are devoid of sculpture decoration and are not a part of the subject at hand.

Hunt in the 1880s and 1890s worked on two monuments with the New England sculptor Franklin Simmons: the Soldiers' and Sailors' Monument in Port-

RETURN TO
Richard M. Hunt, Arch't.

7.33 R. M. Hunt, Wadsworth Memorial Fountain, Geneseo, New York, 1888.

land, Maine, and the General John A. Logan Monument in Washington, D.C. Simmons was an American Italianate sculptor who worked most of his career in Rome. A marginal artist at best, Hunt's relationship with Simmons brought out the best in the sculptor, for the two statues the men collaborated on are among Simmons's finest works. The Soldiers' and Sailors' Monument for Portland (fig. 7.34) was unveiled on 28 October 1891.[46] The memorial is crowned with a colossal bronze figure of a robed woman representing the Union, who wears a liberty cap and a wreath and holds a sheathed sword, a shield, and the olive branch of peace. At the base of the column are two bronze sculpture groups representing the army and navy. In each group an officer is flanked by two of his men and the entire group is backed by decorative flags and surrounded by paraphernalia related to their branch of the service. Hunt's and Simmons's second collaboration, the General Logan monument (fig. 7.35), was unveiled in Iowa Circle in Washington, D.C., ten years later, on 9 April 1901.[47] An innovative monument, both the pedestal and the equestrian statue are entirely cast in bronze. Hunt ingeniously created an elegant pedestal that supports the monumental equestrian statue of Logan, the fluted corner pilasters of which produce a strong vertical thrust and act as frames for Simmons's sculptural decorations. At both ends of the pedestal are allegorical figures representing War and Peace, while on either side are complex three-dimensional relief panels showing on one side Logan presiding over a council of war and on the other the general receiving the senatorial oath of office from Vice President Chester A. Arthur. The monument is an imposing one that produces an impression of dignity and power.

The culmination of Hunt's contribution to American sculpture was realized in the great architectural sculpture projects done with Karl Bitter between 1890 and Hunt's death in 1895.[48] In the fall of 1889, Bitter, a young Viennese sculptor, arrived in America. Penniless, but well trained from his studies in Vienna at the School of Applied Arts from 1881 to 1884 and the Imperial Academy of Fine Arts between 1885 and 1888, and with a driving ambition, he found work in a New York firm that specialized in architectural decoration. In a short time Bitter came to Hunt's attention and they established one of the most prolific collaborative relationships in the Beaux-Arts movement in America. An artist

of enormous energy and talent, Bitter possessed a keen decorative sense and a rare ability to administer the ambitious sculpture programs that Hunt and the other Beaux-Arts architects envisioned.

The most tangible evidence of Hunt's and Bitter's collaborative relationship is seen today in the great domestic architectural projects they did together. The Gilded Age was in full blossom, and America's wealthy families, in an unprecedented show of affluence, built vast and opulently decorated mansions. In 1888 Hunt began three great private houses that included rich decorative sculpture programs: Ochre Court for Ogden Goelet in Newport, Rhode Island; Marble House for William K. Vanderbilt, also in Newport; and Biltmore for George W. Vanderbilt in Asheville, North Carolina. In an act almost incomprehensible to us today, Hunt turned to the young and largely untried Austrian for assistance on the interior decoration of the houses.

For Ochre Court, the large French Renaissance château built for Ogden Goelet, the wealthy New York real estate developer, Bitter probably executed the rich decorative carvings that adorn the interior of the house, including, in the great Gothic hall, the heraldic designs (fig. 7.36) and the twelve large caryatids that support the ceiling.[49] For Marble House, William K. Vanderbilt's birthday gift to his wife, Alva, nine million dollars was reportedly lavished on the mansion's opulent decoration, which included Italian marble, gilded walls, mirrors, large mythological paintings, and sumptuously carved architectural details (fig. 7.37).[50] To honor the architect of Marble House, Vanderbilt had Bitter carve above the windows of the staircase mezzanine high relief medallions of Hunt and Jules Hardouin-Mansart, Louis XIV's principal architect at Versailles. For the double mansion that Hunt was building on Fifth Avenue at Sixty-fifth Street for Mrs. William Astor and her son, John Jacob, Bitter designed for the Ballroom (fig. 7.38) a series of caryatids, heraldic designs, and two large female figures to flank the oval portrait over the fireplace. The sculptor also added a series of caryatids just beneath the vaulted ceiling of the entrance hall that James M. Dennis, Bitter's biographer, asserts gave the space "a German baroque appearance."[51] For the Breakers, Cornelius Vanderbilt's enor-

7.34 R. M. Hunt and F. Simmons, sculptor, Soldiers' and Sailors' Monument, Portland, Me., 1889.

7.35 R. M. Hunt and F. Simmons, General John A. Logan Monument, Iowa Circle, Washington, D.C., 1901.

7.36 *Opposite:* R. M. Hunt and K. Bitter, sculptor, Gothic hall at Ochre Court, Ogden Goelet house, Newport, R.I., 1888–92.

7.37 *Right:* R. M. Hunt and
K. Bitter, interior of William K.
Vanderbilt's Marble House, show-
ing relief medallions of Hunt and
Mansart, Newport, R.I., 1888–92.

7.38 *Below:* R. M. Hunt and
K. Bitter, Ballroom of the Mrs.
William Astor and Mr. John Jacob
Astor IV house, 840 Fifth Ave-
nue, New York City, 1891–96.

mous summer cottage in Newport modeled after a sixteenth-century Genoese palazzo, Hunt again enlisted Bitter. In the arcade opposite the grand staircase is a huge Caen stone fireplace that was decorated by Bitter (fig. 7.39).

The culmination of Hunt's and Bitter's collaboration in domestic architecture was Biltmore.[52] The vast estate, built by George W. Vanderbilt, consists of a huge French Renaissance château, designed by Hunt, on 125,000 acres laid out by Frederick Law Olmsted. For the great Banquet Hall Bitter executed a marble frieze twenty-five feet long representing the "Return from the Chase" for the mantle over the tripart fireplace (fig. 7.40); five relief panels, measuring some forty feet, with approximately sixty figures, decorate the oak balustrade of the organ gallery; and above the door to the hall he carved two limestone statues of the medieval warrior-saints Saint Louis and Joan of Arc. For the Palm Court, the polygonal, glass-domed greenhouse, Bitter modeled a bronze fountain group: a nude boy struggles with two geese, one held in his arms and the other under his feet (fig. 7.41). Bitter's final project at Biltmore was an ornate walnut fireplace in the library complete with large female figures draped in flowing robes and polished steel andirons representing Venus and Vulcan.

7.39 *Below:* R. M. Hunt and K. Bitter, Caen stone fireplace of Cornelius Vanderbilt's Breakers, Newport, R.I., 1892–95.

7.40 *Below right:* R. M. Hunt and K. Bitter, detail of the "Return from the Chase," mantle in the Banquet Hall, Biltmore, George W. Vanderbilt house, Asheville, N.C., 1893–95. Photograph courtesy of Biltmore Estate, Asheville, N.C.

7.41 R. M. Hunt and K. Bitter, "Boy with Swans," detail of Palm Court, Biltmore, George W. Vanderbilt house, Asheville, N.C., 1893–95. Photograph courtesy of Biltmore Estate, Asheville, N.C.

While an enormous amount of time and energy were devoted to these great domestic commissions, Hunt's and Bitter's involvement in three important public projects—the entrance doors to Trinity Church in New York; the Columbian Exposition in Chicago; and the Fifth Avenue facade of the Metropolitan Museum of Art in New York—also had a profound impact on American Beaux-Arts sculpture. The Trinity Church commission was one of Hunt's and Bitter's first collaborations.[53] However, because of the number of other commissions that came to the two artists in the early 1890s it was not actually completed until 1896, the year after Hunt's death. Money for the Broadway entrance to the Gothic-revival church, which had been designed and built earlier in the century by the English-born architect, Richard Upjohn, was given in 1890 by William Waldorf Astor as a memorial to his father, John Jacob Astor. Hunt was selected as the architect for the three bronze doors, the principal

7.42 R. M. Hunt and K. Bitter, Trinity Church doors, Broadway at Wall Street, New York City, 1894–96.

Broadway entrance, and two side entrances. Following a competition, Bitter was chosen to execute the portals for the main entrance, and Charles Niehaus, a Cincinnati sculptor, and J. Massey Rhind, a Scottish sculptor working in New York, were awarded the south and north doors respectively. Bitter's portal (fig. 7.42), executed between 1893 and 1894, consists of a carved limestone tympanum with twelve apostles seated in small cusped arches, above which Christ is shown opening the kingdom of heaven. The bronze doors were inspired by Ghiberti's second set of gates for the baptistery in Florence. The three panels on each door represent the Fall, Redemption, and Last Judgment of mankind. The panels on both doors are framed on the sides by a series of standing figures of prophets and saints set on pedestals under canopies and recessed in niches; alternating between these figures are portrait heads, including Bitter's and Hunt's in the lower right-hand corner of the right door. Above and below the panels are reclining allegorical figures flanking the emblems of the four evangelists. The Trinity Church portals, James Dennis concludes, "represent an art historical synthesis: a study in nineteenth-century revivals. Their architectural setting is Gothic revival in style; the organization of the doors themselves is Renaissance in origin; and the composition of the sculpture is basically baroque."[54]

At approximately the same time that Hunt received the Trinity Church commission, he was also selected to lead the New York contingent of architects at the World's Columbian Exposition in Chicago.[55] Because of his supreme position in the field of American architecture, he was invited to design the Administration Building that was to stand at the end of the Court of Honor (fig. 7.43). Hunt's building, grand in scale and with a great central dome flanked by four square four-story pavilions, was nonetheless a classically reserved building. Structural ornamentation was used sparingly, James Dennis points out, and "therefore, an impression of ephemeral pomp and pageantry befitting an 'overture' to the White City by the Lake became the responsibility of the sculptor in embellishing the Administration Building."[56] Bitter's Austrian Baroque aesthetic was perfectly suited to the task at hand. He flanked the four great arched entrances to the Administration Building with allegorical groups entitled "The Elements, Controlled and Uncontrolled." At the corners of the roofs of the pavilions he designed groups of two figures—an adult and a child—who symbolized Abundance, Unity, Theology, Patriotism, Tradition, Charity, Joy, Liberty, Strength, Truth, Education, and Diligence. At the corners of the octagon colonnade or loggia that supported the dome, more complex groups of three figures represented the eight subjects of Industry, Art, Commerce, Science, War, Justice, Religion, and Peace. Henry Van Brunt, an architect and former student of Hunt's, acknowledged the success of Bitter's sculpture for the Administration Building when he wrote that it was "characterized by great breadth, dignity of treatment, and by that expression of heroic power and fitness which is derived from knowing how to treat colossal subjects in a colossal way, and how to model figures so that they may assist the main architectural thought and not compete with it."[57] The fruit of Hunt's and Bitter's successful collaboration, the lesson in coordination and planning, was one of the great legacies of the Columbian Exposition. Out of the fair came a renewed stimulus to the American Beaux-Arts neoclassical revival and the "City Beautiful" movement that was to dominate American urban planning for the next quarter century.

7.43 R. M. Hunt and K. Bitter,
Administration Building of the
World's Columbian Exposition,
Chicago, 1891–93.

146

For all its influence, the Columbian Exposition had been built of staff, a material composed of plaster and hemp, and it was torn down shortly after it closed. In contrast, the Fifth Avenue facade of the Metropolitan Museum of Art was built of stone and was the culmination of Hunt's and Bitter's collaborations (see fig. 9.2).[58] (For a complete discussion of the subject, see chapter 9.) Tragically, Hunt died in 1895, shortly after the plans for the museum were completed, and not all of the sculpture program that Hunt had intended Bitter to execute had been completed at the time the new museum was opened in 1902.

From the time the museum moved to Central Park in 1880, Hunt, who was on the museum's board of trustees, had hoped to design a portion of the institution's building. His relationship with General Cesnola, the director of the museum, was somewhat strained, and it was not until the 1890s, as the third addition to the museum was being undertaken, that Henry G. Marquand, the new president of the board of trustees and a long-time friend and patron of Hunt's, invited the architect to prepare plans for the proposed enlargement. Hunt's plans were developed and presented to the board of trustees shortly before the architect's death on 31 July 1895. The actual construction of the Fifth Avenue facade was carried out by Hunt's son, Richard Howland Hunt, who was appointed architect.

Hunt's drawings reveal that he was entirely responsible for the sculptural program for the classical Beaux-Arts building. Around the high attic of the central section Bitter executed a series of female masks joined by swags of fruit. For the keystones of the three great arches he carved helmeted female heads, and for the spandrels of the arches medallion portraits of Bramante, Michelangelo, Raphael, Dürer, Rembrandt, and Velázquez. For the attic of the two wings flanking the central section Bitter carved three-dimensional caryatids representing architecture, sculpture, painting, and the museum. Unfortunately, the massive blocks of rough stone over the double columns, which were to be great sculpture groups representing the arts of the four great epochs, were never executed. Less jarring today is the absence of the statues, never executed, intended for the niches between the double columns, which were to represent the four major artistic periods. Although unfinished, Hunt's Metropolitan Museum facade is one of the great monuments of the American Beaux-Arts movement; its success and importance are a fitting testimony to the influence Hunt exerted on American sculpture for over a quarter of a century.

Notes

1. Paul R. Baker, *Richard Morris Hunt* (Cambridge, Mass.: MIT Press, 1980), p. 32. Baker's book is the source for all biographical information related to Richard Morris Hunt in this essay.
2. Ibid., p. 36.
3. Ibid., p. 56.
4. Ibid.
5. Ibid., pp. 58 and 60.
6. See also Baker's chapter "The Central Park Gateways," pp. 146–61.
7. Ibid., p. 154.
8. Ibid.
9. Ibid. There are also three unidentified watercolors in the American Institute of Architects Foundation's collection that are possibly related to the Central Park gateways (78.699, 78.700, 79.3572).

10. Ibid., p. 144.

11. Hunt also executed a watercolor (80.5578) for another monument to Lincoln, which may be a preliminary sketch for the base of Brown's statue, erected in Prospect Park in 1868.

12. George C. Groce and David H. Wallace, eds., *The New-York Historical Society's Dictionary of Artists in America, 1564–1860* (New Haven: Yale University Press, 1957), p. 385, reports that the *New York Business Directories* and *City Directories* for 1854–56 list a Leo J. Larmande and a Alfred J. B. Bourlier as sculptors working in New York City.

13. Lewis I. Sharp, *John Quincy Adams Ward: Dean of American Sculpture* (Cranbury, New Jersey: Associated University Presses, 1985), pp. 170–72. The author's catalogue raisonné is the source for the collaborative relationship between Ward and Hunt.

14. Ibid. See also Baker, pp. 300–314, 587.

15. From "Biography of Richard Morris Hunt" by Catharine Clinton Howland Hunt (Mrs. Richard Morris Hunt), typescript, p. 277, American Institute of Architects Foundation. Paraphrased in Baker, p. 300.

16. Baker, pp. 540, 544.

17. Sharp, pp. 177–81.

18. Ibid., p. 178. Baker, p. 540, mistakenly lists the Shakespeare as having been done by Hunt in 1872.

19. Ibid., pp. 172–77.

20. Ibid., pp. 182–83.

21. Ibid., pp. 314–22 and Marvin Trachtenberg, *The Statue of Liberty* (New York: The Viking Press, 1976). A drawing by Hunt in the Hunt collection corresponds to the Lafayette Monument by Bartholdi that was presented to New York City in 1876 by its French residents.

22. Marie Busco, "Liberty Enlightening the World." In *The Romantics to Rodin*, ed. Peter Fusco and Horst W. Janson (Los Angeles and New York: The Los Angeles County Museum of Art in association with George Braziller, Inc., 1980), p. 123.

23. Baker, p. 318.

24. Ibid., p. 319.

25. Sharp, pp. 207–9.

26. Ibid., pp. 209–13. Drawings in the Hunt collection, dated 30 December 1884, are inscribed that they are for the pedestal for the Washington Monument in Newburgh, New York.

27. Ibid., pp. 141–3.

28. Ibid., pp. 201–4.

29. "The Designs for the Yorktown Monument," *The American Architect and Building News* 10 (15 October 1881): 182–83; illus. 303.

30. Sharp, pp. 220–23.

31. Ibid., pp. 227–28.

32. E. B. Rose, "Soldiers' and Sailors' Monument," *Indiana Historical Society Publication* 18 (1857): 399. The ten American architects were Richard Morris Hunt and George B. Post, New York; Van Brunt and Howe, Kansas City; Cabot and Chandler, Boston; T. P. Chandler, Philadelphia; Frederick Baumann and Burnham and Root, Chicago; James W. McLaughlin, Cincinnati; Adolph Sherrer, Indianapolis; and Peabody and Stearns, Saint Louis. Three unidentified sketches (78.11, 80.5594, and 80.5589) in the Hunt collection are possibly related to the Soldiers' and Sailors' Monument in Indianapolis.

33. Sharp, pp. 215–17.

34. Baker, p. 308.

35. Sharp, pp. 217–18.

36. Ibid., pp. 223–27.

37. Letter from J. Q. A. Ward to R. T. Lincoln, 11 February 1885, Garfield Monument Record Group 42, Public Building and Grounds, National Archives, Washington, D.C.

38. Sharp, pp. 229–30.

39. Ibid., pp. 233–35.

40. Baker, p. 221.

41. Ibid.

42. Sharp, pp. 237–41.

43. Telegram from H. C. King to J. Q. A. Ward, 8 March 188[7], Ward papers, the New-York Historical Society.

44. Contract between the executive committee of the Beecher Statue Committee and J. Q. A. Ward, 6 April 1888, Ward Papers, the New-York Historical Society.

45. Baker, pp. 312 and 314.

46. Wayne Craven, *Sculpture in America.* (New York: Thomas Y. Crowell Co., 1968), p. 299.

47. Ibid., p. 300. See also James M. Goode, *The Outdoor Sculpture of Washington, D.C.* (Washington, D.C.: Smithsonian Institution Press, 1974), pp. 278–79.

48. James M. Dennis, *Karl Bitter: Architectural Sculptor, 1867–1915.* (Madison, Milwaukee, and London: The University of Wisconsin Press, 1967). Dennis's book is the source for all biographical information related to Karl Bitter in this essay.

49. Baker, pp. 348–52.

50. Ibid., pp. 352–62.

51. Dennis, p. 30. See also Baker, pp. 345–48.

52. Baker, pp. 412–32 and Dennis, pp. 24–33.

53. Baker, pp. 373–74, and Dennis, pp. 48–55.

54. Dennis, p. 55.

55. Baker, pp. 392–411 and Dennis, pp. 40–48.

56. Dennis, p. 42.

57. Henry Van Brunt, "Architecture at the Columbian Exposition." *Century Illustrated Monthly Magazine* 44 (May 1892): 92–93, as quoted in Dennis, p. 42.

58. Baker, pp. 442–49 and Dennis, pp. 77–80.

8

Superb Privacies: The Later Domestic Commissions of Richard Morris Hunt, 1878–1895

David Chase

EMINENT in professional circles almost from the day he resettled in America in 1855, Richard Morris Hunt gained his reputation as an architect of wider renown only with the construction of the first of his palatial residences, the New York townhouse of William K. and Alva Vanderbilt, begun in 1878 and completed in 1882.[1] From 1878 until Hunt's death in 1895, his office was engaged in over one hundred commissions. About a quarter were for monuments and tombs, over half were residential, and the remainder were for a broad miscellany of building types, from museums to stables.[2] Obviously, domestic work was the firm's specialty and it is fitting that Hunt's reputation as a practitioner rests here.[3]

Of the fifty-odd later residential commissions, drawings for thirty survive. Fourteen of these dwellings must be considered major projects supervised by Hunt himself,[4] beginning with the W. K. Vanderbilt townhouse (fig. 8.1) and ending with Hunt's Newport cottage, the Breakers (fig. 8.2), commissioned by William Vanderbilt's older brother, Cornelius, begun late in 1892. It is with these mansions that we shall be principally concerned, buildings that differed from Hunt's important early dwellings in a number of fundamental respects and that have stirred controversy since they were built.[5]

Before comparing Hunt's major later houses to his earlier domestic work, and before considering the controversy that surrounds his later houses, it will be useful first to give an overview of these buildings—their physical, social, and economic setting and their formal characteristics in terms of massing, plan, style, and interior embellishment. Despite the fame of these dwellings, aside from the well-known Vanderbilt commissions, Hunt's later houses are not familiar. Those that are known are set apart in a curious limbo, adored and detested by times, consigned to the status of sociocultural paradigms epitomizing "Gilded Age" excess. But they are not *looked* at, not considered.

What is the architectural image conjured up by mention of Hunt? A very large stone-built residence, either in the city or the country, imposing, sumptuously finished, almost regal, carried out in the florid style of François I. This image fits many of Hunt's later houses. But his work is actually more diverse, and some of the atypical dwellings are among his best. The W. K. Vanderbilt townhouse was indeed of the "chateauesque" type, as were the Marquand and Gerry townhouses in New York (see fig. 8.11), the William Borden house in Chicago (see figs. 8.5, 8.6) and (in rather more French Early Renaissance fashion) the Astor double house, also in New York. The only other important

8.1 William K. Vanderbilt house, 660 Fifth Avenue, New York City, 1878–82.

8.2 Cornelius Vanderbilt II house, the Breakers, Ochre Point Avenue, Newport, R.I., 1892–95.

townhouse of this period for which Hunt himself was responsible, the Ogden Mills residence in New York, was more or less Venetian Gothic. Hunt's later country houses are a bit more varied than the city residences. Ogden Goelet's Newport villa, Ochre Court (fig. 8.14), and George Washington Vanderbilt's North Carolina manor house, Biltmore, are Hunt's outstanding French Gothic buildings. For O. H. P. Belmont's eccentric, stable-cum-bachelor's-quarters in Newport, Hunt designed a complex, colorful, mansarded structure in stucco and granite with brick banding and an interior courtyard elaborately half-timbered (fig. 8.3). Alva and W. K. Vanderbilt's Newport residence, Marble House (see fig. 8.17), is loosely modeled after the Petit Trianon. The exterior of Cornelius Vanderbilt's Newport cottage, the Breakers, derives from sixteenth-century Genoese palace design. Three Hunt country places of the late 1880s—all constructed of stone, all massive—are relatively devoid of specific historical stylistic ancestry. They are James Pinchot's Grey Towers in Milford, Pennsylvania (see fig. 8.29); Archibald Rogers's house, Crumwold Hall, at Hyde Park (fig. 8.4); and the Dorsheimer-Busk house, Indian Spring (see fig. 8.20), at Newport. Though each has conical-roofed towers and thus recalls the French Gothic, each is more aptly described as a "modern" house.

8.3 Oliver Hazard Perry Belmont house, Belcourt, side elevation, Bellevue Avenue at Lake Avenue, Newport, R.I., 24 August 1891.

8.4 Archibald Rogers house, Crumwold Hall, Hyde Park, New York, 1886–89.

Together, these fourteen buildings constitute Hunt's most important later domestic work. By fact or courtesy, all were "millionaires' houses" and thus the subject of public fascination and repeated comment in the popular press. In a representative article published in 1890, *The Nation* observed that "the millionaire is the Paladin of our day. . . . The habits of millionaires today excite as much interest and curiosity as those of European royalty."[5] This fascination was not confined to the American public, as perusal of publications like the London *Spectator* and *Cornhill Magazine* attest. In an era before sports heroes, Hollywood, and television, celebrity was largely the province of the rich, and none of the accoutrements of the American millionaire's way of life excited greater interest than his habitation.[6] Nor was the professional architectural community immune to the spell of such houses: in 1885 readers of the *American Architect & Building News* voted Hunt's W. K. Vanderbilt townhouse one of the finest buildings in the nation. (It placed third in a field of ten.[7]) Architect Charles McKim so admired this building that he made a habit of walking up Fifth Avenue late at night just to take in Hunt's handiwork, smoke a cigar, and then turn in.[8]

To a degree, construction of such costly private commissions corresponded with economic cycles. In the prosperous years of the late 1870s and early 1880s, big houses proliferated. In the mid 1880s the American economy suffered severe setbacks and commissions on this scale were few. Some projects such as Indian Spring, the Newport cottage designed by Hunt in 1885 for William Dorsheimer, were never completed because of financial reverses. During the late 1880s and early 1890s, however, the economy flourished and big house projects blossomed, only to diminish again as a result of the severe depression that began in 1892 and continued throughout the last years of Hunt's life. These years were marked by labor strife, agitation by socialists, populists, and assorted other levelers, and debates over a growing American plutocracy and the morality—even the legality—of rich men building lavish houses.[9]

Although by the 1880s, Hunt's reputation was national—even international—his big house projects were carried out for a fairly parochial segment of society: wealthy New Yorkers constituted Hunt's clientele almost exclusively. As this suggests, an overwhelming number of his residential projects were for sites on or just off Fifth Avenue. In addition to his own residence and office in New York City, Hunt had a home and a studio (really a second office) in Newport, and here, too, he had work, a small number of very large commissions, all for New York clients. Only one noteworthy client of these years, William Borden of Chicago, was wholly outside the circle of New York business and finance that patronized Hunt. A real estate operator whose fortune derived from mining investments in Leadville, Colorado, Borden commissioned a demi-château for Lake Shore Drive on which Hunt worked intermittently between 1884 and 1889 (figs. 8.5, 8.6).[10]

The physical setting of all Hunt's townhouses was very circumscribed. They were built on narrow, deep corner lots and occupied the whole of the site, hemmed in by adjacent structures on two sides. Typically, these corner-sited city residences were complex and asymmetrical in massing, dominated by a tower or turret at or near the corner, a common late nineteenth-century motif utilized by speculative builders and sophisticated architects alike. Though pulled back from the corner, the tourelle on the W. K. Vanderbilt townhouse (fig. 8.7) is a case in point: it defines a cardinal viewing point from which the building was to be seen—a diagonal vista, taking in both front and lateral elevations (see fig. 8.1). Hunt turned to this corner tower motif in earlier resi-

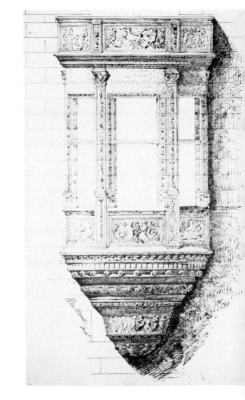

dences as well, for example in the Fisk house of 1871 (fig. 8.8).[11] The importance of this motif as a compositional device is illustrated by a comparison of Hunt's December 1885 perspective of the Borden house, which lacks such an accent (see fig. 8.5), and the corner-turreted building as completed (see fig. 8.6). A number of the many alternative designs Hunt's office produced for William B. Astor, Jr., and his wife, and for their son, John Jacob Astor IV, in 1891–92 are of the corner-towered type (fig. 8.9).[12] Writing in 1895 in his still definitive critique of Hunt, Montgomery Schuyler commented on the architect's happy use of this device in designing the Elbridge Gerry townhouse of 1891–94 (see fig. 8.30), calling it "distinctly the most interesting and the most successful" of these compositions.[13] Hunt's motive for using the corner tower was not practical; he did not seek to provide extra daylight. His impetus was aesthetic. A towerlike corner treatment tied his often disparate elevations together, emphasized the three-dimensional quality of the house, and served to "detach" the building from all-too-close neighboring dwellings. Not incidentally, it also served to draw attention to the building.

The massing of two of Hunt's most interesting corner-sited townhouses does not utilize the modulating tower motif. In the Ogden Mills residence of 1885–87 (a very unusual design for Hunt with an absolutely plain corner), massive twin chimney stacks rising from the walls of each facade close to the corner orchestrate a dynamic, two-front composition with great originality and success (fig. 8.10). The Henry Marquand townhouse of 1881–84 (fig. 8.11), by contrast, exhibits a radical and very unsatisfactory corner treatment. Here the corner is cut away, the bulk of the building carved back to form a reentrant angle. The rectangular space thus obtained is filled with an ill-sorted pile of fussy, minor elements—a first-story conservatory, a second-story dressing room surrounded by a wrought-iron catwalk and lighted by a pair of mean little windows, and, atop all this, a cantilevered third-story balcony. Withal, Marquand's corner has the look of what normally would face an alley rather than a major intersection.[14]

In compositional terms, Hunt's country houses were naturally more diverse than the townhouses. Generally asymmetrical, these houses characteristically

8.5 *Above left:* Elevation of the William Borden house, Lake Shore Drive at Bellevue Place, Chicago, 1884.

8.6 *Above:* William Borden house, 1884–89.

Below: 8.7 Drawing for the oriel window of the William K. Vanderbilt house, 660 Fifth Avenue, New York City, ca. 1879.

8.8 *Top left:* Proposal for Fisk residence, Fifth Avenue near Seventieth Street, New York City, ca. 1871.

8.9 *Top right:* Mrs. William Astor and John Jacob Astor IV house, 840 Fifth Avenue, New York City, 1891–95. The Fifth Avenue elevation drawn on 4 January 1892 shows a corner turret closely related to the oriel window of the William K. Vanderbilt house (fig. 8.7).

8.10 *Bottom left:* Ogden Mills house, Fifth Avenue and Sixtyninth Street, New York City, 1885–87.

8.11 *Bottom right:* Henry Marquand house, 8 East Sixty-eighth Street, New York City, 1881–84.

incorporate major elements, often the most forceful elements of any facade, which articulate only moderately subordinate internal symmetries. On Biltmore's west front, for example (fig. 8.12), semioctagonal towers define an assertive, symmetrical central block set off against large, asymmetrical wings. Biltmore's east-facing entrance elevation (fig. 8.13) presents an intricately modulated asymmetry developed from what is fundamentally a symmetrical scheme.[15] On a much smaller scale, this tension can be seen in the composition of the entrance front of the Archibald Rogers country house, Crumwold Hall (1886–89; see fig. 8.4), where symmetry and asymmetry again interlock. The entrance elevation and ocean front of Hunt's Newport cottage for Ogden Goelet, Ochre Court (1888–92; fig. 8.14), are akin to the major elevations of Biltmore in several respects, yet they contrast with the Biltmore elevations in that the Ochre Court entrance front is more assertively asymmetrical, while

8.12 West elevation of the George W. Vanderbilt house, Biltmore, Asheville, N.C., ca. 1890. Photograph courtesy of Biltmore Estate, Asheville, N.C.

8.13 East elevation of Biltmore, dated 1 July 1890 and initialed W. G. L. Photograph courtesy of Biltmore Estate, Asheville, N.C.

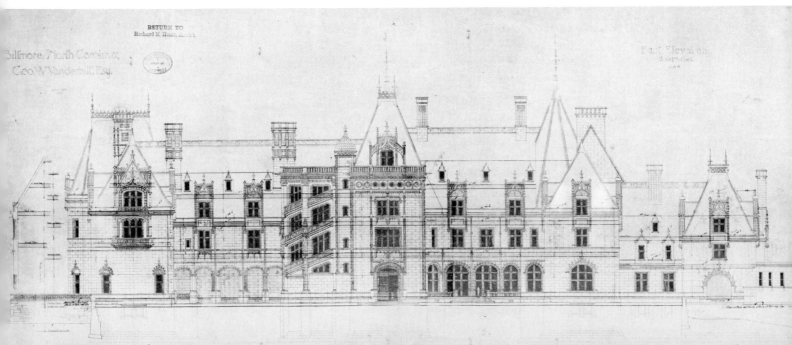

8.14 Ogden Goelet house, Ochre Court, Ochre Point Avenue, Newport, R.I., 1888–93.

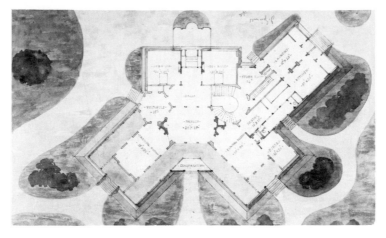

8.15 Preliminary floor plan study for the John N. A. Griswold house, Bellevue Avenue and Old Beach Road, Newport, R.I., ca. 1861.

the corresponding ocean elevation is more assertively regular. Hunt's two classically inspired and fully symmetrical Newport villas, Marble House (1888–92; see fig. 8.17), built by the W. K. Vanderbilts, and Cornelius Vanderbilt's Breakers (1892–95; see fig. 8.2), like Ochre Court, have centrally accented entrance fronts. Likewise, their ocean-facing elevations have matching lateral pavilions bracketing a central loggia, or, in the case of Marble House, a central terrace.

One of Hunt's most admired late projects, the Dorsheimer-Busk house at Newport (see fig. 8.20), in essence follows the same compositional formula: an intermeshing of symmetrical and asymmetrical elements, a central block with contrasting wings, a centrally focused entrance front, and an ocean front with towers flanking a deep porch.

Among the surviving Hunt drawings are a large number of floor plans, most of them unremarkable. An intriguing minority, however, done throughout Hunt's career, are of special note and bear the stamp of Hunt's personal vision. Their common characteristics are the prominence given to nonrectangular room shapes—ellipses, octagons, circular spaces; frequent development of diagonal axes; and a peculiar compactness, a honeycomb-like density. The early J. N. A. Griswold residence at Newport (1861–63; fig. 8.15) has a plan that illustrates these characteristics. One of Hunt's 1861 sketchbooks contains

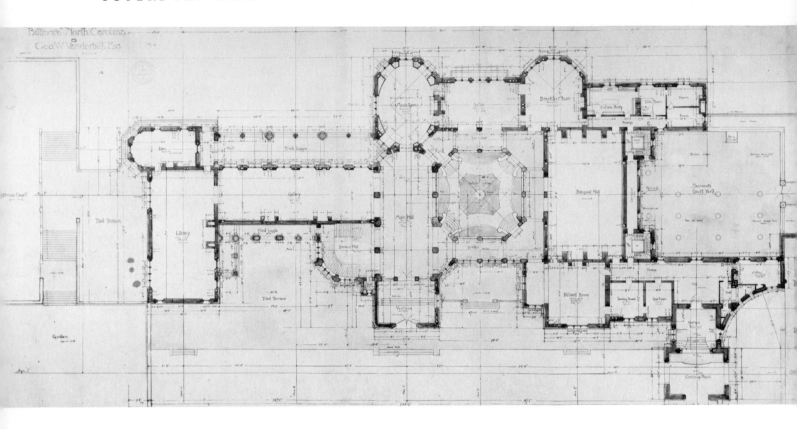

pages of floor plans that document his fascination with these themes. In the Marshall Field house in Chicago (1871–73), Hunt again produced a dense, complexly geometric plan with diagonal axes, octagonal, semioctagonal, and circular spaces. Among the later houses, some of Hunt's many alternative floor plans for the Elbridge Gerry townhouse reiterate these idiosyncracies (see fig. 8.30). And at Biltmore, Hunt's most extensive house, a highly original combination of rectangular and less conventional spaces produce the architect's most spectacular executed plan. On the ground floor there are eleven major rooms: octagonal, semioctagonal, elliptical, square, and rectangular (fig. 8.16). Of all Hunt's schemes of this sort, Biltmore's is the most self-revealing because of the scale of the spaces and the openness created by the arcaded, octagonal winter garden with its ambulatory, from which the rest of the house seems to open up. One is constantly aware of the entirety and its elaboration.

As noted earlier, Hunt's executed designs and surviving drawings in terms of their style, attest to his devotion to French architecture of the late fifteenth and early sixteenth centuries. In particular, transitional late Gothic- early Renaissance châteaux like Chenonceau, Blois, and Chambord provided sources for his work. His efforts to "naturalize" the architecture of the French Renaissance all date to the latter part of his career.[16] Biltmore was Hunt's most spectacular and convincing exercise in the style of François I. Hunt's chief design assistant working on the Biltmore drawings was Warrington Lawrence. While on a holiday and study tour in France in September of 1889, Lawrence wrote to Hunt from Blois: "I don't wonder any longer that you admire so much the François Premier wing, it is undoubtedly a fine piece of design." Lawrence went on to relate how he was making sketches and notes which he hoped would be useful in his work on the Vanderbilt château.[17] Only two months before Lawrence

8.16 First floor in plan for George W. Vanderbilt's Biltmore, labeled "No. 12 First Floor Plan," dated 3 February 1891 and initialed J. A. J. Photograph courtesy of Biltmore Estate, Asheville, N.C.

8.17 William and Alva Vanderbilt house, Marble House, Bellevue Avenue, Newport, R.I., 1888–92.

8.18 Proposed perspective elevation of the Breakers in the French Renaissance style, dated 28 December 1892. The design was rejected by Cornelius Vanderbilt in favor of the one proposed in fig. 8.19.

8.19 Proposed perspective elevation of the Breakers in the style of sixteenth-century Genoese palaces, dated 12 January 1893.

wrote this letter, Hunt himself had returned from a European journey during which he accompanied G. W. Vanderbilt on visits to the famous French châteaux Hunt so admired, visits calculated to inspire ideas for the grand Asheville residence then in the early stages of design.[18]

It is clear that in the latter part of his career, Hunt preferred to design houses in French late Gothic style, which he obviously found sympathetic to his own taste and purposes. He could not always design in the style he favored, however, as Marble House and the Breakers demonstrate. The Petit Trianon guise of the former was determined by Mrs. W. K. Vanderbilt, and all surviving drawings reflect a neoclassical source of inspiration (fig. 8.17). In the case of the Breakers, Hunt presented the Cornelius Vanderbilts two alternative schemes for an extraordinarily grand seaside villa, drawn by E. L. Masqueray in December of 1982 and January of 1893 (figs. 8.18, 8.19).[19] One version of this build-

ing was châteauesque, the other of northern Italian Renaissance inspiration, as the clients had requested. Ultimately, they settled on a revised and scaled-down version of the north Italian palace. Hunt's preference for French late Gothic was not solely aesthetic. Picturesque asymmetry and high roofs had practical advantages when it came to providing the extensive service areas required in the most elaborate late nineteenth-century households. The symmetrical facades of Marble House mask a warren of passages and small service rooms fitted into hidden mezzanine spaces and behind the parapets. At the Breakers these expedients were not available and Hunt was compelled to create a four-story "house" in order to accommodate the program, much to the chagrin of his clients.[20]

Of the three later country houses in which historical motifs are only vaguely alluded to, the finest is the Dorsheimer-Busk residence (fig. 8.20). Probably alone among Hunt's houses, this building has always been commended by architectural critics.[21] It is an exercise in Richardsonian design and, although the fascinating history of the project points out the source of inspiration, there is no explanation of how it was that Hunt achieved such striking success in this homage to his brilliant and very different rival, a rival Hunt esteemed but never imitated before or after.

According to Mrs. Hunt's biography of her husband, the plans for this Newport cottage were originally prepared for the prominent Buffalo lawyer, politician, and civic leader, William Edward Dorsheimer, who died while Hunt was at work on the project. The plans were then taken up by the Joseph Busks. Newport land records and newspaper accounts relate that Dorsheimer purchased a rocky site on Beacon Hill with a fine view in 1885. Frederick Law Olmsted had planned the subdivision in which this property was located, the King-Glover Plat. Between 1885 and 1887 Olmsted's firm laid out the Dorsheimer grounds. When Dorsheimer died, he left unsettled bills for which Olmsted and Hunt never received full payment. As late as May 1890, Olmsted corresponded with Dorsheimer's widow concerning the project. By that December, however, Mr. and Mrs. Joseph R. Busk had taken over the failed project, and Olmsted and Hunt were on the job, working at a new site very similar to Dorsheimer's, located about a mile away. The one-and-a-half-story, turreted, brown-stone-trimmed tan granite dwelling, called Indian Spring and set atop a rocky bluff overlooking Ocean Drive and the sea, was occupied in the summer of 1892.

8.20 Ocean-facing elevation of the Joseph R. Busk house (begun for William E. Dorsheimer), Indian Spring, Ocean Avenue, Newport, R.I., ca. 1890.

8.21 Section, Indian Spring.

William Dorsheimer was an ardent admirer of both Frederick Law Olmsted and Richardson. Why Dorsheimer did not commission Richardson to design his Newport house before the architect's death in 1886 is unknown. Nevertheless, as built from Hunt's plans and erected for the Busks, Indian Spring suggests Dorsheimer stipulated that Hunt produce a design in Richardson's style. The most intriguing explanation for the Dorsheimer design is that the cottage was to be something of a developer's model, meant to attract interest in building in the King-Glover subdivision and to show exactly what would be suitable in this beautifully barren coastal setting. Deeds indicate that William Dorsheimer was closely associated with John H. Glover, one of the investors for whom Olmsted's subdivision plan was prepared. Olmsted's narrative accompanying the plat called for erecting in this ruggedly picturesque area, a setting Olmsted's design carefully preserved, "buildings and garden works consistent with these natural circumstances." Glover erected on a neighboring knoll a stone house designed by McKim, Mead, and White equally Richardsonian (or should one say Olmstedian?).

The involvement of Olmsted in the Dorsheimer-Busk project is crucial, for the subdivision for which it was designed was his creation. He had long been associated with Richardson and Dorsheimer, and it may well have been he who suggested reviving Hunt's Dorsheimer plans when the Busks came to him to lay out their grounds. At this time Olmsted and Hunt were working together on their most famous collaboration, Biltmore, a collaboration that echoed the creative partnership Olmsted had known with Richardson. Whatever the sequence of events and linkages, Hunt created in Indian Spring a fine house in the Richardsonian manner, a house Schuyler thought was perhaps better than Richardson himself might have produced—a well-edited version of Richardson, so to speak. In 1886 the critic Marianna Griswold Van Rensselaer expressed sentiments akin to Olmsted's concerning development of the King-Glover lands, hoping to influence those who might build there to "carefully and artistically preserve its charm," and not attempt to subdue this quality in favor of "neat prettiness." Indian Spring was anything but neat and pretty. It is a house at one with its situation—an extension of its natural setting.[22]

As one might expect to find in a substantial house of the 1890s, Indian Spring's external stylistic purity stopped at the door. The interior boasted a variety of treatments, each room more or less "done" in a different period style— the great hall French Late Gothic, complete with a chapel-like, timber-braced ceiling and enormous hooded fireplace (fig. 8.21); the library Elizabethan; the bedrooms Colonial; and so on. Such a bouquet of styles could be found in all Hunt's major late houses, but much of this interior work was not designed in Hunt's office. It was contracted out to designers like Ogden Codman, who was responsible for bedrooms at the Breakers, or more frequently and spectacularly to the big French and American decorating houses, chief among them Allard.[23] Nevertheless, the Hunt office produced considerable interior design work during the 1880s and 1890s, some every bit as ambitious as that produced by decorators.

The great hall in the Busk house is the smallest and least elaborate of three important late Gothic rooms by Hunt: the others are the banqueting halls for W. K. Vanderbilt's townhouse and G. W. Vanderbilt's Biltmore (figs. 8.22, 8.23).[24] Of more general interest are the entrance halls Hunt's office produced. No matter what other rooms might be turned over to specialists, Hunt seems always to have designed the entrance halls for his houses. Drawings document the lengths taken to try to satisfy one client, Elbridge Gerry, with his entrance hall. At least twelve alternatives were considered and presented in full sets of floor plans, some worked up additionally in sections and perspective studies (fig. 8.24). Despite this effort, Gerry was not pleased with the hall. Soon after the house was completed he had Hunt's entrance hall demolished and hired another designer to create a replacement.[25] Whatever Gerry's complaint, Hunt's assured and authoritative interior work for this and his other later housebuilders would never incite a critic to repeat what was said at least once of typical early Hunt interiors, that they were "cryingly ugly."[26]

Hunt gained a special reputation late in his career for a peerless deftness in the decorative use of marble veneer as an interior finish. Two Hunt-designed marble interiors deserve special note: the dining room at Marble House (fig. 8.25) and the billiard room at the Breakers (fig. 8.26). Both achieve sumptuousness without vulgarity. A drawing for a third marble-sheathed room is intriguing, for it depicts the elevations proposed for Alva Smith Vanderbilt's bathroom in the W. K. Vanderbilt townhouse (fig. 8.27). This is the only

8.22 Study for the W. K. Vanderbilt banquet hall, 660 Fifth Avenue, New York City.

8.23 Banquet hall, Biltmore. Photograph courtesy of Biltmore Estate, Asheville, N.C.

8.24 *Below, left:* Perspective drawing of the entrance hall of the Elbridge Gerry house, 2 East Sixtyfirst Street, New York City, ca. 1891.

8.25 *Right:* Dining room, Marble House. Photograph courtesy of the Preservation Society of Newport County, R.I.

8.26 *Below right:* Wall elevation of the billiard room of the Breakers showing mosaic and marble detail, 4 June 1894.

8.27 *Bottom:* Study for the decoration of Mrs. W. K. Vanderbilt's bathroom, 660 Fifth Avenue, New York City, ca. 1881.

bathroom for which a Hunt design is known and it reputedly set a new standard for luxury and sophistication. It had marble fixtures of Roman inspiration and a marble wainscoting with mirrored walls above, overpainted with flowering vines. Mrs. Hunt recorded that in 1881 she "had the privilege of attending to Mrs. W. K. Vanderbilt's marble bathroom. . . . The Misses Ely, contributors to the Decorative Arts Society, painted the mirrored walls most artistically."[27] These lavish interiors exhibit the flash and brilliance characteristic of the architect's most interesting early work, tempered by a sense of fitness and a self-assurance so complete that Hunt now could venture to the very limits of good taste without overstepping them.

This sense of mastery is not all that sets Hunt's major residential commissions of the period from 1878 to 1895 apart from his earlier production. Stylistic differences, as well as differences in character, distinguish Hunt's early and late work. There are telling differences in Hunt's involvement in the design process and in the participation of his clients themselves, Hunt's relationships with them, and in the scale of their commissions. Most importantly, there are differences in the degree to which Hunt's work was accepted.

Stylistic historicism characterizes nearly all Hunt's work of the 1880s and 1890s, with particularly convincing renditions of the forms and detail of the François I period. Rarely is thoroughgoing historicism encountered in Hunt's early domestic work. His urban dwellings of the 1860s and 1870s are often in the contemporary Neo-Grec idiom. His country houses of the same period are also contemporary stylistically, executed for the most part in the mock half-timbered "Modern Gothic" or, in the case of occasional larger masonry country houses, executed in polychrome brick- and stonework and patterned slate, exemplifying equally contemporary "chalets normands." One may contrast the Brimmer houses of 1870, the Griswold house of 1862–64, and the Appleton cottage of 1870–71 with the W. K. Vanderbilt townhouse of 1878–82 and Ogden Goelet's Ochre Court of 1888–92.

The image these houses present is strikingly divergent. Hunt's early dwellings are essentially upper middle class in character, set off from most bourgeois habitations by their self-conscious, often eccentric aestheticism. They proclaim themselves the dwellings of cultivated people. Hunt's later houses are no less self-conscious, but here the similarity ends. In their size, bearing, and stylistic associations they present themselves not as the homes of the intelligentsia but of a class whose common denominator is wealth and, by implication, power. The houses seem to seek to define a fixed hierarchical social order in which their owners occupy the topmost station. Dynastic symbolism is a natural extension of this imagery. It appears most consistently in Hunt's four houses for the Vanderbilt brothers in the form of ciphers and the decorative and armorial use of the acorn and oak leaf, family heraldic devices selected by Alva Vanderbilt (fig. 8.28).

One Hunt residence is an exception to the generalized "image" Hunt's later houses present, in that its imposing, chateauesque form evoked associations specific to the client and his family: the rubble-walled country house Grey Towers, which Hunt designed for his friend, the prosperous New York merchant James Pinchot, late in 1884 or early 1885 (fig. 8.29). The house was built on forest lands long held by the Pinchots in the hills above Milford, Pennsylvania, overlooking the Delaware. The families were close, and Hunt and Pinchot—both confirmed francophiles—were associated in the erection of the Statue of

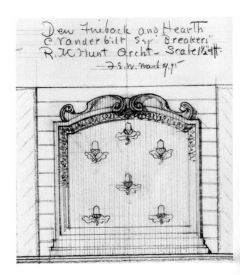

8.28 Study of the "den" fireback, Cornelius Vanderbilt II house, the Breakers, dated 19 March 1895.

8.29 James Pinchot house, Grey Towers, Milford, Pa., 1884–86.

Liberty during the years in which Grey Towers was built. The fortresslike demeanor of Grey Towers recalled for Pinchot his French heritage and more specifically the medieval castle that had protected his ancestral home, Breteuil-sur-Noye. A bust of Lafayette in a niche—the focus of the turret-flanked garden front—made reference to the family's long-standing republican sympathies and to the Pinchots' French-American heritage. Hunt's drawings for Gray Towers were apparently a gift. The project was not supervised by Hunt's office but was carried out under Pinchot's direction. Pinchot modified Hunt's plans somewhat and brought in a little-known English-trained New York architect, Henry Edward-Ficken, to design most of the interiors. All this notwithstanding, Hunt took pride in the result. Richard and Catharine Hunt visited Grey Towers after its completion and Mrs. Hunt recalled later that it had impressed them as having "a character about it quite unlike anything else in America."[28]

Surviving drawings illuminate yet other aspects of the character and quality of Hunt's early and later work, as well as the design process itself. One infers from the dearth of autograph drawings dating to the 1880s and 1890s that Hunt participated less directly in the design of his buildings as his practice and outside commitments grew. Wholly lacking among extant drawings for the later houses are the spirited preliminary sketches routinely produced for buildings like the Griswold house and Jones chalet. Yet, if the quantity and quality of Hunt's graphic production dropped off in the last decade and a half of his life, the quality of the buildings was every bit as good, if not better, than it had been. Perhaps the idiosyncratic, rather private virtuosity of what Schuyler termed Hunt's early "staccato" style was best suited to expression through drawings, but was too cranky, even at times too aggressively ugly, for execution in stone, brick, and wood. Conversely, Hunt's later houses tend to be less appealing on paper but achieve a level of architectural success, as buildings, on an order that often eluded his youthful efforts. Bravado, wit, and excessiveness are qualities appreciated in architectural drawings; harmony, authority, legitimacy, and grandeur—these are virtues appreciated in built form.

Study of the drawings also reveals much about the way Hunt handled his clients. Again, there is a contrast between the architect's early and later practice. During this period Hunt's clients often participated substantially in the design process. For example, clients routinely received a variety of plans and elevations to choose from. For Mrs. William Gammell, Hunt prepared four sets of plans and elevations for a projected Newport house (never built) in January of 1881; for Sidney Webster's townhouse, Hunt drew four sets of floor plans in 1883–85; for William Borden's Chicago house, completed in 1889, Hunt prepared two separate schemes, each with a series of alternate plans and elevations; the Frederick Bronson house of 1889–90 went through at least five sets of plans, including an unusual study in the Colonial Revival style; Mrs. William B. Astor, Jr., in December of 1891 and January of 1892, was sent no fewer than seven alternate designs for the front of her proposed townhouse; during February and March of 1893, E. L. Masqueray drew at least a dozen floor plans for the Breakers. During these years, Hunt provided what amounted to a multiple-choice design service, having evidently taken to heart his own oft repeated maxim: the architect's job is to provide what the client wants and make a success of it.

In this limited sense at least, Hunt was an indifferentist.[29] One might broaden the definition of the term usefully in Hunt's case: his was the indifferentism of an architect who cared little for architectural theory, who dreaded speech making, who habitually had nothing insightful to say about his work, but who cared deeply about architectural practice, about creating buildings.

In general terms, the differences between Hunt's early and later clients are very marked. During the 1850s, 1860s, and 1870s, Hunt's residential commissions tended to come from family members and friends. Many clients were members of a close-knit, monied but not remarkably rich, old-guard social and intellectual elite, a class into which both Richard and Catharine Hunt were born. Starting with the first Vanderbilt commissions in the late 1870s, Hunt's patronage became increasingly restricted to a small circle of extremely wealthy clients with whom he had few social connections and who were not associated with the intelligentsia. There were, however, a few crossovers. The most remarkable of these was Henry Marquand, a highly successful New York businessman with a passion and talent for art collecting who served as president of the board of trustees of the Metropolitan Museum of Art. Marquand commissioned major houses from Hunt in 1872, for Newport, and in 1881 for New York (as well as a number of other projects of various types over the years). Marquand's artistic interests may explain the design of his townhouse, with its seemingly haphazard assemblage of bits and pieces piled up at the corner like a stack of gifts under a Christmas tree. The exterior was but a wrapping for a diverse series of exquisitely furnished rooms reflecting his eclectic and tireless connoisseurship. George Washington Vanderbilt may also be judged a man of substantial intellectual and artistic interests, whose relationship to Hunt became very close.[30] Yet this is not at all evident in the baronial house Hunt designed.

The esteem George Vanderbilt and Hunt's other Vanderbilt patrons felt for the architect is revealed in the extraordinary steps each took to commemorate his exertions on their behalf. For Biltmore, George Washington Vanderbilt commissioned life-size portraits of Hunt and of Frederick Law Olmsted. Under the patronage of Cornelius Vanderbilt at the Breakers, a series of allegorical reliefs in the great hall depicting the arts and sciences incorporates into a relief devoted to Architecture Hunt's portrait and a view of his Chicago World's Fair Administration Building of 1893. Above the landing of the main staircase at

Alva and William Vanderbilt's Marble House is a portrait bust of Louis XIV and above it on the wall, borne aloft by gilded spirits, are portrait medallions of Hunt and J. H. Mansart (see fig. 7.36). The first and best known of these *hommages à l'architecte* was the half-size stone figure of Hunt in mason's garb that perched atop the gabled dormer crowning the Fifth Avenue facade of the W. K. Vanderbilt New York townhouse. Hunt was so fond of this image of himself that he kept a cast of it in his Newport studio.

Such tributes from Vanderbilt patrons did not come without effort. Judging solely from marginal inscriptions on surviving drawings, one may guess that these were Hunt's most demanding clients. Notes regarding the preferences of all the third-generation Vanderbilts survive—George Washington Vanderbilt, Cornelius Vanderbilt, W. K. Vanderbilt, and, most demanding of all, Alva Smith Vanderbilt, who, during the time she employed Hunt, was married to W. K. Vanderbilt. Hunt is said to have had high regard for Alva Vanderbilt's talents and taste, but he surely found this imperious woman difficult as well.[31] Two drawings capture this client-architect relationship with wonderful economy. They are a pair of alternate studies for wainscoting in a second-floor corridor at Marble House. On one the exasperated Hunt scrawled, "This absolutely disapproved by Mrs. Vanderbilt," and on the other he wrote, "This accepted by Mrs. Vanderbilt."

Whatever Mrs. Vanderbilt's opinion in this instance, the problem for anyone considering Hunt's later houses generally is that, as a body of work, as a class, they have been "disapproved." They are so grand, so palatial, that they are judged to be alien to American culture, and for this they are condemned. Few critics since Montgomery Schuyler's day have been able to overcome this bias and evaluate these dwellings dispassionately.

When the W. K. Vanderbilt townhouse was completed in 1882 the initial response took note of its merits. *Harper's Weekly* published a very positive review by Montgomery Schuyler. He liked the "power and massiveness" of a structure richly embellished yet unblemished by profusion or ostentation. A contrary view was expressed in the *North American Review* by the critic Clarence Cook (long a Hunt detractor), who decried this "copy, and a slavish one, of the architecture of the time of Francis I, with its entrance an adaptation of a French Renaissance chimney-piece!"[32] Writing in 1886, Marianna Griswold Van Rensselaer, though critical of the building's "too profuse and delicate ornament," declared it to be the most beautiful house in New York, and presented it as proof that "lavish art may be as refined as modest art."[33]

By the mid 1880s, however, a different viewpoint was already being expressed. The townhouse was condemned in print as "socially inappropriate" because "W. K. Vanderbilt indulges in aristocratic appendages and poses as the herald of our future nobility. . . ." Dwellings on this scale prompted the Senate Committee on Education and Labor in 1885 to consider legislation putting a cap on the amount a millionaire could spend on his house.[34] A decade later, as Hunt's most costly houses neared completion during a period of severe economic hardship and social turmoil, a torrent of condemnation found its way into the periodicals. E. L. Godkin's 1896 article "The Expenditure of Rich Men" is representative. Godkin held that affluent Americans faced a problem unknown to their European counterparts: how to spend their money. Here the wealthy had to decide for themselves what abroad was dictated largely by tradition and descent.

That, under these circumstances, they should, in somewhat slavish imitation of Europe, choose the most conspicuous European mode of asserting social supremacy, the building of great houses, is not surprising. But in this imitation they make two radical mistakes. They want the principle reasons for European great houses. One is that great houses are in Europe signs of either great territorial possessions or of the practice of hospitality on a scale unknown among us.

The other reason, said Godkin, and the most serious argument against the building of great houses in America, was that dwellings "should be in some sort of accord with national manners" and palatial residences were not. Joseph Lee, writing for *New England Magazine*, carried this line of reasoning still further, expressing the opinion that great houses were a blight "out of harmony with the spirit of American institutions and sooner or later one or the other must go."[35] In the *Theory of the Leisure Class*, Thorstein Veblen's satirical social critique issued in 1899, the author cites residences of Huntian magnificence as examples of "conspicuous consumption," a phrase he was the first to use.

During the opening years of the twentieth century, Henry James continued this litany of reproach. He described Hunt's Newport mansions and their kind as white elephants, and cheerfully pitied "their averted owners [who], roused from a witless dream, wonder what in the world is to be done with them." For James, these vast habitations would ever stand as reminders of "the peculiarly awkward vengeances of affronted proportion and discretion." They were mistakes, and so too, he felt, were the grand but "flagrantly tentative" New York townhouses, so "discernibly deficient in reasons." It was the lack of an established stratified social order that made the presumption implicit in the image of these houses impossible to sustain.[36] Twenty years later Hunt's reputation was so diminished that Lewis Mumford, in his highly acclaimed book *The Brown Decades* (1931), which was devoted to analysis of late nineteenth-century American art and architecture, could dismiss Hunt with a single slighting reference. Henry-Russell Hitchcock's monumental 1958 publication, *Architecture: Nineteenth and Twentieth Centuries*, still the standard work on the subject, deals with Hunt's later houses as nothing more than a "curious episode." And John Burchard and Albert Bush-Brown, in *The Architecture of America: A Social and Cultural History* (1961), conclude that Hunt's W. K. Vanderbilt townhouse was based on false premises. In their view, it was "a first-class development of a theme which had no relation to the real meaning either of the society or the owner."[37] Such views continue to this day. Hunt's great houses are still not accepted.

But "acceptance" here must be defined in terms linking it to critics, to opinion writers, as opposed to the public at large. Great houses in this country are popular successes—they always have been, and the attendance statistics for such Hunt mansions as the Breakers and Biltmore attest to their abiding appeal.

In a tribute to Hunt written soon after the architect's death in 1895, his former student Henry Van Brunt regretted that his master had not had greater opportunity to design civic buildings and national monuments. Nevertheless, Van Brunt declared that the "superb privacies" Hunt created for Vanderbilts, Goelets, Gerrys, and Astors had done much in the cause of a higher aesthetic standard in America.[38] These private houses stood as public monuments. This

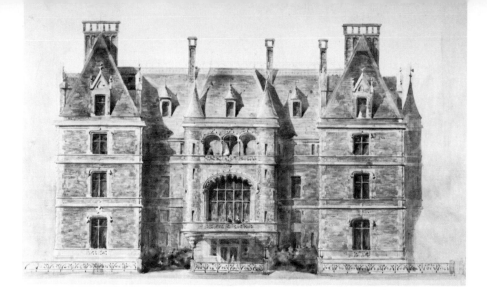

8.30 Elbridge Gerry house, 2 East Sixty-first Street, New York City, 1891–94.

is the real difference between Hunt's early and later domestic work. Before 1878, his houses were essentially private in character, many built for Hunt intimates, many expressive of an extreme and rather hermetic architectural taste. After 1878, Hunt's domestic work became less personal, his clients were less likely to be close friends, the aesthetic was more accessible to the public, and, in effect, in its scale and design, the work *was* civic. Despite Elbridge Gerry's protest to a *New York Times* reporter that his imposing new house was not a palace at all "but simply a comfortable modern home," Montgomery Schuyler correctly concluded that it was one New York's "public possessions" and thus a palace in the true sense after all (fig. 8.30).[39] Sadly, the value and lesson of this building and the others like it Hunt produced in the last fifteen years of his life are preserved for us now largely through photographs. Fortunately, through the drawings that survive, we can come to appreciate their genius and quality more directly. Indeed, they were superb.

Notes

I would like to express my appreciation to William Jordy, Richard Chafee, and the late Paul Molitor for reviewing earlier drafts of this essay.

1. Joy Wheeler Dow, *American Renaissance: A Review of Domestic Architecture in America* (New York, 1904), pp. 123–24. Three exhibition catalogs have in the past decade made limited use of the AIA Foundation's Hunt drawings as a key to the analysis of Hunt's later houses: Richard Guy Wilson et al., *The American Renaissance* (Brooklyn, 1979); Damie Stillman et al., *Architecture and Ornament in Late Nineteenth-Century America* (Newark, Del., 1981); and William H. Jordy and Christopher P. Monkhouse, *Buildings on Paper: Rhode Island Architectural Drawings* (Providence, 1982). The only other substantial collection of Hunt drawings in addition to that at the AIA Foundation is in the Biltmore House Archives. It was analyzed by Susanne Brendel in a Columbia University Preservation Thesis (April 1978) entitled "Documentation of the Construction of Biltmore House through Drawings, Correspondence and Photographs."

2. Paul R. Baker, *Richard Morris Hunt* (Cambridge, Mass., 1980), pp. 544–49. Numbers are approximate; there are several valid ways to compute these figures.

3. Montgomery Schuyler, "Work of the Late Richard Morris Hunt," *Architectural Record* 5, no. 2 (October–December 1895): 126.

4. Projects like the William V. Lawrence residence, although very well represented through drawings in the Hunt collection, are excluded from this list because they were supervised by Hunt's son Richard Howland Hunt. Richard Morris Hunt's participation must be considered minimal, based on his own testimony. See Catharine Clinton Howland Hunt's typescript biography of Richard Morris Hunt (1907), transcribed by Alan Burnham, p. 245.

5. "Millionaires," *The Nation* 50 (2 January 1890):7–8.

6. For example, two articles concerning houses several Vanderbilts were to build in New York: *New York Times*, 9 December 1879, p. 8, col. 2; and 14 July 1880, p. 2, col. 1.

7. *American Architect and Building News* 17 (13 June 1885):282.

8. Charles Moore, *Daniel Burnham, Architect, Planner of Cities* (Boston, 1921), 1:116. In 1904, McKim's partner Stanford White designed a suitably French Gothic companion dwelling beside the Hunt-designed townhouse of 1878 for W. K. Vanderbilt, Jr.

9. Charles Hoffman, *The Depression of the Nineties* (Westport, Conn., 1970), pp. 26, 47–96; "Mr. Vanderbilt's Expenditure," *The Spectator* (London), 26 January 1895, pp. 128–29. It should be pointed out that, as in so many other ways, Hunt's Vanderbilt commissions did not correspond with economic cycles. As the wealthiest family in America, other factors prompted the timing of Vanderbilt projects. W. K. Vanderbilt's townhouse was built immediately after the settlement of grandfather Commodore Vanderbilt's estate. The Hunt-designed townhouse was but one of three impressive Vanderbilt residences begun simultaneously on Fifth Avenue, the others being George B. Post's house for brother Cornelius and the double house designed by J. B. Snook, commissioned by their father, William H. Vanderbilt. Marble House and Biltmore were begun in the boom years of the late 1880s; Marble House was completed just as the depression of 1892 began but the construction of Biltmore, house and grounds, continued for years at a reported cost of $45,000 per week—a cost that finally overtook George Vanderbilt's income (Laura Woods Roper, *FLO: A Biography of Frederick Law Olmsted* [Baltimore, 1973], p. 456). The Breakers was built after Cornelius Vanderbilt's first Newport summer house burned to the ground late in 1892. The new house was erected during the depression, which diminished Cornelius Vanderbilt's immense income from the New York Central Railroad.

10. Baker, pp. 288, 544–549.

11. Hunt Collection drawings 81.6572, 81.6573, 81.6616.

12. For example, William B. Astor, Jr., Scheme C, 4 January 1892 (79.3090); Scheme for J. J. Astor IV, 22 January 1892 (79.3083).

13. Schuyler, p. 131.

14. For a more positive assessment, see Schuyler, pp. 131, 165; also Baker, p. 295.

15. Biltmore House Archives, drawings 8 and 9, catalog nos. 6 and 7.

16. *The Inland Architect* 26, no. 1 (August 1895):4, quoting the *New York Times*.

17. Warrington G. Lawrence to Hunt; letter dated Blois, 15 September 1889; AIA Foundation Hunt collection. This document is so telling it is worth printing here in full:

My Dear Mr. Hunt

We have been some time getting here—but now we are here, and I have seen the *Chateau Blois*—and am now ready to die—it is grand. I wish I could tell you all I feel regarding it—I don't wonder any longer that you admire so much the Francis Premier wing[,] it is undoubtedly a fine piece of design, my preference is still for the Louis XII—I think that brick and stone combination on the Court one of the finest things I have ever seen, and by the way we have seen some fine things since we left home.

We took a nice little trip through Holland and Belgium—spent two weeks in Paris—and are now on our way down the Loire— We have been to Mamtenon (what a beautiful chateau it is), to Chartes [sic]; to Orleans—where we saw that beautiful renaissance work in Diana Portiers, and Agnes Sorrels houses, also Beaugency—where we saw some fine work in the Hotel de Ville, to Vendome, and now at Blois. We have had a fine time and have seen many beautiful things, made some sketches and taken many notes which I hope will be very useful to us in our work by and by. We went to Versailles one Sunday and saw the water works—it was a great sight—enjoyed it immensely[.] Was very much pleased with the rooms in the Grand and Petit Trianon. We went also to Fontambleau [sic] where we again saw some fine rooms—I think tho. the finest room I have yet seen is in the Royal Palace in Amsterdam—perhaps you remember it—it is a room 56′ × 120′ and is 100′ high with a barrel ceiling. I will stay here about a week. Then we leave for Tours and the other places of interest.

I hope you are well—and that the work is progressing on Mr. V's chateau, I am very anxious to see what changes have been made.

Kind regards to Mr. Fornachan and the office.

Respectfully

Warrington G. Lawrence.

18. Catharine Hunt, pp. 210–17; Baker, pp. 331—33.

19. Illustrated and discussed briefly in Wilson, *The American Renaissance*, pp. 97–98. The rather uninspired preliminary sketches for Marble House are discussed by Jordy in *Buildings on Paper*, pp. 94–97. In comparison to Hunt's outstanding selection of monographs on French architecture, his volumes on Italian architecture were few. He did, however, own a copy of Rubens's *Palazzi di Genova* (1622).

20. Antoinette Downing, response to Leonard Eaton's piece, "Should the Breakers be preserved," in *Architectural Preservation Forum* (Bulletin of the Society of Architectural Historians' Preservation Committee) 1, no. 1 (February 1979): 2.

21. See, for example, the comments by Schuyler, pp. 126–29; and Vincent Scully, *The Architectural Heritage of Newport* (New York, 1967), p. 165.

22. Catharine Hunt, p. 222; Baker, pp. 340–41; Newport Land Evidences 55/261, 59/241, 62/422, 63/109, and 63/369; *Newport Mercury*, 29 August and 3 October 1885, 2 July 1887, 16 July 1892; James F. O'Gorman, *H. H. Richardson and His Office* (Cambridge, Mass., 1974), pp. 32, 122; Olmsted Associates project files 681, 1073, 1299; Library of Congress, Frederick Law Olmsted Papers, correspondence, microfilm reel 52; Frederick Law Olmsted, "King-Glover Subdivision Plat Report" (1885); Schuyler, p. 129; Marianna Griswold Van Rensselaer, *Garden and Forest*, 5 December 1888, p. 483.

23. On Codman's work at the Breakers, see Pauline C. Metcalf in Jordy, *Buildings on Paper*, pp. 51–52, 211. On Allard and Hunt, see James T. Maher, *The Twilight of Splendor* (Boston, 1975), pp. 51–57, 271, 275–80. Maher is presently working on a book that will deal more directly with Hunt's major late houses and the involvement of such decorating firms in their design and execution.

24. Two other Gothic rooms in Hunt houses are less successful: the Gothic salon in Marble House and the Gothic ballroom in Belcourt. Drawings 78.803–78.805 indicate that the Marble House interior was designed by Moreau Frères of Paris. The Belcourt ballroom designed for O. H. P. Belmont is attributed to the Hunt office; however, no drawings for it exist, and it is so Gothic Revival that one wonders if, perhaps, someone else was responsible for it.

25. Catharine Hunt, p. 252. Baker, p. 343.

26. Joy Wheeler Dow, p. 122.

27. Catharine Hunt, p. 162.

28. "Grey Towers," Historic Structure Report, United States Department of Agriculture, Forest Service, October 1979, pp. 1–31.

29. Peter Collins, *Changing Ideals in Modern Architecture, 1750–1950* (Montreal, 1967), p. 117.

30. Baker, pp. 240, 412–32.

31. Catharine Hunt, p. 233; drawings 79.3682 and 79.3683.

32. Montgomery Schuyler, "The Vanderbilt Houses," *Harper's Weekly* 26, no. 42 (21 January 1882). Clarence Cook, "Architecture in America," *North American Review* 310 (September 1882): 250.

33. M. G. Van Rensselaer, "Recent Architecture in America. V. City Dwellings," *The Century Magazine* 31, no. 4 (February 1886): 555.

34. Unidentified clipping ca. 1884, AIA Foundation Richard Morris Hunt Collection, scrapbook entitled "Architectural cuttings from 1860 to 1897," p. 54; John Burchard and Albert Bush-Brown, *The Architecture of America* (London, 1966), p. 86.

35. E. L. Godkin, "The Expenditure of Rich Men," *Scribner's Magazine* 20, no. 4 (October 1896): 497–500. Joseph Lee, "Expensive Living, the Blight on America," *New England Magazine* 18 (March 1890): 54.

36. Henry James, *The American Scene* (New York, 1967), pp. 224–25, 161–62.

37. Henry-Russell Hitchcock, *Architecture: Nineteenth and Twentieth Centuries* (Baltimore, 1958, 1968), p. 457. Burchard and Bush-Brown, p. 111. An even more condemning tone pervades Leonard Eaton's piece regarding preservation of the Breakers, published in the Society of Architectural Historians' *Architectural Preservation Forum* 1, no. 1 (February 1979). Denigration of Hunt and his work is especially harsh in the writings of such social historians as Russell Lynes in *The Taste-Makers* (New York, 1949), pp. 131–32, 140–41, 144; and J. C. Furnas in *The Americans: A Social History of the United States, 1587–1914* (New York, 1969), pp. 595, 765, 771–73.

38. Henry Van Brunt, "Richard Morris Hunt," *Architecture and Society, Selected Essays of Henry Van Brunt* (Cambridge, Mass., 1969), p. 336.

39. *New York Times*, 15 May 1892, p. 16; Schuyler, p. 131.

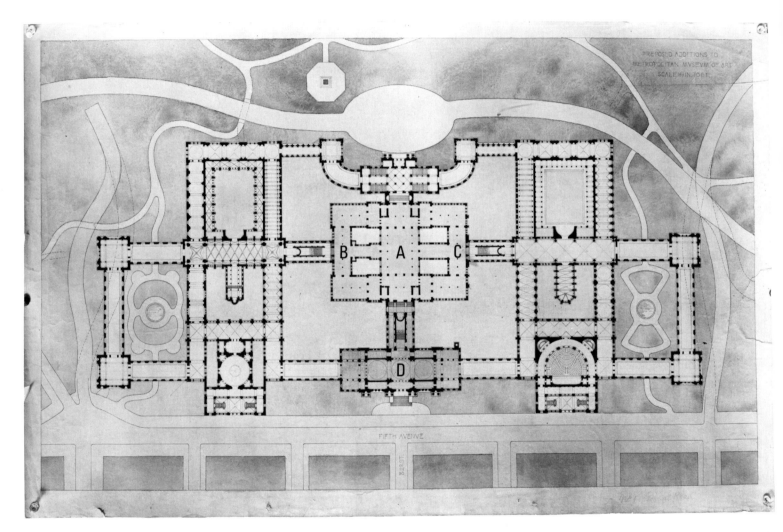

9.1 The Metropolitan Museum of Art, plan of proposed additions, probably April 1895. Photograph courtesy of the Metropolitan Museum of Art.

9

Hunt and the Metropolitan Museum of Art

Morrison H. Heckscher

HEN RICHARD MORRIS HUNT'S great entrance wing to the Metropolitan Museum of Art was opened to the public on 22 December 1902, a fellow architect described it as "the best classic building in this country" (see fig. 3.30).[1] Indeed, it was a building of superlatives: Hunt's last project and his most famous public building. If the plan had been executed in its entirety, it would also have been his largest commission. It was, as the president of the Museum noted at the time of Hunt's death, his monument.[2] Furthermore, the Museum building symbolized a number of things: the ultimate triumph of French classicism over the English High Victorian Gothic that had dominated American public buildings during the 1860s and 1870s, the acceptability of the placing of great museum buildings prominently in public parks, and the recognition, perhaps, that such large and complex buildings should only be designed by architects of the highest standing.

Hunt's involvement with the architectural history of the Museum was of long standing, going back to the institution's founding in 1870. For a quarter of a century he served on the Museum's board of trustees, often advising on architectural matters, and enduring the frustrations of watching a magnificent opportunity given to men he saw as less competent and professional than himself.

On 23 November 1869, the Art-Committee of the Union League Club of New York organized a meeting of prominent New Yorkers to consider the founding of a Metropolitan Art-Museum. William Cullen Bryant presided; and Hunt, as president of the New York chapter of the American Institute of Architects, served as one of nine vice-presidents. In a short speech Hunt claimed, with characteristic directness and vigor, that

> the Society of Architects . . . commenced some ten years ago with the idea of establishing a National Museum . . . it is our aim to have, at no very future period, a museum similar to the Kensington Museum in London. . . . But there is one thing that we must have first, and that is the building itself; because, when you catch a bird you need a cage for it. And besides, I believe it will be much more difficult to fill the building when we have it, than it will be to get the funds to erect it. . . . The first thing we need is a building; and as far as the architects of the country are concerned, I can promise they will do their best to put the building up when you are ready for it.[3]

Hunt himself was an inveterate collector—of paintings, objets d'art, antique furniture—and recognized the need for an art museum in New York. He was also quick to see that the museum building held the promise of being one of the great public commissions of the era. His speech was an open offer to take it on.

The Union League meeting resulted in the formation of a Committee of Fifty, including Hunt, which was empowered to prepare a constitution, apply for a charter, and so on. On 31 January 1870, John Taylor Johnston, the railroad executive and art collector, was chosen as president of the Museum, and Hunt was appointed to the Executive Committee. In May, Hunt was elected a trustee for a four-year term—a position he was to retain for the rest of his life. In addition to his interest in the building program, Hunt was to make financial contributions and lend paintings and casts from his own collection.

In 1870 Hunt's career had just entered high gear. Among American architects, the extent of his training at the Ecole des Beaux-Arts was unique. He was forty-three years old; he was comfortably off and, through his marriage to Catharine Clinton Howland, well connected with the seats of social and commercial power in New York and Newport. At the time he had more than two dozen commissions under design or in construction—private houses and public buildings alike. Hunt had been active in the American Institute of Architects since its founding in 1857. On the New York architectural scene, he was a rising star: Richard Upjohn and Alexander Jackson Davis were past their prime; and James Renwick, a decade older than Hunt, was at the peak of his career (his Gothic Revival masterpiece, Saint Patrick's Cathedral, was half built). Furthermore, Hunt had designed the Studio Building (1858) for John Taylor Johnston, now the Museum's president; and James Lenox, his client for both the Presbyterian Hospital (nearing completion) and the Lenox Library (just begun), was on the Provisional Committee for founding the Museum. Hunt was a perfect candidate for the Museum commission.

But since the building was to be located in Central Park and paid for with public funds, the Museum was not a free agent in choosing the designer. It was entitled to recommend architects from whom the Board of Commissioners of the Central Park would make the final selection. The Museum would then oversee the design, which the Park Department (in 1871 renamed the Department of Public Parks) would approve and execute. The choice of Calvert Vaux, Hunt's contemporary and a fellow activist in the American Institute of Architects, was therefore not surprising. After all, the Park had been laid out in 1858 by Vaux and the landscape architect Frederick Law Olmsted. The two men had supervised execution of the plan until, in the early 1860s, they went their separate ways. In 1863, the Central Park commissioners approved a competition for the four south entrances to the park, which Hunt won. (See chapter 4.) Hunt's splendid classical designs, reflecting his Parisian training, were in direct conflict with the English landscape tradition that the Park embodied; and in 1865, after intense controversy, Vaux managed to have the designs laid aside. In July the Park commissioners rehired Olmsted and Vaux. When it came to building the Museum in the Park, therefore, Vaux was clearly acceptable, Hunt equally clearly not.

The site chosen for the Museum was on the Fifth Avenue side of the park, bounded on the north by Eighty-fourth Street, on the south by Seventy-ninth Street, and on the west by the Croton Reservoir. The Park commissioners had sought legislation, made law on 5 May 1869, "to erect, establish, conduct, and maintain on the Central Park a Meteorological and Astronomical Observatory, and a Museum of Natural History and A Gallery of Art, and the buildings therefor. . . ." On the commissioners' map for 1869, an immense building complex is outlined in the space and described as "Proposed Art Museum and Hall."[4] It faced Fifth Avenue. At the incorporation of the Metropolitan Museum in April 1870, the trustees petitioned for the erection of the authorized building. In June of 1871, the Museum's Committee of Architects, led by Hunt, met with Parks Department representatives to urge that the plan be made simpler and less expensive, more in the manner of the South Kensington Museum in London. In November they conferred with Vaux and Olmsted directly.[5]

Preliminary building plans were reviewed by the Museum's Executive Committee in July 1872. Members of the Committee attended Mr. Vaux in his office on two different occasions; at the first, Vaux expressed himself unable to reconcile their suggestions with his own views; at the second, a scheme acceptable to both parties was devised. Excavation work was begun in 1873, construction in 1874. In December of 1875 members of the Executive Committee visited the site to consider further changes. A special committee—consisting of Johnston, Hunt, and another trustee architect, Theodore Weston—met with Vaux in January regarding the changes.[6] Construction dragged; not until 30 March 1880, was the wing opened to the public.

Vaux's building was a simple rectangular block, with walls of granite and brick, pierced by pointed-arch windows. The ends of the long walls were unfinished, in anticipation of additions; but, at least at the beginning, Vaux only intended short stubby wings.[7] Perhaps this lack of a comprehensive plan for long-term growth was one reason why both Johnston and Hunt were soon to call Vaux's building a mistake. Another reason must have been the building's ambivalent relationship to the Park. The Vaux and Olmsted park plan specifically excluded all buildings except for necessary small structures (such as bridges and gazebos) in suitably picturesque styles. Vaux was not comfortable with the idea of a large museum building in the park; in spite of an effort to please the Museum representatives, he treated the building as an overgrown park pavilion—sited as far into the landscape as possible and entered on the park side through a rustic, wooden, covered staircase.

The Museum, growing rapidly, undertook construction of a second wing (Wing B) immediately after the first one (Wing A) was completed. In place of Vaux, a man from within the Museum family was chosen. He was Theodore Weston, like Hunt a founding incorporator and trustee of the Museum as well as an architect. Weston had been actively involved with architectural questions at the Museum: in 1872 with the Committee of Architects; in 1873 with planning the Museum's temporary home; and between 1876 and 1878 as an adviser on the Vaux wing. He had the support of the director, and he was approved by the Parks commissioners who, in 1884, were to make him "Constructing and Superintending Architect."[8] About the only printed record of his architectural activity, however, is the legend "Architect and Civil Engineer" on the top of his note paper. The choice of Weston over Hunt must have involved personal rather than professional judgments.

In December 1880 Weston was asked to prepare preliminary drawings. In 1881 a Special Committee of Advisory Architects for the Museum—consisting of Hunt, Weston, and James Renwick—was appointed to decide on the plan for the new addition.[9] Weston was sandwiched between two of America's leading architects, hardly a position calculated to instill confidence. Nonetheless, in 1883 Weston was officially appointed Museum architect, a position he was to hold until 1890. His selection appears to have owed much to the flamboyant new director, Louis Palma di Cesnola. In August 1883, Weston declared "I have begun actively in making the ground plan sketches. . . ." In September he drew up an alternate scheme suggested by Cesnola, and readily agreed with Johnston that it was better than his own! He told Cesnola of criticism by a Mr. Fornan (doubtless Hunt's chief assistant, Maurice Fornachon), but brushed it aside. In October yet another new scheme was begun: "A beautiful result can be obtained, dignified and most satisfying to my artistic feeling."[10]

The final plans and specifications were readied and approved in the spring of 1884. Weston later thanked Cesnola in the most heartfelt way for his help: "Your telegram & letter this morning has given me new life—I owe you much for your affectionate sympathy . . . now the work will have the time of hearty encouragement which alone could restore the strength almost gone."[11] Hardly a professional architect-client relationship Hunt would have approved.

Meanwhile, Johnston had appointed a Building Committee consisting of himself, Cesnola, and Hunt, to review additional facade sketches that Weston had prepared. The problem was one of harmonizing the facades of the new and old buildings. (Wing B, an E-shaped addition to the south of Vaux's wing, was similar to it in scale and materials, but not in fenestration.) Hunt was out of town, but when he returned the next month he could contain his professional dismay and personal displeasure no longer. "It will neither be convenient or agreeable for me to serve on the building committee," he wrote Cesnola, "as the plan of the proposed addition does not meet with my unreserved approval." Cesnola gave the letter to Weston, who replied: "I return Mr. Hunt's note, which apart from its discourteous tone, seems to have presumed that no opportunity was to have been afforded for suggestion or criticism on his part. . . . I am certainly sorry that we shall not have the benefit of his artistic advice."[12] Johnston, seeking to restore peace, wrote to Hunt at Newport. On 10 July Hunt replied:

> Naturally, I was surprised when informed that I was requested to serve on the building committee of the proposed addition to the Museum. As this important matter has been before the Trustees for a year or more, during which time plans were prepared and assorted—subject it is true to modification— without any consultation with me on the subject—which seemed to me not a little strange feeling as I naturally did that the professional difficulties of the problems were better comprehended by me than by the other members of the board: Knowing too that the Trustees generally felt that the problem was one which required the services of an educated and experienced architect.
>
> Had such a person, not a member of the Board, been appointed I could not have objected however much my professional pride might have been wounded at being ignored after a professional career of forty years, & being one of the original trustees—
>
> When the design of the original building was adopted I alone formally protested, & it was not until this building was well nigh completed that the Board recognized that I was right. A work of such importance should only be entrusted to a person of recognized ability in the profession.
>
> If such were the case my services would not be required. Besides, feeling as I do in regard to the project, the responsibility is greater than I wish to assume. Regretting to be obliged to refuse any request of yours I [remain?] Yours truly.[13]

Johnston passed Hunt's note to Cesnola, ruefully noting: "Our first building was a mistake, there must be none about the second." Cesnola in turn shared the letter with Weston, who replied: "I return our friend Hunt's unhappy letter—the whole thing looks so like pique and jealousy that it is entirely unworthy the man. . . . I propose that we have a sensible, simple as well as artistic building, thoroughly correct architecturally. I do not believe that Mr. H is the only man in the country who is capable of carrying it out."[14] Hunt had made no such claim, but it soon became a question whether Weston was capable of carrying out the project.

Construction of Wing B began during the winter of 1884–85, and there were numerous problems. Damage to Wing A was caused by blasting for the foundations and by the resulting excavations being left open all winter. Then, in December 1885, the Parks Department stopped the work, claiming that the plans were not clear. Weston reminded the commissioners, to no avail, that they had approved the plans eight months earlier. Apparently Hunt, thoroughly disgusted, had raised questions with the Parks Department, and in November Charles deF. Burns, secretary of the Parks commissioners, had requested an opinion on the plans from Maurice Fornachon, Hunt's chief assistant. Fornachon sent a list of necessary changes to Henry R. Beekman, president of the Department of Public Parks, with a copy to Henry G. Marquand—a Museum trustee, and friend and frequent client of Hunt.[15] Robert W. deForest, secretary of the Museum's board, was outraged at Hunt's end-run action. To Marquand he wrote: "In view of the architect's relation to you and his professional relation to a brother architect it seems extraordinary that he should have written such a letter to the Department of Public Parks without first seeing you or Mr. Weston. . . ."[16]

The Parks commissioners were persuaded to begin the work again toward the end of January. Nearly three years later, Weston and his associate, Arthur Lyman Tuckerman, completed the building for the public opening on 18 December 1888.

Marquand succeeded Johnston as president of the Museum in 1889, and early in 1890 convened the Building Committee (consisting of trustee Heber R. Bishop, chairman; Cesnola; and Marquand himself) to discuss the construction of Wing C on the north side of Vaux's building. On 20 January "the question of recommending a new architect to the Parks Commissioners was fully discussed and Mr Marquand promised to obtain certain information concerning the ability of a candidate which the Building Committee has in view to recommend." (On 12 January 1890 the *New York Herald* had published a sketch of Weston's and Tuckerman's proposed overall plan—an endless extension along Fifth Avenue of the uninspired Wing "B" facade—but that hardly pleased anybody.) At the request of the Parks commissioners, the Committee proposed three architects in order of preference: R. M. Hunt; Messrs McKim, Mead, and White; and Robert H. Robertson. This was on 17 February.[17] The next day Hunt wrote Marquand: "I beg herewith to tender my resignation as trustee of the Metn Museum of Art to take effect when I may be appointed architect of said confirmation [*sic*]."[18] The way seemed finally clear to hire an architect of superior training and experience, one, in addition, deeply committed to the Museum. In March Weston submitted his resignation to the Parks commissioners, who promptly requested the Museum to supply them with the names of additional architects for their consideration. Marquand had the Executive Committee prepare a list at once, which included George B. Post (one of Hunt's most distinguished pupils), James Renwick, and last, Arthur Tuckerman, Weston's associate and the manager of the Museum's art schools—only to discover that the Parks commissioners had already chosen Tuckerman, a promising young man but an architectural nobody, over perhaps the five most prominent firms in New York![19] Had Weston arranged this succession with Cesnola? Or had Vaux insisted that the job be taken by someone who would respect his building? Whatever the reason, Marquand must have been distressed, Hunt outraged.

On 18 April Tuckerman made the first of a number of reports to the Building Committee on the design of Wing C. In August he reported having prepared plans and specifications "in constant conference with the Chairman of the Building Committee and the Director of the Museum." On the twenty-eighth the plans were approved and presented to the Parks Department.[20] Tuckerman, whose art school was to be housed in the new building, had so exhausted himself by his obsessive labors that a few months later he was dead. He was succeeded by Joseph Wolf, who, as superintending architect, oversaw construction of Wing C, which opened to the public on 5 November 1894.

Hunt attempted to resign from the Board of Trustees in January 1891, claiming the press of business. Marquand must have dissuaded him, however, because in November the Building Committee, now including Hunt, met in the latter's office to discuss modifications to the plans of Wing C. In addition, Wolf was instructed to submit the plans for the proposed boiler house to Hunt for his approval. When the committee met next, on 22 January 1892, Hunt reviewed the boiler house plans and moved its location westward, "so as not to cut out the light from the future building on the east side of it."[21] This is the first indication that Hunt had an idea for an overall architectural plan for the Museum; it is also more than a little suggestive that he expected a large role in the next phase of the Museum's expansion.

Hunt's expectations were well founded. The Building Committee that Marquand convened in January 1894 for preliminary discussions about the Museum's fourth building campaign had a power and unity of purpose heretofore lacking. Its members were Marquand, Cesnola, and (in the chair) Hunt. Marquand and Cesnola worked perfectly as a team, and Marquand had long championed Hunt. Just back from the triumph of the 1893 World's Columbian Exposition, where he had served as president of the Board of Architects and designed the Administration Building, Hunt was at the height of his fame. If ever a building committee had a chance to make its mark, this was it.

Not surprisingly, the Committee recommended that the new building face east and be in the shape of a T, with the boiler house behind it to the north and with a library building behind it to the south. Wolf, as superintending architect, was requested to produce a ground plan for submission to the Executive Committee.[22] On this basis the application for public funding could begin. The Building Committee met again officially on 20 January 1895, supposedly to decide if the plan prepared the previous year, "which was laid on the table for future consideration," could in any way be improved. In fact, at Marquand's express request, Hunt had been hard at work for the past year on an overall plan for the Museum. On 5 April, the Building Committee met at Hunt's office to see the drawings (see figs. 6.24, 9.1, 9.2). In the words of the minutes, Hunt "had, for several months, been studying and preparing a set of plans showing the entire architectural style of a building which, in his opinion, should be

9.2 The Metropolitan Museum of Art, preliminary study for the entrance facade, East Wing, 1894–95.

erected on the whole area which the City set aside for the Metropolitan Museum of Art, and had also prepared a plan showing the elevation of a portion of the East Side."[23]

Anticipating, momentarily, the appropriation of building funds, the committee agreed to send the drawings in their present unfinished state to the trustees for their approval. They were taking no chances on another architect being considered. On 16 April, the legislature in Albany passed the bill appropriating $1,000,000 (but no more than $200,000 in any one year) for the construction of the Museum's East Wing. The spring trustee meeting was scheduled for 20 May, which coincided with a visit Hunt had to make to the Vanderbilt project at Biltmore in North Carolina. Hunt therefore instructed his son Richard Howland Hunt, who had joined the firm in 1887, to make the presentation on his behalf. Seven finely rendered drawings were delivered to the Museum on the seventeenth: an overall plan for the Museum (see fig. 9.1), and three elevations (fig. 9.3), two sections, and a floor plan (fig. 9.4) for the East Wing.[24] The trustees, after lengthy discussion, referred the drawings back to committee for further study.

Hunt, however, was never to return to New York. He died suddenly on 31 July 1895, before the designs for his last great project were completed and approved. Cesnola summarized the situation in a letter to the president:

> Mr. Hunt's unexpected death will place our Building Committee in a very difficult position. How far his plans of our new wing have progressed since we last saw them I do not know; but if they have advanced sufficiently, I think our Committee ought to stick to them, if we do not I am sure that some of our trustees will recommend their own architects and finish by selecting one of them, and all of the work already done will go for nothing . . . we ought to be prepared to recommend the adoption of Hunt's plans, if after examining them

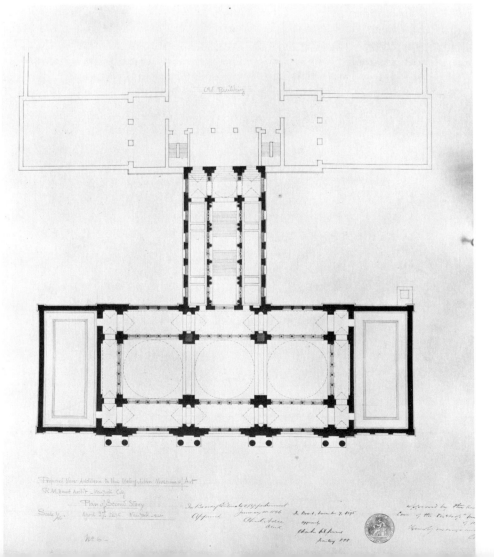

9.3 The Metropolitan Museum of
Art, presentation rendering of the
entrance facade, East Wing, April
1895. Photograph courtesy of the
Metropolitan Museum of Art.

9.4 The Metropolitan Museum of
Art, presentation rendering of the
second story plan, East Wing,
drawn by E. L. Masqueray,
27 April 1895. Photograph courtesy of the Metropolitan Museum
of Art.

very carefully, our Committee is satisfied that Fornachon and Hunt's son could finish them exactly as Hunt intended to have them. . . . I write to you all this confidentially—Personally I did not care much for Hunt but for his architectural ability I always had the highest esteem." [25]

Marquand's reply was unequivocal: "I expect to carry out the Hunt design— He went all over the work with Richard his son and had given much thought on the subject for a year—there will be no chance for any body else to come in and snatch his monument—I fancy some of the members will advocate Mr. Ware [William R. Ware, a pupil of Hunt's and founder of the department of architecture at Columbia College] to take the vacancy on the Building Comm—he has good taste but poor business capacity—." And, two weeks later: "Mr Hunt had the whole matter in his mind for 18 mos & we conversed about it often. It has been my wish to have a well digested plan made for 2 years past—I find that Mr. H went over with his son & Fornachon the entire scheme. So that they understood it fully & can carry it out." [26]

Marquand, for whom Hunt had designed houses in Newport and New York, as well as the Marquand Chapel at Princeton, had greatly liked and admired Hunt, and would see to it that the Museum project got built. Two months later, in October 1895, the Executive Committee met and approved the Hunt plans for the East Wing; on the thirtieth the trustees approved them. [27] That same day Marquand himself wrote the letter of transmittal of eight drawings—one elevation (see fig. 9.3), two sections, and five plans (see fig. 9.4)—to the commissioners of the Public Parks:

> In accordance with Chapter 347, Laws of New York of 1895, the Trustees . . . submit to you for your approval, the plan for the extension of the east side of the present Museum building. The prevailing style as seen in the elevation herewith submitted is intended to be carried out hereafter throughout the whole structure covering the 18 acres so that the same general architectural character shall be preserved in future additions. The Trustees intend that the principal entrance to the Museum should be at this eastern extension when completed. [28]

Thus were decided the major questions that had plagued the building program for a quarter of a century: What is the appropriate architectural style? Where should the entrance be? What should the extent of the plan be?

On 5 November, Cesnola reported to Marquand on his conversations with Charles deF. Burns, secretary of the Parks Department. Burns recommended that Marquand and R. H. Hunt appear with Cesnola at the hearing on the seventh. In Cesnola's words:

> He also tells me that the plans were referred to Mr. Vaux and that he is 'kicking about them' (these are Mr Burns' words). He says that Mr. Vaux 'is dead against the general plan of the Museum.' This the Trustees can well understand because the plans which Vaux made in 1878 for the whole Museum building accepted and placed on file at the Park Dept have been ignored, and will be superseded by these new plans of Mr Hunt. Mr. Burns, however, does not think that Mr. Vaux's opposition will carry any weight. When we told Mr Vaux that the general plan was not officially before the Board and there was no action to be taken on it, Mr. Vaux got angry and said that the front of the projected wing was a part of the general plan, and for that reason objected to it." [29]

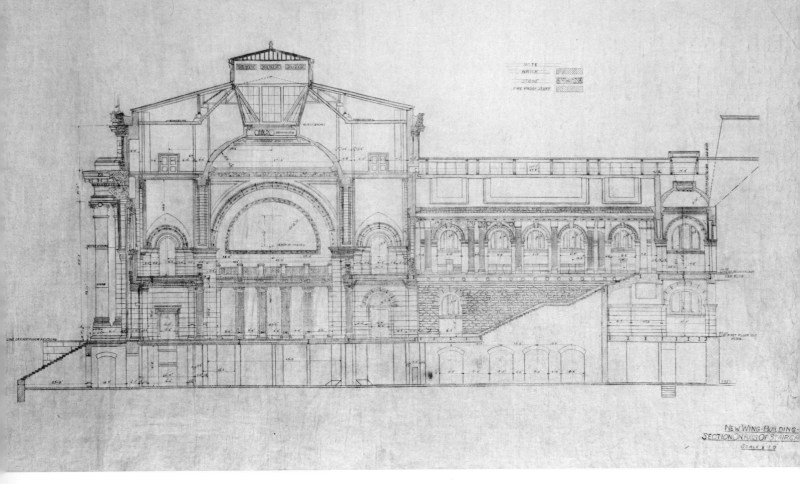

At the meeting on the seventh, the plans were approved. Burns signed the drawings on behalf of the Parks commissioners, Marquand on behalf of the Buildings Committee of the Museum. On 10 January 1896, the final approval was secured when Charles V. Adee, clerk, signed them on behalf of the Board of Estimate of the City of New York.[30] The next day the Buildings Committee instructed R. H. Hunt to prepare working drawings for the new wing; the first nine numbered drawings are dated in late January and February. The first and second, facade elevations, were approved by the Buildings Committee on 17 February, and so inscribed.

Meanwhile, a dispute developed between the Museum trustees and the Parks Commissioners. The Executive Committee refused to take full responsibility for Hunt as sole architect, and insisted that a consulting architect be chosen to assist him, an understandable request considering Hunt's relative inexperience and the magnitude of the project. The Building Committee suggested the firm of McKim, Mead, and White, but the Parks people balked, preferring Hunt alone. In April, a compromise was reached when George B. Post, now one of the city's leading practitioners, agreed to be consulting architect.[31]

On 12 November 1896, ten months after beginning the working drawings, Richard Howland Hunt presented twenty-nine sheets of meticulously prepared pencil-on-linen drawings (fig. 9.5) to the Building Committee;[32] that same day they were ordered printed, and on the twenty-fourth a set was delivered to Cesnola. The Committee examined them, authorized a number of changes, and unanimously approved them on 5 December; and on the twelfth the trustees adopted the plans.[33] Post reviewed structural and engineering questions—for example, in July a study of the roof trusses was reissued with the notation "Revised according to the suggestion of the Consulting Architect"—and complimented Hunt "upon the artistic way in which he had provided to carry out the designs of his father."[34] Finally, on 19 August 1897, Cesnola inscribed his name, the date, and the approval of the Building Committee on each drawing in one complete set.[35]

The Parks commissioners approved the architectural specifications in September, and on 31 December 1897 construction contracts were let. The excavations had already been completed, and in 1898 the structure had reached half of its final height. There was a long strike in 1899, but the fabric neared completion by the end of 1900. After a year for the stonework to dry out, the interiors were fitted up for the grand opening on 22 December 1902.[36]

The Museum's new entrance building was executed very much as originally designed by Richard Morris Hunt. Hunt, however, had intended the facade to be of white marble, with an extensive ornamental program of inscriptions and figural sculpture. (For Hunt's association with sculptors, see chapter 7). This was the design approved by the Building Committee on 17 February 1896 (see. fig. 9.3) It included thirty-one pieces of sculpture: above the paired columns, monumental figural groups; between them, relief panels and niches containing freestanding statues; in each arch, a keystone with a helmeted female head and, in the spandrels, two portrait rondels; over the windows in each wing, three relief panels separated by caryatid figures. None of the sculptural subject matter had been specified. The attic groups, for example, are all of the same design, though every other image is reversed. The design also included six panels with inscriptions—three in the attic and three within the arched openings—and on them the wording was all spelled out. The attic panels had a running text:

ANNO DOMINI MDCCCXCV IN URBIS NOVI YORKI CONCILIORUM ALBANI LEGES EX
AUTORITATIS DE HANC NOMINATIONE IN DE CONCILII ET PAR AUTORITATE ETATIS
HUNC ANNO LIBERTAS MUSEUM ARTIS ET SCULPTURI ET PICTI EREXIT PUBLICUM
ARMA VIRUMQUE CANO TROJAEQUE PRIMUM ARBORIS ITALIAM FATO PROFUGUS
LAVINIAMQUE VENIT QUE.

Those in the arches had lists of names, mostly famous Renaissance painters and architects (including Raphael and Michelangelo, Bramante and Scamozzi). There were also the names of a number of contemporary architects: Garnier and Lefuel from Paris; R. M. Hunt, R. H. Hunt, and from their office, Fornachon and the draftsman E. L. Masqueray. (The home team was well represented.) In the drawings revised by Richard Howland Hunt in November 1896 the text of the attic panels and the six sculptural relief panels in the side wings were omitted (fig. 9.6).[37] In the final version, that approved by Cesnola in August 1897, the name panels have also been deleted; instead a profile relief portrait bust of R. M. Hunt, done by the sculptor Karl Bitter in 1891, is employed as one of the rondels.[38] Such representation continued an ancient and honorable tradition, and one not new to Hunt: a near life-size effigy of Hunt as a stonemason served as a rooftop finial on his William K. Vanderbilt house (1882); and Hunt's head is incorporated in Bitter's bronze doors at Trinity Church, New York (1894).

In July 1898, R. H. Hunt proposed letting a $10,300 contract for the carving of Bitter's four caryatids (representing Painting, Sculpture, Architecture, and Music) and six rondels, but it was only in November that the Building Committee decided on whom the latter were to represent (Bramante, Michel-

angelo, Raphael, Dürer, Rembrandt, Velázquez).[39] Had they been deadlocked about whether or not to include Hunt? At any rate, the facade was simplified in execution for purely budgetary reasons: Indiana limestone replaced marble;[40] and, with the exception of Bitter's keystones, rondels, and caryatids, all the ornamental inscriptions and sculptures were left undone. A certain surface richness—the reflective qualities of marble and the chiaroscuro effects of ornamental carving—was undeniably lost. The building had to depend instead upon the perfect scale and proportions of its parts.

Hunt's East Wing (Wing D) was conceived from the start as being the main entrance to the Museum and the central focus of a long Fifth Avenue facade. As such it required a certain imperial grandeur while remaining inviting. All Hunt's preliminary facade studies employ a massive central block flanked by low, set-back wings and large end pavilions. The central entrance block in the early studies is square, with a domed interior space, sometimes expressed on the outside. In the later studies Hunt had decided on a rectangular central block with a tripartite facade expressing a triple-domed interior space. He played with single free-standing columns flanking wide low arches, with double columns on high plinths flanking wide arches (see fig. 9.2), and finally settled on tall columns and narrow arches (see fig. 9.3). The change was from a squat, Roman-bath look to an elegant eighteenth-century classicism.

Hunt's facade is a characteristic Beaux-Arts design, combining arches, architectural orders, and sculptural decoration; so are his drawings—plans, elevations, sections, but no perspectives. In 1853, as a student at the Ecole, Hunt had prepared designs for a Ministry of Justice (see figs. 2.28–2.30); in certain respects its facade prefigures that of the Museum: it has arched bays separated by columns above which, in the attic, are inscribed panels separated by sculpted fig-

9.6 The Metropolitan Museum of Art, rendering of East Wing, drawn by E. F. Hunt and Charles E. Mach, probably November 1896. Photograph courtesy of the Metropolitan Museum of Art.

ures. In general arrangement and in scale (except for the paired columns and the attic treatment) the Museum facade approximates that of Paul-Henri Nenot's 1877 Grand Prix design for an Atheneum.[41] The double-column motif had been used by Lefuel in the additions to the Louvre on which Hunt had been employed (1854–55). At the Metropolitan, however, Hunt combined paired columns with triple arches so successfully that they were soon to be found cropping up everywhere, including the New York Public Library and Grand Central Station.

Hunt's plan (see fig. 9.1) was designed around the rectangular block comprising the existing Museum buildings (Wings A–C). The old buildings were to more or less float in an immense rectangular court. The new East Wing (Wing D) was joined to it by a monumental staircase wing that formed the central axis of the whole plan. The rest of the immense project, which never got beyond the schematic plan stage, consisted of large, projecting library and auditorium wings facing Fifth Avenue, and long, low wings or pavilions enclosing six subsidiary courtyards.[42] The whole, with an overall symmetry and the juxtaposition of axes and spaces, is thoroughly in the Beaux-Arts manner. A number of features even suggest specific prototypes. The massive library and auditorium wings juxtaposed with low pavilions create a rhythm in spirit not unlike that of the famous 1855 Grand Prix design for a Conservatory of Music and Oratory by Hunt's fellow pupil at the Ecole, Honoré Daumet.[43] The semicircular auditorium with semicircular apses in the corners was a popular motif in Beaux-Arts designs, one Hunt had employed in his 1851 project for a theater for a little village (see figs. 2.9–2.12). And in the case of the chapels that extend into the center of the two interior courtyards, one cannot fail to note the similarity with Labrouste's celebrated 1824 Grand Prix for a Supreme Court.[44]

We have seen that Hunt was involved with the Metropolitan Museum, off and on, for the last twenty-five years of his life—years that span the prime years of his highly successful career. Until the end of this period, he was utterly frustrated in his hopes to get the Museum commission. It seems to have been a combination of politics and personality, on the one hand, and conflicting design tradition on the other. It is idle to speculate about the building he would have designed in 1872 or 1880 or 1890; but it seems certain that, whatever it was, it would not have been the total success, then and ever since, of his 1895 design. Hunt's classical designs for the Central Park gates (1863) were ahead of their time; his Gothic designs for a New York Historical Society building (1866) and his Second Empire designs for a Museum of Natural History (1872), both on park sites, went unexecuted. If built they would probably, like so much else of Hunt's work, have long ago been demolished as inadequate and ugly. By the time that Hunt, with Marquand's help, finally cornered the commission, the pendulum of architectural taste had swung firmly into the classic camp—in good part thanks to Hunt's influence.

Though executed posthumously, Hunt's design for the entrance wing of the Metropolitan Museum was faithfully adhered to by his son. Praised the day it opened as "the most outstanding building of its kind in the city, one of the finest in the world,"[45] it continues to serve perfectly its original intended function—as the grand ceremonial entrance to a vast museum complex—and this in spite of numerous changes over the years made in the general plan. What more fitting conclusion to the career of one of the leading figures in American nineteenth-century architecture and the first dean of the profession?

Notes

Unless otherwise noted, all manuscript material referred to is in the Metropolitan Museum of Art Archives.

1. Anonymous, "The New Metropolitan Museum of Art," *Architectural Record* 12 (August 1902): 306.

2. Letter, Marquand to Cesnola, 7 August 1895 (B868).

3. W. C. Bryant et al., *A Metropolitan Art-Museum in the City of New York: Proceedings of a Meeting* (New York, 1869), pp. 17–18.

4. *Thirteenth Annual Report of the Board of Commissioners of the Central Park for the year ending December 31, 1869.* (New York, 1870), p. 24; ibid., fold-out plan of the Central Park, dated 1 January 1870.

5. Executive Committee Minutes, 28 June, 27 November 1871.

6. Ibid., 10, 13, 16 July 1872; 6, 13, 20 December 1875; 17 January, 7 February 1876.

7. One of the Vaux drawings for the Museum, now at the Municipal Archives, New York City, is a "General Ground Plan" (undated) showing four wings, each but thirty-eight feet long. Other drawings for the building are signed by Vaux and Jacob Wrey Mould, associate architect in the Parks Department.

8. Executive Committee Minutes, 27 November 1871; 11 June 1872; 7 January 1873; 7 January, 15 April 1878. Trustee minutes, 2 July 1884.

9. Executive Committee minutes, 13 December 1880; 22 December 1881.

10. Letters, Weston to Cesnola, 14 August, 7, 12 September, 20 October 1883; Johnston to Cesnola, 6 September 1883 (B868).

11. Letter, Weston to Cesnola, 4 April 1885 (W529).

12. Letters, Hunt to Cesnola, 5 July 1884; Weston to Cesnola, 11 July 1884 (B868).

13. Letter, Hunt to Johnston, 10 July 1884 (B868).

14. Letters, Johnston to Cesnola, 11 July 1884; Weston to Cesnola, 19 July 1884 (B868).

15. Letters, Cesnola to Parks commissioners, 16 November 1885; Johnston to Weston, n.d.; Burns to Fornachon, 20 November 1885; Fornachon to Beekman, n.d.; Fornachon to Marquand, 1 December 1885 (B868).

16. Letter, deForest to Marquand, 2 December 1885 (B868).

17. Building Committee minutes, 20 January, 17 February 1890.

18. Letter, Hunt to Marquand, 18 February 1890 (H913).

19. Executive Committee minutes, 31 March 1890.

20. Building Committee minutes, 18 April, 12 May, 2, 28 August 1890.

21. Ibid., 25 November 1891; 22 January 1892.

22. Ibid., 14 January 1894.

23. Ibid., 5 April 1895. A number of Hunt's facade studies are in the Hunt Archive at the AIA. See catalog nos. 79.1375–77, 80–81; 80.6104–6106; 81.6103, 6107, 6108, 6108a.

24. Letter, Cesnola to Hunt, 20 April, 10 May 1895; Hunt to Cesnola, 7, 13, 15 May 1895 (B868).

25. Letter, Cesnola to Marquand, 2 August 1895 (B868).

26. Letters, Marquand to Cesnola, 7, 24 August 1895 (B868).

27. Letter, Marquand to Executive Committee, 24 October 1895 (B868).

28. Letter, Marquand to Parks commissioners, 30 October 1895 (B868).

29. Letter (draft, with corrections), Cesnola to Marquand, 5 November 1895 (B868).

30. None of the presentation drawings that were duly signed and approved have been located; however, there are photographs of the Fifth Avenue elevation and of the basement, first-, and second-floor plans; the section through the great room was traced to make working drawing no. 8.

31. Building Committee minutes, 30 March–28 April 1896.

32. Seventeen of the twenty-nine original drawings—plans, framing plans, and sections, but no elevations—are on file at the Museum.

33. Building Committee minutes, 12, 24 November, 5, 12 December 1896.

34. Drawing no. 18A, on file at the Museum. Building Committee minutes, 11 December 1896.

35. The blueline prints of this set, mounted on linen, are now divided between the Municipal Archives of the City of New York and The Metropolitan Museum of Art.

36. The Metropolitan Museum of Art, *Annual Reports* (1898–1903).

37. The rendering (fig. 9.6) was the centerpiece of the Architectural League exhibition of New York in 1899. Illustrated in situ in A. D. F. Hamlin and F. S. Lamb, "New York Architectural League Exhibition," *The Architectural Review*, n.s., 1 (1899): 39.

38. Drawing no. 24 (copy at Metropolitan Museum); ordered printed 12 November 1896; corrected and printed 11 August 1897; approved by Cesnola, 19 August 1897.

39. Building Committee minutes, 13 July, 19 November 1898.

40. Letter, R. H. Hunt to Marquand, 14 November 1895 (B868).

41. Arthur Drexler, ed., *The Architecture of the Ecole des Beaux-Arts* (New York, 1977), pp. 258–59.

42. In the Hunt Collection at the AIA Foundation are a number of studies for the plan of the library wing.

43. Drexler, p. 224.

44. Ibid., p. 157.

45. Quoted in Winifred E. Howe, *A History of the Metropolitan Museum of Art* (New York, 1913), p. 277.

Index